now i see the moon

harperstudio

An Imprint of HarperCollins*Publishers*

now

i

see

the

moon

A MOTHER, A SON, A MIRACLE

elaine hall

with elizabeth kaye

The names and identifying characteristics of some individuals
discussed in this book have been changed to protect their privacy.

HarperCollins books may be purchased for educational, business, or sales promotional use. For information please write: Special Markets Department, HarperCollins Publishers, 10 East 53rd Street, New York, NY 10022.

To book Elaine Hall for a speaking engagement, visit www.harpercollinsspeakers.com.

For more information about this book or other books from HarperStudio, visit www.theharperstudio.com.

FIRST EDITION

Designed by Eric Butler

Library of Congress Cataloging-in-Publication Data

Hall, Elaine, 1956–
   Now I see the moon : a mother, a son, a miracle / Elaine Hall. — 1st ed.
   p.   cm.
   ISBN 978-0-06-174380-1
   1. Hall, Neal—Health. 2. Hall, Elaine, 1956– 3. Autistic children—United States—Biography. 4. Autistic children—Family relationships—United States. 5. Mothers of autistic children—United States—Biography. I. Hall, Neal II. Title.

RJ506.A9H17 2010
618.92'858820092—dc22
[B]

2009052443

10 11 12 13 14   OV/RRD   10 9 8 7 6 5 4 3 2 1

Dedicated to Sol and Betty—
who gave me life and taught me how to live

And to Neal, who taught me unconditional love

There are only two ways to live your life.

One is as though nothing is a miracle.

The other is as though everything is a miracle.

ALBERT EINSTEIN

Barn's burnt down—

now

I can see the moon

MIZUTA MASAHIDE

contents

now i see the moon

overture

SOMETIMES NEAL IS right there with you, his almond-shaped, hazel eyes gazing deep into yours as if he's seeing the insides of your soul.

At other times, his eyes focus on something distant. His hands flicker up and down like static on a television screen. He seems sequestered in his own private world.

To reach him, I had to enter that world. When he stared intensely at his hand, I stared at mine. When he screeched, I screeched. When he spun in a circle, I took his hands and spun with him, round and round for as long as he wanted, until the two of us were breathless and laughing, connecting, daring, relishing our special haven, and our own, unique version of "Ring Around the Rosie."

All this led to a progression of days and experiences that were novel, magical, amazing. Bit by bit, Neal relinquished his solitary world. Gradually, the miracle happened and he merged into another world: mine.

My world. What can I tell you about it? I am the mother of Neal, a nonverbal teenager with autism whom I adopted from a Russian orphanage when he was a toddler. I am director of The Miracle Project, a theater and film program for children with autism and their typically developing peers. I also lead a bar mitzvah and bat mitzvah program for children with autism and other special needs. In between, I go to my weekly dance and yoga classes, attend a spiritual support group, see friends and family, and try to get the occasional pedicure.

My life took a surprising turn in recent years when The Miracle Project was filmed for the HBO documentary *Autism: The Musical*. The documentary won two Emmy Awards and, since then, both it and The Miracle Project have garnered international acclaim.

Because of this, I've traveled throughout the United States and Canada to speak of my work with autism. I've received honors from a variety of organizations including Autism Speaks, Autism Society of America, and The Doug Flutie Jr. Foundation. I've walked the "red carpet" several times with paparazzi flashing away as I drag my shy, reluctant new husband along. I was even invited to speak about autism at the United Nations. Sometimes I just can't believe that this is my life.

My son, who at one time was considered a hopeless case of severe autism with low cognitive ability, has surpassed all expectations. Today, Neal is a beautiful teenager, still nonverbal but capable of expressing profound thought and understanding. Today, our struggles are much like those of any parent with a teenager—rebelliousness often outweighs autism.

Neal has been my greatest teacher. From him, and because of him, I have learned patience, understanding, and compassion in ways that I never imagined. I have had to reach down inside to find strength within me that I never knew existed. I have screamed out to God for help; I have gratefully accepted guidance and assistance from others.

Like many women of the millennium, I often feel like that guy on the old Ed Sullivan shows who twirls plates on sticks, and tries to get one plate twirling before another plate comes crashing down. My life, and maybe yours, is about keeping all those plates going at once.

What keeps my life from whirling out of control is a connection to something greater than me. That "something" is a force, a power that I consciously contact every evening before I go to sleep and every morning when I awake. It is my connection to this force that has brought me through my darkest times and guided me to my greatest joys.

As I write these pages, I reflect back on times of struggle and happiness, times when I didn't know if I could go on, and times that I wished would never end. Though I didn't know it then, I can see now that every seemingly meaningless event lined up to perfection, creating the life that I share today. I welcome you to join this journey with me, to learn of my world, and of Neal's. I offer this journey to you in hope that it will, perhaps, help guide you with yours.

phase one:
my child

I get up. I walk. I fall down. Meanwhile, I keep dancing.

DANIEL HILLEL

AS A CHILD, all I ever wanted was to fit in. Growing up as a Jewish girl in the non-Jewish suburbs of Washington, D.C., "fitting in" was always a challenge. Being quite petite, with a large nose and a long name (both of which are now shortened!), did not help things along. I was constantly teased, my family received threatening Nazi phone calls, and my best friend insisted that I go to the bathroom before swimming in her pool because her dad didn't want any "Jew pee" in it.

I longed for normal. You know: the *Father Knows Best* and *Gidget* kind of normal. But "normal" did not seem to be what I was destined for. And so, at a young age, I retreated into my own whirlpool of imagination. I had an imaginary friend, "Susan," who knew the ropes and walked with me everywhere. Susan was my fashion police. She was my dark angel. My internal humorist.

To calm myself before I went to sleep at night, I would climb onto my bed, open the curtains, pull up the blinds, and talk to the moon. I had a language of signs and symbols that I would "write" on the fog-breathed window, as I told the moon all about my day, and shared my fears and my dreams. I even discussed what dress I wore that day to school and what shoes I was going to wear the next. The moon was more than a light. It was an energy that seemed to connect directly to my heart. It gave me a sense of belonging to something larger and grander that, in those days, I didn't feel at other times or in other places.

The windowpane would get smudged as I engaged in my nocturnal musings, but I didn't notice. My mom would come in the next day and ask, "Why are your windows such a mess?"

"I dunno." I'd shrug, and deny any part of the crime.

Now I'm on a plane, about to embark on what will be my life's greatest journey. I look out the window into the darkness and there

I see my old friend, the moon, guiding me to Russia, where I will meet my child and bring him home.

"My child." Those words reverberate in my mind and heart. They have always been magic for me. I had wanted to bear children, to be sure. But I had also wanted to adopt a bevy of kids. I've fantasized about this since I was a little girl. I would live on a ranch near the ocean. I'd have two biological children and a dozen or so adopted ones: all shapes, sizes, races, creeds. We'd have a mini–United Nations in our backyard. I'd be like the Old Woman Who Lived in a Shoe with so many children she didn't know what to do! Some of my kids would have disabilities: as I imagined it, one was in a wheelchair, one was blind. This didn't make me love them less. It made me love them more. Yet, had I known Neal had autism, I might have been too afraid to adopt him. Thank God I didn't know.

2.

WHEN I WENT looking for my son, I had been married nine years, though, in retrospect, I almost always felt like a single parent. My marriage had begun brightly enough, but over time, as we traveled, ate at great restaurants, and stayed in fancy hotels, our relationship seemed more like an extended Saturday-night date than a true partnership. It slowly devolved, as marriages often do, from a union into a circumstance. Union was something I yearned for; and I would find it, but only after my marriage ended.

We waited a few years before trying to conceive, never suspecting that we would have "trouble." In my mid-thirties I began to have the usual apprehensions about time running out. So we started "trying."

In those days, I was an A-list acting coach for children. A "baby wrangler" they call it. This work required me to wake up at 5:00 A.M. every morning and be on a movie set coaching young children in feature films. I totally enjoyed my work—the people, the creative energy . . . the movie magic. I got to work with the best and the brightest kids and to be around gifted adults, among them Elizabeth Taylor, Rosie O'Donnell, and Emma Thompson.

When I became pregnant, I was working on the film *The Flintstones*. I'm convinced that these two things weren't unrelated. In movies they usually cast twins to play little kids, so when one gets tired the other can work on the set. The two sets of twins who played the roles of Pebbles and Bam Bam were so absolutely adorable that I wasn't the only one who looked at them and yearned to have a child: Rosie O'Donnell adopted her first child soon after shooting ended.

Pebbles was played by a set of precocious, blond, four-year-old girls who had to dye their hair red for the role. One was named Melanie, the other Elaine. They were fun, and playful. Whenever the director called "my" name, little Elaine would run up to him. To end the confusion, the twins' mom dubbed me "Coach E." The name stuck.

Bam Bam also was played by four-year-old twins—Hlynur and Marino—who came from Iceland and were exotic-looking, with blond hair and high cheekbones. The boys were just learning English, so I became both their acting coach and, in many ways, their interpreter. When they were overstimulated by the lights, cameras, and constant activity on the set, I taught them to focus solely on me so they wouldn't get overwhelmed. I loved every minute of working on this film: imagine getting paid to go to Bedrock every day!

In this movie, Bam Bam is the adopted son of Barney and Betty Rubble. He doesn't speak except to say, "Bam, bam." Later, I would joke that Neal was my own Bam Bam: he was adopted, exotic, strong, blond, athletic, and, like the movie's Bam Bam, he spoke few words!

Midway through the *The Flintstones* shoot, I noticed that tastes had become more pronounced, and that I was exceedingly sensitive to smells. One night, while I was painting my toenails, the fumes made me nauseous. Even before the test strip turned blue, I knew that I was pregnant. I felt pregnant. I loved the feeling. There was a slight swelling in my breasts and a new energy in my heart. After years of working with other people's children, I was going to have my own.

——————————— 3. ———————————

I WENT FOR a routine physical checkup, thrilled at the prospect of seeing an ultrasound image of my baby. The doctor was enjoying my excitement. But as she scanned my belly, her face paled.

"Let me try this again," she said.

She circled the ultrasound wand over my belly. Again. Then again. There was no sign of the baby. It wasn't there. I couldn't understand this. I had taken two pregnancy tests—one at home, the other in the doctor's office, both of them positive. I knew I was pregnant.

The doctor put me through another series of tests that had a higher degree of accuracy. I lay on the table, panicked. Finally, the doctor said, "The egg is lodged in one of your fallopian tubes. You're having an ectopic pregnancy."

There was no possibility, she said, of the fetus becoming a baby. But the fetus would grow and as it did, it would burst the organ that contained it and could endanger my life. I pleaded with her to take the fetus and put it in my uterus where it was supposed to be. But that, of course, was impossible. There was only one remedy: the pregnancy would have to be terminated immediately. It was surreal. I had come into the doctor's office expecting to celebrate, and I left to be rushed into surgery. There was no time even to try to process what was going on.

Afterward, I experienced a depth of sadness that I never felt before. My friends, my mother-in-law, and my family tried to comfort me, saying the usual, "It's okay. You'll get pregnant again."

I wanted to believe them. But somehow, for some indefinable reason, I knew this wasn't true.

"Hurry and get well," they would say, "and then you'll have fun trying again."

My favorite cheer-up, from my aunt Sue, actually did make me laugh: "The best thing about having children is having children," she said. "The worst thing about having children is having children!"

But it hurt to laugh. Inside and out. So I cried. I cried a lot.

One afternoon, in the midst of this sorrow, a friend came over with her six-month-old child. She placed him in my arms. Holding her baby provided me with a sense of wholeness, of healing. I'll never forget that act of loving-kindness.

— 4. —

MY HUSBAND HAD difficulty with my sadness. My parents, when they came to visit, had never seen me so down. My dad and I usually share a joie de vivre, a sense of optimism, a light even when there is darkness. He often said that people referred to him as a Pollyanna. Me, too, I suppose. But not now, not this time.

My dad got me out of bed. Each day, he insisted we take a long walk. The incision hurt. The emotions hurt more. As we walked, my dad pointed out the beauty around us: vibrant cascades of scarlet bougainvillea, golden sunlight filtering through giant eucalyptus trees. He encouraged me to feel the warmth of the sun and the wind on my face, to pet neighborhood dogs, to smell the roses. God forbid we'd stop beside a genetically engineered rose that didn't smell. My dad had a thing about "pretty" roses that had no scent; don't get him going!

He whistled as we walked. My favorite memory of childhood was taking walks with my dad when he came home from work. It was lovely to feel small again, to be nurtured and entertained by him. All this both calmed and stirred me. Soon, I was ready to return to the world, back to work, back to Bedrock.

— 5. —

WHAT A RELIEF it was to be on a movie set again, where there is fun, lively discussion, and where the day's most important task is to get the shot, a task that is actually achievable! Combine this with being surrounded by a whole cast dressed like cartoon characters and it's impossible to feel sad.

My first day back, I rehearsed a scene where Barney Rubble is playing baseball with Bam Bam, his young adopted son. In the script, Bam Bam is supposed to hit the ball so hard that it comes soaring through the sky over Barney's head.

The challenge was that my two precious Nordic twins, Hlynur and Marino, didn't know from baseball. Soccer, yes. Baseball, no. So I had to teach them what a bat and a ball are. Then I taught them how to swing a bat and how to hit a ball, and finally, how to pretend to hit it really, really hard. Imagine the set that day with lighting designers, grips, gaffers, and me all trying to teach two little boys the fundamentals of baseball!

Looking back, I can see that it was precisely this breaking down of a task into small, dissectible parts that I would do one day with Neal, so that he could learn even the most rudimentary skills. To me, there's something preordained about the fact that so much of what I did intuitively as a kids' acting coach would come to serve me so well later.

Each day, I would think how lucky I was to have work that I found so utterly absorbing, to have colleagues who gave me such joy and support! Rosie O'Donnell as Betty Rubble was wonderful to work with. She was great with the kids. So loving and funny. You'd think the Bam Bams were really her own. I'd become very close friends with the Bam Bams' real family. They were warm and encouraging.

John Goodman as Fred Flintstone was such a nice guy. So down to earth. He would wait in line each day with the rest of the crew by the lunch truck, never playing the "star" card by insisting on being first in line. Everyone was nervous the day Elizabeth Taylor was going to be on set. Yet she was so lovely, so kind to the crew, to me, and especially to the kids. She actually pointed out to the lighting director that she was blocking Pebble's light and wanted to make certain that the little girl could be seen well! What a class act.

I worked steadily that year on a number of films, and also taught private acting classes and coached kids for several commercials. It was an engaging, active time, yet as May approached, my spirits dipped again, for May was the month in which my child would have been born. That very month—May 6, 1994, to be precise—a child was born in Russia and named Nial. As things turned out, he was my child, though it would be a while before I knew this.

— 6. —

MY DOCTOR INSISTED that I undergo a series of tests to determine what went wrong with my pregnancy. She injected me with dye, then took pictures of my uterus and fallopian tubes. I was looking forward to this. I needed to know what had caused the problem, and I was curious to see all of my internals in living color and looking like those plastic, see-through man/woman models you put together in science class.

Here's what I learned: a normal uterus is shaped like a triangle. Mine is shaped like a "T." Usually, a woman with a T-shaped uterus can carry a child to term. However, the doctor said, my T was so small that there was no space for a fetus to develop. I stared at her, disbelieving.

She picked up my chart and read, "It says here that your mom took D.E.S. when she was carrying you."

"Yes." I knew that. I also knew that D.E.S was given to women in the 1950s to guard against miscarriages or premature deliveries.

"Didn't anyone ever tell you," the doctor asked, "that if your mother took D.E.S. there's a small but distinct possibility that your uterus will be T-shaped?"

I continued to stare. Here we go again, something about me is not normal.

"No," I said finally. "No one told me."

In the following weeks, I did my best to come to terms with the impossible. I went to movies with friends, took yoga classes, and attended a therapy support group. I told myself it was going to be okay.

I thought, there has to be some purpose in this pain. Many people go through life without having children. I'm busy; I have a lot of good stuff on my plate. I'll be fine.

Yet at work, on a movie set, a two-year-old in a tutu would send me into tears. It just didn't make sense. I had worked with children all my life. Why wouldn't God want me to give birth?

In the evenings, I would sit by the window, staring at the moon, waiting for it to guide me in a new direction. The same thoughts went through my mind night after night: I will never pass on my grandfather's gray-blue eyes, my grandmother's creamy skin, my dad's musical ability, my mom's warmth and kindness.

Friends suggested that I try a surrogate pregnancy. However, in order to impregnate a surrogate, you must first take fertility drugs to increase the number of eggs that might be fertilized. After the effects of D.E.S. on my body, I was afraid to put more drugs into my system, even though the jury is still out as to whether or not the combination of these drugs can cause future harm to a woman's body or to the unborn child.

It also felt a little hubristic for me to deem my genes so critical to the human race that I needed to artificially ensure that they would be propagated. "No," I'd say, trying to joke, "I don't want to try surrogacy. Any child born to my husband and me is bound to be cursed with his proclivities for accidents and my lousy sense of direction."

When I wasn't attempting jokes, I was raging. I raged at God, at fate, at the pharmaceutical industry.

-------------------- 7. --------------------

YOU WOULD NEVER have guessed my actual mood had you seen me then, out in the world, where I always managed to maintain a positive aura. I started work on a new sitcom, *Grace Under Fire,* coaching toddler twins. They were absolutely beautiful boys, with golden hair and a beautiful energy and light around them.

Television has a different flavor than film. There are shorter hours, and longer employment. Generally speaking, the week on a sitcom goes like this: day 1 is a read-through of the script; days 2, 3, and 4 are for rehearsals onstage; on the evening of day 5, they shoot the episode with three cameras on a live sound stage in front of a full audience.

The producers of *Grace Under Fire* had called me in to fix a difficult situation. Apparently, whenever one of the twins was called onto the set for a taping, he started to cry, making it impossible to shoot as well as embarrassing the actress who was playing their mother. What I realized in a very short time was that, in the hustle and bustle of the production schedule, time had never been set aside for the actress "mom" to get to know her theatrical "babes."

The only time they saw each other was under the pressure of lights-camera-action. So I just arranged some private quiet play and bonding time with no one else around on the set, just the "mother" and one twin at a time. We also worked it out for the kids to be taped earlier than the rest of the cast so only they and their "mother" would be on the set without the pressure of an audience. From then on, there was never a tear. And those boys were on their way to becoming major, future heartthrobs for adolescent girls.

I LOVED THIS new job, the kids, their parents. At work I was happy. Yet at home, where contact with my husband was increasingly strained, I would lie on the couch, crying and alone, a secretly emotional mess staring into the middle distance. Here I am, I would think, Coach E—the person everyone relies on to be joyful and positive.

I couldn't stand being depressed and was embarrassed by my inability to snap out of it. One day, as I was lying on the couch, literally in the fetal position, I heard a voice inside me cry out, "ENOUGH! No more despairing! Get out of the dumps!"

Until now, I never wallowed in self-pity. My way of being in the world was to seek solutions rather than to stay stuck in the problem. Okay, okay, I told myself, It's time to get into action. And being a "multimodality" kind of girl, I chose to push out of this grief in a variety of ways.

First, I called my friend Kathleen, who is a professional storyteller. I asked if she would help me create a ceremony that would give me some sense of closure about my unborn child. She agreed. We met near her home in the Santa Monica Mountains and hiked to a beautiful oak grove. Under the glistening sunshine, I literally danced my grief, creating a physical interpretation of my sorrow and loss. We then "buried" my unborn child at the foot of an old oak tree. It was a solemn yet joyous ritual, full of respect for the miracle that is life and for the inevitability that is death.

As the wind blew through the trees, I heard the whispers of my grandmothers and aunts, several of whom had died when I was a child. In their Eastern European accents, they guided me to heal, to move on, to let go and be part of life again.

Next, I met with my holistic doctor, who is also one of my spiritual mentors. "Elaine," he said, "you've been pregnant in many lifetimes. In this lifetime you have other lessons to learn. Soon they will become apparent."

8.

MY DAD CAME to visit again. As always, I marveled at how connected he is to the simple, lovely aspects of life. He would say, "Let's get some chocolate ice cream," or "Let's go to the beach and collect seashells," or "Hey, listen to the radio, they're playing Louis Armstrong's 'Wonderful World.'" My dad has a genius for finding joy, for recognizing the most fundamental and satisfying ways to be happy.

We went to Back on the Beach, one of my favorite spots for lunch, and one of the few reasonably priced restaurants in L.A. where you can order a sandwich while actually sitting on the beach. Normally, with sand on my feet, waves crashing, and my beloved, playful dad sitting across from me, I would be in great spirits.

"Dad," I asked, "will I always feel this sad?"

"The sadness will always be there, sweetheart," he said, "but you will have so much joy around your heart that you will have to search for it."

I believed him. My dad is the wisest person I have ever known. I guess that it's no mistake that his name is Solomon.

With all this support and healing, I began to trust that there really was a purpose to my pain. I had faith that the pain would lead me from where I was to wherever I needed to be.

Still, I wasn't quite ready to take the actions required to move on. For me, action always starts from an internal motivator. As much as my dad's message gave me hope, it didn't yet solve an essential dilemma.

9.

MY JEWISH TRADITION dictates "Be fruitful and multiply." I could do neither. And I thought of little else at the start of the Jewish high holidays when we celebrate Rosh Hashanah, the Jewish New Year. For this holiday, there is a traditional reading that tells of Hannah and her inability to give birth. Hannah goes to the temple every year and prays to God to give her a child. One year she prays, "If you give me a son, I will give him back to you, to serve you all his days."

She prays with such intensity this time that her mouth moves but words do not come out. Her prayer is so fervent that the high priest mistakenly thinks she is drunk. She tells him that she is not drunk but that she is pouring her heart out to God. When he sees her authenticity, he apologizes and gives her a blessing. Soon after, she gives birth to a baby boy. She names him Samuel, which means "asked from God." When Samuel grew up, Hannah kept her promise and brought him to the temple to be of service to God.

During the New Year's religious service, I cried Hannah's tears. My rabbi saw me crying. He gave me the Torah to hold. This was startling. In the strict reaches of the Jewish faith, where I was raised, the Torah—the Holy Book of God—is held only by men.

The Torah is huge: nearly three feet high and a foot wide. I did not know how to hold it. My rabbi saw me struggling. He told me, "Hold it like a baby."

Later, I met with the rabbi. I confided to him what I had been unable to communicate to anyone else. "All my life, I have felt like an outsider. As a child I could not fit in because I was Jewish; now I don't even fit into Judaism. I cannot be fruitful nor can I multiply. I am a failure as a Jewish woman."

He asked if I had considered surrogacy, and I told him my true feelings about this. I also said that since there are so many kids in the world who need a family, why would I feel the need to conceive artificially? Why wouldn't I want to adopt one of the unwanted children?

So the rabbi asked the obvious: "Why not adopt?"

"Because," I insisted, "I am stuck. I am stuck on my command as a Jewish woman. I am not fruitful."

The rabbi was comforting. Being fruitful and multiplying, he said, does not need to be taken literally. The creative work I do with children is being fruitful. The plays that I've written for children's drama groups, the programs I've created to enhance the self-esteem and self-expression of children are all ways of being fruitful. The ways that we give to the world, such as teaching, or nursing, or volunteer work, or any way of doing good deeds—all of this brings fruit into the world.

He said that, in ancient times, we needed to multiply to help our families in the fields. Lots of bodies were required for that kind of work. More recently, with so many Jewish lives lost, it was important to multiply to keep our culture going.

But he also told me something that I had never heard before, something that would change my life forever. He said that adopting a child is among the greatest blessings in the Jewish tradition.

"To adopt," he said, "is to be fruitful and beyond multiplying." With that, I understood where I was being led. The rabbi had solved my dilemma. I told him, "I am going to adopt a child."

Suddenly, where there were no possibilities, the possibilities were endless.

When I make a decision, I become unstoppable. That, for as long as I can remember, has been my chief asset . . . and principal liability. As soon as I decided to adopt a child, every remnant of depression left me. In its place came excitement, wonderment, reading books, talking to people who had adopted, talking to people who had been adopted, going to workshops, researching, gaining information. What became clear to me was that I didn't want to adopt an infant here in the United States where there are many prospective parents looking for infants. In fact, with infertility rates rising, there are waiting lists of people who want to adopt infants. My feeling was that if I was not able to give birth biologically, then there had to be some meaning in the struggle. I wanted to adopt a child that most people didn't want. I wanted an older child, a toddler that would be around the same age as my child, had it come to term.

I prayed to God and asked for guidance. I prayed that my child would come into my arms. Finally, I felt like myself again: the person who'd been given the I Dare You award in high school because I'd refused to acknowledge any limits.

10.

ADOPTING IS NOT a simple process. In addition to endless paperwork, there are background checks, and personal and financial evaluations. You need letters of recommendation. And you have to write pages on why you want to parent a child. I loved this. It should be required, I thought, of every prospective parent.

God should say, "Okay, you want to have a baby—take this exam first and see if you qualify." Wouldn't that be an interesting change? How many fewer unwanted children would there be, how many fewer abused and neglected children? How many fewer drug addicts, depressives, and inmates would exist if their parents had to ask themselves why they wanted their child before they conceived?

The main adoption center in Los Angeles is Vista del Mar Child and Family Services. It's been described as the "last place you want to need and the first place you call." To adopt through Vista del Mar, you're required to attend a six-week workshop where you can process your feelings and concerns about the adoption process. This workshop is much like a support group, in which each member helps the others through pending adoptions. One couple I met there, Alice and Greg, still among my closest friends, adopted two children from China.

On my first day at Vista, I was walking down a long hallway when I passed a sign that gave the time for a presentation about Russian and Eastern European adoptions. I knew instantly that I wanted to attend. My heritage is Russian. If I couldn't actually pass down my family's genetic history, at least I could connect with the place from which they came.

At the first presentation, parents talked about how swiftly their Russian-born children adapted to American culture. Within two months, they marveled, their children were speaking perfect English and singing Disney songs. "Wow!" I thought. "Instant preschoolers."

Other stories had a different flavor. One woman had adopted a little Russian girl who had no legs. She spoke of Russian kids with special needs. If they are not adopted, she said, they are sent away as adults to horrible conditions.

Another woman recalled the day that she was to take her Russian child home. That very afternoon, she had learned that the little girl had heart disease.

"How do you feel about the child?" her mother had asked.

"I love her," she said.

"Then she's your child," said her mother. This story remained with me.

"How great is the power of love," I thought. Once you know a child is yours, you accept them whether they are sick or well. That child is your child. When I, too, came to love a Russian child with special needs, the story of this woman would bring me comfort. It brought to mind my childhood fantasy in which I had tons of kids, some with special needs—every one of them special. I left that first meeting knowing that I would adopt a child from Russia. Fortunately, my husband agreed.

Within weeks of completing the paperwork, I was receiving manila envelopes from an international adoption agency, each of them filled with photographs of dozens of kids. I had learned that, for several years, the doors to Russian adoptions had been closed. Now they were recently opened, and there were hundreds of children just waiting for a family to adopt them.

In the photographs, I saw the faces of real children who were alone in the world. I looked at each picture with curiosity and love. These were sweet children. Still, I would look at a picture and say, "That's not my child."

One photograph that gave me pause was of a boy with strong, handsome features. He was about three years old and had an angular face, and a strong jaw. Alex was his name. Yet while I admired his beauty, I knew that he wasn't mine.

A few weeks after I began looking at pictures, my husband and I flew to Washington, D.C., where we would meet with the director of the international adoption agency. In the course of this meeting, I would find my son.

11.

IN MY RUSSIAN-JEWISH culture, dreams are not merely fleeting nighttime fancies. They hold meanings used to make predictions and important decisions. Take the story of Joseph and the coat of many colors. His brothers hate him because he tells them a dream of his future greatness, yet this same talent for dreaming and dream interpretation garners the attention of the Pharaoh and allows Joseph to rise to an esteemed position in Egypt.

Learning from Joseph, I've always given credence to my dreams, my visions. I've even felt the presence of unseen beings surrounding me. I know this sounds a bit bizarre. Believe or disbelieve as you may—but this is my truth. It's something I've lived.

On the morning of our meeting at the international adoption center, a strange thing happened. In the predawn hours, as I drifted between consciousness and sleep, I became aware of three beings standing in my room. Somehow, I knew that they were angels, though they didn't have wings or long white robes or halos like you see in movies. But they did have an aura that was holy, peaceful, and nurturing.

The first was a man who wore doctor's scrubs. The second, also a man, looked like Paul McCartney. The third was a dark-haired woman with an intense but loving manner.

I felt their presence for a moment. Before I fell back to sleep, I said aloud, "There are angels in this room." I wanted to mark the moment as a truth. At sunrise, I awoke feeling joyous, centered, and serene. Unbelievable as it may seem, in my real, waking life, I would see each of these angels again.

----------------------------------- 12. -----------------------------------

SHORTLY BEFORE THE meeting with the director of the international adoption agency, I felt a sharp cramp, as if someone had socked me in the stomach. Then the pain was gone.

"It's nothing," I told my husband. Thinking I was getting my period, which was a few days overdue, it seemed logical that I was having menstrual cramps. It was easy to ignore them. The only thing that mattered was the meeting.

The director showed us a scrapbook filled with more photographs of children. There were pages and pages of wide-eyed, beautiful kids. Girls, boys, all sizes and shapes. These children had already been adopted. The point was to get a sense of what sort of child I was looking for.

As I looked through the book, I kept being drawn to the boys. Especially boys of around two or so years old.

She showed us two videos of two little boys. One was very active, talkative, and had a cleft palate. The other had blond hair, large dark eyes, and a sweet yet serious expression. I looked at the video of this second boy three or four times. His name was Nial. Though I didn't know why, I was especially drawn to him.

Yet, I also noticed that he didn't walk well. This troubled me.

"But he's so beautiful," my husband said.

I looked at the video again. At one point, Nial's shoe fell off. He sat down and put his bare foot up against the camera lens. It was as if he was saying, hey, help me out here. It was charming. The more I looked, the more I felt for him. This was a child I could love to hold, to play with, to nurture.

We decided to show the video to our pediatrician and to several other doctors back home. We'd call the international adoption agency in a week, we promised, and let them know our decision. As we were about to leave the office, my cramps returned with a vengeance.

I called my doctor in Los Angeles. "Do not get on the plane," she told me. "With your history, this may be another ectopic pregnancy."

She insisted that I call a local doctor immediately. I picked a number from the phone book at random. The doctor turned out to be the head of gynecological surgery at George Washington University Hospital.

Twenty minutes later, in the emergency room, the doctor confirmed that I was suffering another ectopic pregnancy. One of my fallopian tubes was bursting. Had I gotten on the plane, I could have died. He said that he would have to operate immediately. As I was about to be given the anesthesia, he asked for permission to tie my tubes.

"I don't want this to ever happen to you again," he said.

I gave the permission. How kind he seemed, this doctor in scrubs. How fortunate that I had picked his name out of hundreds in the phone book. I took a long look at him and was amazed by what I saw. He was the first angel from my dream.

After surgery, I was taken to a private room. When I awoke from the anesthesia, the first thing I saw was Nial. His little face looked down on me from the television on the wall. My husband had taken the videotape of him and had it put on a loop so that it could play over and over. As I looked at Nial, I felt as if I had given birth. There he was, that adorable little boy. If I had had any doubts before, they were completely gone. This was my son.

I was so grateful to my husband. Now, when I look back at the intense challenges of our marriage, I recall this time and his capacity for selfless acts of kindness.

Gazing into Nial's solemn hazel eyes, I knew that I had a single mission: to get well so that I could travel to Russia and pick him up.

"Please," I said to friends who called from Los Angeles, "say healing prayers for me."

Two days later, I was wheeled out of the hospital. I held on to the video as if I were holding on to my child. It was as if I had had a cesarean birth and was leaving the hospital with my baby. My belly ached from the surgery. But my spirits were high.

—————————————— 13. ——————————————

AT HOME, I rested and regained strength. Friends brought me breakfasts, dinners, and lunches. I was consumed with going to Russia and adopting Nial. I dreamed about him every night. I felt that we were "meeting" each other in our dream state. I felt a powerful energy in my heart unlike anything I'd ever experienced.

Some of my friends expressed concern that I was jumping too quickly into adopting Nial. "You need more time," they would tell me, "both emotionally and physically."

I didn't listen. I couldn't listen. This was my child and I knew it.

STILL, THE CONCERNS remained. I was reluctant to share them, so as not to alarm others. I had not forgotten that Nial didn't walk well. I showed the video of him to several doctors, as planned. I was afraid they would tell me not to adopt him when, in my heart, he was already mine. One, my pediatrician friend Sandy, worried about the possibility of cerebral palsy. Another expressed concern that Nial was not speaking, although he was almost two years old. I knew I had to listen to the professionals. This meant we would not adopt him. I sank into intense depression. I wanted this boy. I wanted Nial.

I became determined to adopt him. "Slow down," my friends urged me. My neighbor, born and raised in Russia, was full of dire warnings: many Russians are alcoholics, he said, prior to commencing an endless lecture about fetal alcohol syndrome. This got my attention. I showed the video to specialists who reassured me that Nial did not have the appearance of an alcohol-damaged child.

To allay my few lingering doubts, we arranged a phone consultation with a Russian interpreter and "Doctor Maria," administrator of the orphanage in which Nial lived. Doctor Maria was a combination of warm and friendly mixed with tough and to the point. She was the first person I spoke to who actually knew Nial. I listened intently to her answers as I asked the relevant questions.

"Is Nial able to walk?"

"He is running around in front of me right now," said Doctor Maria.

"Does he have any significant developmental delays?"

"Nothing more," she said "than any other children here."

That was that. Decision made! The international agency let me know that the orphanage was in serious need of essentials: first-aid creams, Band-Aids, alcohol, ointments, aspirin, cough medicine, vitamins. You name it, I bought it. I also bought a T-shirt with an American flag on it and tiny sneakers and jeans for Nial.

I was told to bring "American gifts" to give to the caretakers at the orphanage and to the government workers who would be processing and signing our paperwork. On Venice Beach, I bought California-themed T-shirts and sweatshirts, and Gap jeans. Russia was in the early stages of glasnost; with communism ending, anything that sug-gested the West was a prized commodity. So I bought T-shirts and mugs from the CBS sound studio where I worked, and lots of movie posters and posters of rock-and-roll bands.

The night before I was to leave, I panicked. I couldn't pack. My friend Liza came over. She had made a journey similar to the one I was about to embark on when she went to China to adopt a little girl. Daniela, then three years old, was a beautiful, talented, terrific "poster" child for adopting internationally. Liza and Daniela had long been my inspiration.

"What if I'm not up to this?" I asked her.

"Look," she said, "your friends are here for you. We are here for you now. We're here for you if you choose to bring a child back. And we're going to be here for you if you come back without a child. So get on that plane. And enjoy the ride."

14.

NOW, ON THE plane, I recall Liza's words. I think of my grandfather who began life, as Nial had, as an orphan in Russia. My grandfa-ther had come to America on his own when he was fourteen years old. He spoke no English, but carried with him an abiding belief in the dream that America represented. Even as a young man he was a spiritual, religious being. As he aged, he became known as one of the most honest men in Washington, D.C. He took pride in the fact that he always paid cash and never owed anyone anything.

Every Sunday we went to his house for dinner. I would sit at his feet and he would tell stories about his life that gave me hope and taught me to share his view that anything is possible. After dinner we watched *The Lawrence Welk Show* and then I'd put on a show for him, directing my older brother and younger sister to perform the songs and dances we'd just seen.

My grandfather loved these shows. He'd watch us with a big smile on his face and a twinkle in his gray-blue eyes. He died when I was thirteen. My father told me that in his final moments, my grandfather had looked up into the sky and asked, "Sol, is this the Yiddisha Gut?" using the Yiddish words for "Jewish God."

"I guess so, Pop," my dad replied.

"Good," said my grandfather.

Then he smiled one final time. He closed his eyes. That was it. Good-bye.

Now, here I am, heading halfway across the world to adopt my child from the same part of the world that my beloved grandfather came from.

------------------------------ 15. ------------------------------

WE ARRIVE IN Moscow in the early evening. That night, my husband and I stay in the Savoy Hotel, a spectacular place where everything that isn't gilded is crystal. Unable to sleep, I sit at the window, staring at the moon, willing the hours to pass. Morning cannot come quickly enough. In the morning we will fly to Yekaterinburg, in the Ural Mountains of Siberia, where I will meet my son.

Yekaterinburg is one of the largest cities in Russia. Many extremely intelligent and talented people live there because Siberia is where many artists and intellectuals were sent when they spoke out against the Soviet government. Yekaterinburg is also a town with a distinct history. It is named for a member of the Russian royal family, Catherine the Great, and it is where Catherine's great-grandson, Tsar

Nicolas II, was killed by Bolsheviks. Also killed that night were the tsar's wife and four daughters—including Anastasia, later rumored to have been the rout's sole survivor—and the heir to the Russian throne, the young Tsarevitch Alexei.

Reaching Yekaterinburg from Moscow is none too pleasant. In the Russian airport, the X-ray machines are so old that I can hear them. The sound they make is an ominous *k-clink, k-clink, k-clink.* I've been told to pack snacks, as the food in Russia is expensive and not especially tasty. I've packed boxes of cereals, granola bars, bags of pretzels and chips, but the machine dispenses a level of radiation so extreme that it contaminates my snacks and makes them inedible.

The plane is terrifyingly dinky. It features lumpy, narrow seats, no seat belts, and no overhead bins to keep luggage stable. As we chug along through the air, luggage shifts noisily above our heads.

Yet, amazingly, the food served on the plane is absolutely fantastic. I cut into my chicken Kiev and watch my plate fill with melted, golden butter. "Everything must be okay," I tell myself, "'cause we're going to eat well."

We land at a tiny airport. No one speaks English. It seems to me that other travelers regard us with suspicion. Outside, everything is dark, gray, and icy. I look for the greeter from The International Children's Alliance. He isn't here.

For an hour and a half, I walk aimlessly through the terminal, trying to spot a friendly hostlike face. I am met with glares that make me uncomfortable. I have no phone number to call. I don't even know the name of the person I am supposed to meet. As the minutes tick by, my panic increases. I go into the bathroom and pray. "Dear God," I say, "please help. Show me what to do."

The moment I walk out of the bathroom, I see a sweet-faced man standing a few feet away, holding a sign with my name on it. His name is Alexei. He apologizes profusely for being late and says that when he didn't see me at the gate something compelled him to go and wait outside the bathroom.

My prayer has been answered. I realize that this is a sign to remember. I am not in charge here. God is in charge. I am going to be okay.

I keep looking at Alexei. He seems so familiar. Then I realize why. He looks like a forty-something Paul McCartney. He's the second angel from my dream.

16.

THE ORPHANAGE IS an old redbrick building surrounded by a high metal gate. The yard is piled high with soot-blackened snow. It is April, spring to Siberians, but winter to me. I am wearing layer upon layer of clothes: thermal leggings under my ski pants, a turtleneck, a sweater, scarf, hat, and parka.

Suddenly, fifteen naked toddlers come darting across the porch. I am startled and amused by this unexpected scene. I will soon learn that running in the dirt-crusted snow is part of their daily health regimen. It looks like they are having fun; the cold doesn't seem to bother them.

Inside the orphanage, all is bright. Walls are painted in rich colors; there are elaborate murals and elegant Persian carpets, accoutrements befitting an institution known as a favorite charity of Boris Yeltsin's wife.

The place is a curious mixture of new and old; I had been told that the children's histories are stored in the "vault." I pictured this vault as a giant steel fortress with a huge lock. But the "vault" turns out to be a couple of state-of-the-art Pentium-chip computers.

I am met in the office by a petite, dark-haired woman. Her name is Anastasia. She is the social worker responsible for connecting overseas prospective parents with children in the orphanage. As she extends her hand, we move closer and, instead, we embrace. I look at her and realize that she is the embodiment of the third angel from my dream.

I feel that she and I are family. She tells me a little about Nial. She says he is their favorite. She's not sure how he will respond to new people. But they have been preparing him.

In a few minutes that seemed like an eternity, she reenters the office, holding the tiny hand of a blond-haired "little man" dressed in black-and-white plaid overall shorts. As soon as he walks into that room, any concerns or doubts I have harbored evaporate instantly. He seems so familiar. I feel as if I have known him his entire life and that I am just remeeting him, or picking him up after day care.

Nial is beautiful. He gazes at me, timid, reticent, and curious, all at the same time. He is tiny, the size of a one-year-old. Here is my child. My son. I truly believe that all my years of working with children have led me to this place, this child.

I don't force myself on Nial. I ask if we can move into another room, one that's familiar to him, as he seems a bit overwhelmed and uneasy with all the office equipment. Turns out this perception is accurate: he's never been in that space.

They take us to a large playroom where there's a Persian rug and a piano. Nial is still holding Anastasia's hand. I sit on the rug, away from them, giving him space. I am bursting with love, yet I know better than to push myself on him. I sit and I wait. I look at him. Nial looks at me. In a moment, he runs into my arms. I fall over backward, gleeful, and we roll together on the floor. We laugh, we play, we giggle, we coo. We hold each other. No longer strangers, we are playmates. We are mother and child. This is the most wondrous moment I've ever experienced. I believe in love at first sight.

Later that day, I learn more about Nial: he was born prematurely, with no oxygen to his brain. He weighed three pounds. At three months old, he contracted pneumonia and severe ear infections. He remained in a hospital for six months. Imagine that degree of isolation. Imagine the loneliness, the sense of abandonment. Did anyone ever hold him, or run their fingers through his hair, or caress his face or stroke his brow?

Any child born seven weeks prematurely has a difficult time, even with two devoted parents sitting by the incubator day and night, watching over their ailing infant, praying for his survival. Imagine that same infant with no parents, subsisting for months in a lighted box, shut off from a world in which no one cares if he lives or dies. Yet Nial lived. And now, here he is, this amazing, valiant, tiny survivor who triumphed over an impossible beginning only to be delivered into my arms.

———————————— 17. ————————————

I HATE LEAVING Nial at the orphanage, even for a night. Yet there are procedures that must be followed and I have no choice. For distraction, we go to a concert. Though my husband sits beside me, I feel alone. The hall is packed. I look around at the gathering crowd. I am seized by a single thought: Nial's biological mother is here. I visualize her. She is tall, beautiful, with classic features and thick blond hair. I am curious as to what she might say or do. I want to thank her, to help her if I can. How I wish that I could go home with her and see her other children, the seven that she kept.

I fantasize about what it would be like to meet her. Would she detail for me Nial's family history, that vanished trail of health, hopes, and striving, of holidays shared, of summers spent, of birthdays, weddings, and burials? Would she be like the other people I've met here in Yekaterinburg, inhabitants of a cold land who are now proving to be the warmest people I've ever met?

When I return the next morning, I begin to see the orphanage for what it is. Sure, there are Pentium-chip computers, gilded furniture, and Persian carpets. But there is terrible scarcity and need amid the unnecessary splendor. I learn that more than one hundred children are living here.

They do not allow visitors to see beyond the office area, the eating area, and the common playroom. I can only imagine what the living conditions are. Dozens of little beds, side by side in one sparse room.

I know that there are not enough clothes for the children, since Nial is dressed today in a girl's blouse and shorts.

The food they feed the kids is a huge pot of clear "slop." The kids are taught at a young age to feed themselves with a spoon. When they eat they look like little robots. There are not enough hands to go around so that they can be fed in the way that most babies are fed. There is no "open wide," no "here comes the airplane into the hangar." These kids fight for their food, for every morsel. As soon as the bowl of "slop" is poured into their bowl, they dig in and devour it.

When we get Nial home, I will let him play with his food with his hands since he has never had this luxury. It will take years before he can execute the necessary steps needed to reach for a fork, put the prongs into a piece of chicken, and place it into his mouth without the food falling off onto the plate or the floor.

The Russian nurses at the orphanage are warm and loving, but there are not enough of them. The children don't get diapers because there aren't enough staff members to change the diapers. Potty training starts at age one: every child squats on a potty at the same time. Children who mess their pants are punished. Yet they don't cry. Orphaned children don't cry because they've learned that their cries will go unnoticed.

Some of these children are born with AIDS. Others suffer from maladies so severe that, if not adopted soon, they will die. I watch Nial among these children. He is controlled. One of the masses. A good little soldier. Like the others, Nial has old eyes.

These children have been required to develop self-sufficiency as toddlers; they have experienced way too much. They look like little Holocaust survivors. They are lost souls, obeying all commands, all hoping, looking, longing for something, someone to hold them, embrace them, to heal their sorrows, their loneliness, to take them home. I can see them looking over at me. Many have dark eyes and black hair. They are children of Gypsies, I am told. If I could, I would bring all of them home with me. I want them all. Every child.

One dark-haired girl approaches me, she circles around in a dance-like fashion, then forlornly shoots me an expression that says, please, take me home. I learn later that she is one of those born with AIDS. For months to come, I will see her and the others in my dreams, where they will appear as gentle, heartbreaking apparitions.

18.

YEKATERINBURG IS A whirlwind of taxis, paperwork, and borscht. Before I can take Nial home, I need to fill out a mountain of official documents and go through a series of steps that leave me feeling like a character in a Russian spy novel.

"You will see a tall woman with blond hair waiting beside a black taxi," I am told. "She will have your papers. You will walk to the steps of the large gray building. At the steps you will meet a woman named Svetlana. She will be wearing a black coat and a red hat. Sveta will give you a blue notebook with green papers in it. Take the papers to the second floor. Someone will be waiting for you." That's how it went.

To adopt a child from a Russian orphanage every single document you're required to fill in must have an official stamp. In each department, only one individual is authorized to use that stamp. Many papers must be signed. And they need to be signed in order. If you miss one document or if someone is on leave or on vacation or out sick, you must wait for them to return and sign the requisite paper before your child can be released. The "gifts" that the international adoption agency told me to bring—those previously mentioned T-shirts, baseball caps from movies and television shows, and souvenirs of Venice Beach—are actually "incentives" to make sure all the paperwork goes through.

Three days after my first meeting with Nial, every single document is duly stamped and signed. Apparently, the government workers like our Hollywood paraphernalia. I am beyond relieved. I had heard maddening stories: one family had to wait in Russia for a month to get a single document stamped and signed. Evidently, the official who was supposed to stamp it had a death in the family and didn't come to work for a month. Finally, the head of the international agency flew from Washington, D.C., to Russia, found the guy's home address, and brought the papers to his house.

The night before I am to pick Nial up, I am sleepless again. Having learned that he was born prematurely, that no oxygen flowed to his brain at birth, I'm faced with the fact that now, at two years old, he does not speak except to utter a few random sounds. Am I doing the right thing to bring him home? Can my already troubled marriage handle the added stress of a child, especially a child who may have special needs? That night, I write down my hopes and fears. I write to God. I ask for guidance.

"Dear God," I begin. "Please tell me what to do. I am scared. I feel alone. Can I do this? Am I up to this?"

In the wee hours of the morning, the answer comes. As I write my question, the answers flow through my fingers to my pen. "Yes, yes. You must bring Nial home. This will not be without sacrifice, but it will bring you the greatest joy you have ever known."

I awake with confidence that this is meant to be. This is my journey, my destiny, my spiritual quest. He is my son, already. In my heart and in my soul, I know that whatever my fate, whatever God puts in front of me, I am willing to accept it.

----------------------- 19. -----------------------

I ARRIVE AT the orphanage in the morning, bringing with me some new clothes and a tiny, bright orange snowsuit that once belonged to my nephew. The clothing that Nial is wearing will remain at the orphanage where other children need it.

I want to take something of his from the orphanage as a memory for him. But he has nothing of his own. I ask what his favorite toy is. It's a box of Lego-like building bricks. They let me take them. I don't know why this is so important to me. I guess I just want him to know that he had a life before me, and that this life was valid. I dress Nial for the very first time. I'm awkward as I take off his little secondhand clothes and put him in his Gap jeans and American flag T-shirt. He looks so cute. Like an all-American boy. Nial is uncomplaining, helpful.

How do I put these little socks on him? Oh dear. I haven't ever dressed a toddler before. On the shoots I work on, the kids come in all diapered and dressed. I am a novice. I tell Nial that I am new to this and ask him for patience. He seems to understand me. Already.

This, the first mother-type thing I have done with him, feels so natural and yet so foreign. I enjoy every single second of the ritual and take deep pleasure in the symbolism of pulling off his old clothes, and putting him in these new ones. Over his T-shirt and jeans, I put him into the orange snowsuit. The suit doubles his girth. He looks like a miniature astronaut crossed with the Pillsbury dough boy.

I take his hand. We walk out the front door. We turn back to look at the orphanage one final time. We wave back to the nurses who look on from the windows, waving good-bye. I wonder how many children they care for and love and feed and bathe, only to say farewell to them?

Nial looks back at the nurses. As we drive away from the orphanage to the airport, he gazes at them through the car window with a bewildered look on his face.

———————————————— 20. ————————————————

IN MOSCOW WE go directly to the American embassy. It is time to deliver all the signed, sealed papers to them so that Nial can travel to the United States. While we wait our turn to get his passport, Nial stands patiently in the line beside me.

We watch other Russian citizens get their photos taken and sign papers for their passports. Soon it is our turn. There, without being told, Nial goes directly to the chair where he will have his passport picture taken. He sits there, like a Hollywood actor awaiting his close-up.

The passport people tell me they've never seen anything like it. They ask me to spell his name. "N-E-A-L," I say.

From now on, Nial is officially Neal. Neal, since it is close to the name Nial. Neal is also the name of the sweet, loving rabbi—Neil Comess Daniels—who encouraged me to adopt. How perfect, I think, for Neal's name to have such a lovely association. Also, it is a name with a Celtic origin and has several meanings: "Champion" or "Cloud," or "Passionate One." Well, he truly is a champion and is quite passionate. His aura is cloudlike. The name fits him perfectly.

His middle name will be Weston, which is the maiden name of Neal's new paternal grandmother. I also like it because of "West," as in Neal is going West. Go West, young man. Neal will later be given a Jewish name, Mordechai, named after my grandfather Marcus (Mordechai) Goldenberg. Throughout the day Neal stays by my side, as if we'd been a family forever.

In the late afternoon, we enter the ornate lobby of a magnificent hotel. It is an extraordinary place, with massive crystal chandeliers, golden ormolu sideboards, and ornate enameled vases. Neal walks in smiling, as if he owns the place. I imagine him saying, "Yes, I have come to where I belong."

Neal has the eyes and bearing of an adult. When we enter the hotel restaurant, people literally stop and stare and comment on his beauty. At one point, the prime minister of Canada, who is visiting Russia on official business, comes over to Neal and says hello. I can't believe his manner: it's not like he's talking to a child. It's as if he's paying tribute to a head of state. Neal seems perfectly at home there, so comfortable with his new social status; he's like a little prince who's returning home in glory after a war. Much later, I entertain the fanciful thought that my beautiful boy, who was born in the town in which the thirteen-year-old tsarevitch Alexei was murdered, is the reincarnation of the young Russian prince. Silly thought. Still, I can't help noting that the woman who brought Neal to me at the orphanage was named Anastasia—the name of the prince's older sister—and that my airport angel was named Alexei. Weird coincidence? I wonder. Or merely coincidence? Or merely weird?

21.

ON THE PLANE ride home, I hold Neal as he sleeps. We're both tired from the intensity of the past few days. He sleeps soundly as I hold him on my chest. His breath joins my breath. One would never know we'd just met.

"What a beautiful boy," says a stranger.

"He's going to be really tall," prophesizes a passing teenager, "look at the size of his feet."

This surprises me, since Neal is 90 percent below the percentile in height and weight for a boy almost two years old. Me with a tall son? Uh-oh. I'm barely four feet ten inches in high heels. Neal will surely alter the Goldenberg gene pool.

We have a four-hour stopover in Germany before boarding the plane to the United States. Neal sticks close to my side at the airport, but then waltzes away from me, a bold little adventurer. I wait to see what he will do. When he gets a few feet away from me, he scurries back.

On the plane to Los Angeles, he sleeps most of time. I feel such joy. Such peace. The years of childlessness have led to this moment. I have been waiting for Neal just as he has been waiting for me. In the coming years, I will learn that autism is defined as an inability to make human connections. Yet Neal and I are connected from the start. That connection, the force of it, will be more than simply therapeutic. It will be redemptive.

————————————————— 22. —————————————————

SUDDENLY, I AM the forty-something mother of a two-year-old child. This would be daunting were it not for the fact that years of coaching small children have lent me the confidence and experience I need. However, even with all of my training, parenting a toddler is not without challenges. Oh, how I wish sometimes that kids would come with a set of instructions.

My mom visits and helps me learn to diaper, to bathe, and to feed. I now understand why in the old country, entire families lived in the same neighborhood or even in the same building. Grandparents and uncles and aunts have already mastered how to navigate the early stages of a child's life. What is so new to me is ancient history to my mom; and we bond in a way we never have previously.

————————————————— 23. —————————————————

ONE THING I learn right away is that the day you bring your child home is the day your dog becomes a dog. Luckie is definitely my first child. She's part saluki, the breed that sultans kept in their tents to chase out rodents, and part Australian shepherd, a herding breed. At the dog park we've always had playdates with other dogs. Luckie is the fastest dog there.

She's also the smartest dog I've ever seen. Once, when a friend knocked on my front door, Luckie pushed down on the door handle and let the friend in! From that day on, I always let the door be opened by our "butler" dog.

Now I am concerned about how Neal will take to Luckie. It's no problem for Neal. But Luckie is jealous. "Who is this new creature in my territory?" Luckie sniffs Neal. I think she is wondering when this new "thing that walks on two legs" will go away.

One night, she growls at Neal. I look her straight in the eye and say sternly, "You will NEVER growl at the baby again. NEVER," and she doesn't EVER. However, like a firstborn sibling, she remains wary of Neal getting too much attention. So we find activities that Neal and Luckie can do together. We take Neal to the dog park and teach him to throw the ball for Luckie. Neal loves to watch her run and catch and play with the other dogs. We also take Luckie to our local kids' park.

Neal is still not accustomed to all the goings-on at the park. My mother-in-law, his grandma Dorothy, helps him walk in the sandbox. My dad will help him learn to swing. One day my husband and I bring Luckie and Neal to the park and try to teach Neal how to climb up the ladder and go down the slide. He secures Luckie on her leash to a nearby tree.

"Neal, just put one foot on the step and then bring the other one up to it," I direct. Cautiously, Neal takes one foot after the other but gets stuck at the top and will not go down. Finally, Neal summons up his courage—he walks up the slide himself and slides down to the bottom.

"Yay, Yay! Neal!" I applaud, jumping up and down.

Luckie has had it. She's tired of Neal getting all the attention. She wiggles out of her leash, runs up the ladder, and slides herself down, awaiting her own applause! What a dog!

----------------------- 24. -----------------------

IN ADDITION TO being very small, Neal walks bowlegged and is more like a new walker than most children his age. He also has high fevers and green gook coming out of his nose. I take him to two doctors, a homeopathic practitioner and a traditional pediatrician. From them I learn that Neal has parasites, liver toxicity, scurvy, and malnutrition. Given what I saw at the orphanage this is no surprise.

The state of Neal's health concerns me, but I'm not alarmed mostly because Neal doesn't seem bothered by these maladies. His energy is strong. I see him as curious, playful, and aware. I trust his process and I have great confidence in my holistic doctors. I know they will help me through this. Give him good nutrition and herbal remedies, I think, and in time Neal will become healthy and catch up. And in time, Neal did become healthy. But he did not catch up.

—————————————— 25. ——————————————

I LEARN TO ask for help early on. One day when Neal's fever is high and I am awaiting a call back from his pediatrician, I get help in calming him from my neighbor, an extremely bright and mature thirteen-year-old who wants to be a doctor when she grows up.

Although I am in a steep learning curve for the "basics" of child care, I see repeatedly the ways in which my years as a baby wrangler have prepared me for my new life. They taught me to see the world through a child's eyes; they taught me to speak to a child's highest level of intelligence. These simple yet significant precepts will be the gateway to my future.

In the days and months when most babies are coddled and cuddled, Neal had been alone in an incubator. So at night I try to give him the nurturing he's never had. I hold him in my arms, rocking him and singing to him. I hold him close to my breast like a newborn baby. I wish that I could nurse him. Instead, I snuggle him ever closer. I breathe and he breathes and our breath makes us one. Our hearts beat the same. It is as if his soul has entered my soul. In the process, something greater than either of us is created.

Each night, Neal and I run and jump and wrestle. Neal loves to play with me. We are wild and reckless. I don't notice that he doesn't look me in the eye, or that his smiles are minimal. Not ever having a child of my own for comparison, I just enjoy these special moments together.

He wraps himself in the bedroom curtain as I sing, "Where is Neal? Where is Neal?" We play like this until he goes, unbidden, and brings me the stack of flash cards my cousin gave us. I can see that

Neal wants to learn. He wants to know about this new world. The cards have pictures and words on them: dog, cat, house, sun, sky.

I hold them up and say each word. He makes a little sound and nods his head. Every night we go through the entire stack of cards. It really doesn't worry me that he cannot talk. In the morning hours, I catch him babbling. Repeating sounds: "bbbbb" and "ppppp." I am convinced that in time Neal will be just like all the other kids adopted from Russia who soon are singing Disney songs.

When we arrived home from Russia, I opened my door to find gifts from friends and family from all over the country. Baby supplies, toys, games, clothes, books. Throughout the next year, the gifts keep coming.

One of our favorites is a huge three-foot-high Richard Scarry book titled *Cars and Trucks and Things That Go.* Sometimes we use it as a wind machine: Neal loves it when I open the first big page and fan it to create wind. The rest of the time, Neal looks at the pictures. Each page has dozens of images.

I ask, "Where's the helicopter, where's the airplane, where's the fire truck, where's the bicycle?"

He always points to the right ones. That is, he always points to the right ones when I'm alone with him. As soon as I want to show off to other people how well he's doing, he won't point at all. As much as I would love for Neal to show others what he knows, I've got to admire my little guy for having the will to thwart me—his acting coach mom—by refusing to perform on cue.

One night I show Neal the moon. I hold him up to the window and point to the gleaming gray-white orb in the summer sky. Neal stares at the moon. He points to it, too. Will the moon someday be a friend we share?

That night he hugs me tight and won't let go. I feel his little arms tight around my neck. I smell the baby shampoo in his hair. It is a closeness I have longed for. The embrace lasts, and lasts. And yet, finally, the intensity is too much for me. I let go. Afterward I am

ashamed. The next morning, as soon as he awakes, I hold him tight.
I vow: I will never let go first again.

26.

NEAL LOVES TO climb up on me. When we go outside, he jumps
onto my chest and wraps his legs around my waist. He clings to me
so tight that I don't even have to use my hands to hold him. My
friends joke that we look like a monkey mom with her baby. He
makes sounds like "ee ee!" I soon call him "my little monkey."

At home the little monkey is in perpetual motion. When I'm trying
to make dinner, he's pulling on the curtains, knocking over chairs,
climbing over things. He opens and closes cabinet doors, jumps on
tables. Nothing is sacred.

When I'm watching TV, Neal does somersaults into my chest
while Luckie licks my face. So, with Neal diving into me and Luckie
licking me, we all roll and play on the floor. Not much TV watching going on.

I try to help him sit still, to focus, but I realize it is not his style. I
figure he needs this time of exploration and will eventually settle in.
To others, we must seem wild and disorganized. As I see it, we are in
our own sweet little world together.

People comment about his lack of eye contact and that his face is
absent of expression. Grandma Dorothy notices that he doesn't respond immediately to his name. Again, I am neither surprised nor
alarmed. He's been living in an orphanage; I tell myself, and others,
what do you expect?

27.

NEAL'S FAVORITE FOOD turns out to be broccoli. He stuffs it into
his mouth with his hands. He goes to bed with his cheeks full of
broccoli. Fearing that he will choke, I try to get it out of his mouth.

At the same time, I understand what he's doing: he's storing and hoarding food because there was never enough to eat in the orphanage. You could imagine what he went through there. One pot of soup and bread for twenty toddlers. No eating when hungry, only when food was put out and then never getting enough.

Now he has a ritualistic way of eating. He eats a few bites, then tosses some food on the floor. After the meal, he crawls on the floor and scoops up the crumbs. I surmise that he must have done this in the orphanage: thrown food on the floor so it looked like the food was gone, then gathering it and storing it for those lonely, hungry moments between feedings. I applaud him for being such a canny survivor.

At the same time, I need to reassure him, to help him see that things are different now and that he won't ever be deprived of food again. I take him to the grocery store.

"Look, Neal," I say. "Look at all the apples, the bananas, the oranges. Look at the milk. The bread. See, we can come here anytime and get food for you."

At home I open the refrigerator. "See, Nealie. You can have this food whenever you want. There is enough here for you." He looks stunned. I am certain that he understands, yet he can't yet trust. For months to come, he will continue to hoard. A friend dubs Neal's behavior "the broccoli response." We define it as repeating behaviors needed for survival when they're no longer necessary.

----------------------------- 28. -----------------------------

BECAUSE I UNDERSTAND what occasioned the hoarding, I convince myself that there are similar explanations for other aspects of Neal's behavior.

When he spins in circles, climbs over chairs, bangs on doors, and pulls things off walls, I tell myself that he's exulting in his newfound freedom. When he stares at his hand for hours and hours, I assume

that in the orphanage his hand was his primary toy. He'll stop staring at it, I reason, when he realizes that he now has so many other
toys.

Soon he does become interested in toys, which leads to another
ritual. His toys of choice are matchbox cars and toy airplanes. Hours
pass as he lines them up in rows and stacks them one on top of the
other. When Neal lines up his little cars and planes, he is intense,
absorbed, immovable. This is classic autistic behavior. But I don't
know from autism.

My friends, who have their own children, see Neal playing. Some
gently suggest that something seems wrong. I know they mean to be
helpful, but here's the truth: I don't want to hear it.

The more people tell me that something seems odd about Neal,
the more I cling to something that others don't see. When Neal hears
a child crying, he goes to them immediately and offers comfort. I
wonder if, in the orphanage, he took on the role of a little caretaker.
Or is it that he relates to other children's tears? Since orphans don't
cry because their cries go unanswered, I was told that when Neal
starts to cry at home, I should take it as a sign that he's settling in.
Neal still doesn't cry, yet he responds instantly to the cries of others.
I wonder what goes through his mind as he comforts another child.
Neal is very solemn at such moments. It moves me to see him so
gentle, so sweet.

29.

NEAL CAN'T SLEEP. He runs back and forth in his crib until he
passes out. When he's big enough, he climbs out of his crib each
night, then runs into the bedroom and gestures to me to pick him
up. No matter how many times I reconfigure the crib he manages to
find a way out. It reminds me of the scene in *The Flintstones* cartoon
where Fred Flintstone picks up the saber-toothed cat and puts him
out the door, only to see the cat come in through the window.

My doctor tells me to lock the door and not let Neal in. I hate the idea but I try it. I know that there is this theory of "sleep training" that originated in the 1950s. The theory is that you should let a child "cry it out" and not comfort them. This theory has since been updated. Now it is known that a child needs first to learn how to comfort and soothe themselves before they can fall asleep on their own. There are doctors who actually help babies "find their own thumb" to suck and to comfort themselves. But our doctor recommended the tough love approach.

Desperately needing a good night's sleep myself, I decide to try my doctor's methods. I put Neal in the crib, kiss him good night, and lock the door. I wait on the other side of the door. I hear Neal climb out of his crib and hear his feet hitting the floor. Boom! He runs to the door and tries to open it. Since I have never locked him in his room before, he doesn't understand. He pulls at the door, then bangs on it, louder and louder, then he throws himself onto the floor, screaming. I listen at the other side of the door as Neal cries and screams. It's horrible. Inhumane. I open the door, embracing him apologetically. I never try it again.

A friend lends me a book called *The Continuum Concept,* about a method of child care practiced by Indians in South America. I learn that they hold their babies for the first three years of their lives. Finally, a way of mothering that makes sense to me.

Here's how I see it: after two years in the orphanage, attached to no one, Neal has been able to attach to me. So when he runs into my bedroom and gestures to come into my bed, the right thing to do is to pick him up and wrap the covers around his little shoulders. He sleeps soundly on my chest throughout the night.

The first night, I stay awake looking at him. I love the feeling of his head heavy on my body. I love gazing at his beautiful, tousled blond hair and peaceful face. He looks like an angel. My husband isn't thrilled with this new development. It annoys him so much that soon he stops sleeping with me.

—————————— 30. ——————————

RELIGIOUS TRADITION AND spirituality are a huge part of my life. They connect me to my heritage, my culture, and have much to do with how I view myself and how I see the world.

Neal was born Tatar, which means that he is Muslim by birth. At the orphanage, he was baptized Catholic. It's important to me that he be converted to my religion, Judaism. Before Neal can be converted, he must be circumcised. Most boys are circumcised shortly after birth. Besides being important to me religiously, I also feel a responsibility to Neal. You see, I don't want him to be in high school and pissed off at me because other teenage boys are teasing him in the locker room for having a different-looking penis!

First, I take Neal to our pediatrician to make sure he's healthy enough for this procedure. The doctor is impressed by how strong and healthy Neal has become. The herbs and nutritious food have cured all his physical maladies. But other matters seize the doctor's attention.

"Look, Elaine," he says, "Neal really should have caught up by now. This is more than just predictable developmental delay due to being in an orphanage. We need to get him checked out. Something else is going on."

"No," I say. "This isn't possible. Nothing is wrong with my kid."

I want to say, "Something must be wrong with you." But this is my trusted, beloved doctor. I have to listen. And I will listen. But not now.

"I can't deal with this until after the circumcision," I say. "Please. I just can't."

The doctor signs the health release for the procedure and kindly lets me off the hook, telling me that I can call him when I am ready to discuss Neal's developmental issues. I am relieved and put it out of my mind. I want to celebrate, darn it! And I don't want anything to get in the way. Not now. Not yet.

————————— 31. —————————

BECAUSE NEAL IS two and a half years old his circumcision will be performed in a hospital by a pediatric urologist and a mohel, the individual responsible for this ritual. I also invite the *beit din*, a "court" of rabbis, to authenticate the event.

As much as I want this, the prospect fills me with apprehensions: what if the procedure hurts, what if it makes Neal angry with me, what if this ceremony, intended only to bring us closer, pushes us apart?

I'm so nervous that when the anesthesiologist gives Neal the "cocktail" that will put him to sleep, I pass out. In my stupor, I am taken to lie down on a couch in the waiting room. By the time I wake up, the procedure is mercifully over, and the scene around me is nothing short of bizarre. Here I am, in the chilly white annex of a hospital recovery room, surrounded by a group of rabbis with long, dark beards and the trailing sideburns known as *peyes,* wearing large black hats and long, dark jackets. I feel as if I'm in a Woody Allen movie.

Neal wakes up out of the mild anesthesia. He motions for me. I hurry to his side. Thank God, I think, he isn't angry. He points to the Band-Aid on his penis. He looks at me quizzically as if to say, what the heck is this?

The next step in the conversion process is the mikvah. My family flies in from D.C. to be part of the event. At the mikvah, Neal will be gently immersed in flowing water while prayers are said to bring him into the Jewish faith. I follow my rabbi's suggestion that we practice dunking his head in the bathtub at home so that the ceremony will not be traumatic for him. Neal is fine with the dunking. Me, too. However, I feel pressured throughout to get back to work. On this of all days, the leading actress on the set has refused to get out of her trailer to tape the scene with the kids. I have to hurry through this beautiful occasion and get back to work.

If I had known then that this would be my last "normal" ritual with Neal, I never would have rushed. Today I know not to rush through ANYTHING. I know that every moment with our children is a precious one to be cherished, and the most important part of the rich and lovely tapestry that is our lives.

But then, I just thought this was going to be one of many special occasions—like his first day at kindergarten or high school graduation. So I hurried back to work, leaving Neal with my family. I simply did not realize the significance of this event. At work I joked, "Neal has been clipped and dipped."

phase two:
neal has autism

When one's expectations are reduced to zero,

one really appreciates everything one does have.

STEPHEN HAWKING

NOW COMES THE reckoning. I am not ready for it. I do not accept that anything is really wrong with Neal. I see his soul. Neal's soul is whole. Why would anyone imply that he is broken and needs fixing?

My doctor orders a series of psychological and developmental tests. I cannot believe how many tests there are. Test, after test, after test. These assessments are conducted in cold rooms with linoleum floors and blank walls, rooms that give a new dimension to the meaning of "sterile." Therapists with lots of letters after their names study Neal as if he's a laboratory rat.

I am becoming more and more concerned. I watch Neal as he sits cross-legged on the floor, tiny victim, stacking blocks as neurologists, psychologists, and occupational therapists look on.

I feel helpless, like Elliot in *E.T.* when his little alien friend is taken from him by government minions and he cannot do anything but observe. All I can do is assure Neal that he is safe. I tell him, "Mommy is here. These people just want to see how smart you are. Show 'em your stuff!"

Neal puts brightly colored beads on strings. He is asked to repeat words and sounds. Neal has no words. He doesn't respond immediately to questions.

"Is he hearing impaired?" they ask.

I don't think so, I say.

They tell me to have him tested by a pediatric audiologist. The diagnosis: his hearing is fine.

I answer question after question. "Yes, he was adopted from a Russian orphanage."

"No, he was not healthy at birth." How many times do I need to say these things?

Finally the report: Severe sensory dysfunction. Severe autism. Mental retardation. Then another question: Didn't they tell you? And a suggestion: Send him back.

--- 2. ---

I'M REELING FROM the diagnosis, yet I'm convinced the doctors are wrong. True, Neal is not like other children. He does not engage in typical play with other kids his age. Sure, he doesn't sit still, but boys are generally more active than girls, aren't they? Okay, he may not speak, but I know how smart he is. And I know that he has his own special sort of intelligence. Take the day he dumped all the pieces from ten wooden puzzles into the middle of his room.

"Nealie, what are you doing?" I had asked, knowing that it would take me hours to put the puzzles back together.

But it was Neal who put every single piece where it belonged. Within five minutes. Or take the time he found my car for me when I couldn't remember where I was parked. Or . . . or . . . I could go on and on with stories about the innate intelligence I know for a fact is in my little boy. But all of my efforts are met with sorrowful looks and pitying nods.

Later, I will come to love the mystery that is autism. I will see infinite hope in every modicum of progress. But for now I can only think that there has to be a way to reach him. Yet, in truth, I am not sure. What will happen to him? I wonder. Will Neal ever fit in with other kids? Will he ever be "normal"?

There it is, that word again: "normal." The one thing I've wanted since I was a child trying desperately to fit in. Now, in the name of normalcy, I reject the prospect of autism. This is just a stage, I tell myself, like the scurvy and the malnutrition. He'll get over it. With the right therapies, we'll soon be on our way to normal. Car pools, PTA, and soccer games.

A few days after the diagnosis, I do one of the things I love most: I take Neal's little clothes out of the dryer and fold them. The blue sweater my mom knitted for him; the Mickey Mouse T-shirt, the tiny Gap jeans. Tiny shirts and shorts with anchors and stripes on them. Tiny blue socks. I love folding Neal's clothes, making life neat for him. I love the way the folding makes me feel like a mom.

But this day, as I fold, I begin to weep and cannot stop. I want to believe that I am above caring about being normal. But I'm not. I care about it for me, and more than that, I care about it for my son. Will my boy have anything normal in his life? Will he have friends? Will he ever play baseball? Will he graduate high school or go to college or have a bar mitzvah? Will he experience the joy of work? Will he bring home his future bride? Will he experience any of the passages we regard as normal and therefore take for granted? Or will that rushed mikvah ceremony be the last bit of normalcy we share?

3.

IN LOS ANGELES, even dinky apartment houses have swimming pools. My little swimming hole in the courtyard of our town house units becomes my sanctuary. At night for the next three weeks, I go there to grieve.

I grieve for all the memories I will not have, for all the dreams that will never come to fruition. I cry, I mourn, I let myself go as deep into despair as I need to. And then in my usual fashion, one night, as I look at my sad reflection in the pool, I realize—I'm done. It's time to go into action again.

Much more is known about autism today. Back then, it was a secret that went largely unmentioned, as if it were shameful. My only reference to autism is Dustin Hoffman's performance in *Rain Man*. I spend hours on the Internet reading everything about autism that I can find.

As I look back now, I see that, perversely, it is my commitment to normalcy that will lead me to unravel the intricacies of my son's autism and to overcome them. It is my desire to fit into the world that will drive me to learn everything I can about this condition. What I didn't know, starting out, is that I would come to love the autism I so desperately feared.

Today I can say that I find people with autism to be the most extraordinary people I've ever met. I see autism as a different and fascinating way of being. But that is now. It was not then. Now I believe that normality is overrated. But at that stage, being normal was all that I wanted for Neal. And if I was being honest about it, I would have told you that being normal was what I wanted for me.

4.

WHEN YOU HAVE no idea how to proceed, it's easy to give in. So I follow the doctor's suggestion and enroll Neal in a preschool for kids with autism. When we walk in, we see kids screaming, throwing tantrums, biting. Some wear helmets. There is no eye contact. Teachers grapple physically with resistant kids. It is the preschool version of *The Snake Pit,* a 1960s movie about mental illness.

My first and only thought is: Neal doesn't belong here. I hold on to his hand, vowing not to leave his side. But at this preschool, there are rules. Rigidity and rules. One of them is that overly protective, doting moms cannot stay. "Okay," I say when asked to leave, "but I will be close by."

You may wonder why I was willing to leave at all. Because I have been told to do so by professionals I trust. And mostly because I don't know a way that is different or better.

I take a walk around the block and come back every half hour to make sure that Neal is okay. The owners of the preschool are sick of me already. The school has one classroom that mixes kids who are typically developing with kids who have slight developmental challenges. An inclusion classroom, they call it. You know how parents pray for their kid to get into Harvard? I pray no less hard for Neal to get into that inclusion class.

But Neal doesn't get in. Instead, he's put into a class for the most severely autistic children. There, he's "rewarded" with M&Ms for sitting still. When I pick him up at the end of the day, teachers tell me how great it is that he put a blue stick in a blue hole or sat still for five minutes. The way Neal is treated at school runs counter to everything I have ever believed about working with children. It's all about rote behaviors. It gives me the willies.

In my own work with kids, I always set meaningful and appropriate boundaries, but I also let them be themselves. I respect their innate intelligence. I treat them as people. To me, the approach used on Neal is barely one step above bad dog training.

His teachers tell the class, "Quiet hands."

This means place your hands in your lap. When Neal hears "quiet hands," he places his hands on his ears. I love Neal's cleverness. He's one step ahead of his teachers. They don't catch it, but I do. Neal is understanding everything. It's just that autism is a protective barrier of sorts, and he's sequestered inside it.

5.

WHEN NEAL HAS been in the school program for three months, the faculty of his preschool attends a conference on the East Coast. It is led by Dr. Stanley Greenspan, a child and adult psychiatrist and psychoanalyst who specializes in children with autism and other special needs. After listening to Dr. Greenspan and considering his methods, the faculty members come to an astonishing conclusion: everything they've been doing for Neal is wrong. It is as if having always believed the Earth was flat, they are told by Dr. Greenspan that it is round. Much to their credit, they believe him.

Dr. Greenspan rejects the notion that a child needs to conform to our world by learning rote behavioral tasks. Instead, he says, a care-taker should follow the child's lead, should see what he's interested in and be curious about it. In other words, if Neal wants to throw pil-lows, we should throw pillows with him and turn the activity into a playful pillow fight. If he wants to run in circles, we should do the same and make a chase game of it. In this way, we will connect with Neal by entering into his world, by meeting him where he lives. The idea is that children like Neal do not progress by learning "good be-havior." They progress by forming relationships.

Through relationships, children can develop everything they need: they can learn to engage with others, to communicate with gestures, to use ideas creatively, to think and reflect. Dr. Greenspan's method shifts the focus from narrow, behavioral goals to broad foundations that he calls "milestones" for healthy development.

Dr. Greenspan emphasizes how important it is to recognize and honor the individual differences in children. Children with autism spectrum disorders or other special needs are by no means the same. Some are overreactive to touch and sound; some are underreactive. Some have good visual perception while others do better with au-ditory information. There is no set way to treat these children. The only essential is to tailor the learning environment to the child's individual profile.

Neal's teachers give me some newsletters from a publication called *Zero to Three*. These newsletters describe a child with autism who had been engaged in classic autistic behaviors: opening and closing doors, spinning in circles, banging things, flapping his hands like a bird, walking on his tiptoes. Rather than coerce this child to stop these behaviors, his therapists entered his world: they flapped their hands like birds as if playing a game; they banged the cabinet doors open and shut to make a session of hide-and-seek; they walked on tiptoes to make a game of pretend tightrope walking.

In a few years, the boy began to relate to people around him. He was able to attend a typical kindergarten. He became what is called "mainstream." In time, in other words, his life included the simple, basic, vital things—the normal things, school, friends, sports, activities—that I want for Neal.

———————————— 6. ————————————

I HAVE TO learn more about this method. I call Dr. Greenspan's office. A pleasant secretary apologetically tells me there is a year wait to see the doctor. I tell her my situation and beg for an appointment. Determined, persistent, I call every day for a month until there is a cancellation and I get one.

Dr. Greenspan's office is in Bethesda, Maryland, near where I was raised. The appointment they give me coincides with my mother's seventieth birthday. For the occasion, my sister has rented a beach house on the Delaware coast where the family will spend the week. I've been longing to join them. Now I can. It seems like serendipity.

But first we have to get there. I'm thinking, how can I get this three-year-old on an airplane? He's bigger now and more active than he was when I brought him from Russia. I picture nightmare scenarios of Neal running up and down the aisles or flailing or knocking over the flight attendant's tray.

Friends suggest I dose him with Benadryl to make him sleep. But Benadryl could also make him superhyper. I don't want to risk it. Instead, I figure out a way to keep him occupied throughout the five-hour flight: I go to a party supply store and buy bags of party favors. I find packages with little matchbox cars; little airplanes; bubbles on a string; Disney characters; plastic pretend food.

I take these items out of their packages and wrap them individually in aluminum foil. The way I figure it, unwrapping each package will take up to three minutes. Then there's another three minutes for him to play with the toy car, spin the wheels, flicker it in front of his eyes, and then line it up on the tray before it bores him. It isn't real play. It's more a matter of looking at the object, then tossing it away. Then I give it back and he tosses it again.

I also wrap Neal's favorite foods in little packages: two crackers here, a piece of string cheese there, three apple slices. During the flight he will have individual packages to open, like little gifts. As it turns out, the most difficult part of the flight is takeoff. Neal holds his hands over his ears and snuggles into me. Once we're in the air, he's intrigued and distracted by his little presents. Once in a while he runs up and down the aisle. I run with him. I'm not surprised that he doesn't sleep for a single second.

———————————— 7. ————————————

THIS IS THE first time that I have brought Neal home, the first time that he's meeting my sister's kids, his cousins. Kira is four and Max is three, yet they sense that Neal is different. At first, they're excited. "Neal's here!" they shout. "Neal's here!"

It matters so much to me that Neal be seen as one of the family. So I'm pleased that they are excited to see him. Neal is a bit dazed from the travel, but does his best to be present with his cousins. My sister, always the thoughtful one, has bought him some match-box cars. He sits on the floor and begins his stacking and lining up. This might seem like a good thing, but the immediate excitement of "Neal's here!" soon drifts to "Neal's there" as he retreats into his iso-lative play. His cousins sit beside him, trying to play with him. I sigh deeply as they look back toward us with bewildered glances.

Though Neal doesn't play with his cousins, he follows them around from time to time. I like that he is interested in them. I wish that they could play more. At one point, Kira calls, "Mom, I like our other cousin Brandon better." This shouldn't hurt—she's only four years old—but I have to admit, it does.

Like every brother and sister, Kira and Max have their battles.

Max slaps Kira as Neal watches from a few feet away. Kira starts to cry. Neal glares at Max, then marches over to him and whacks him on the hand. It's Neal's Clint Eastwood moment. After that, Max stops picking on Kira, at least when Neal's around.

It's moments like these that buttress my conviction that Neal is more than the sum of his autistic tendencies. There is more to him than people see. He has a heart. He has conviction. He has a mind with the capacity for connection, awareness, sensitivity. It's in there. Perhaps it takes a mother's eyes to see. I hope that next week, when we go see Dr. Greenspan, he can confirm my beliefs.

We pile into the car and head for the beach house. Neal begins to cry and doesn't stop for the duration of the four-hour journey. His already shaky popularity takes a dive, to put it mildly. When we get to the beach, it doesn't help that Neal is petrified of sand, of water, of anything to do with the beach.

"Listen," I tell my sister, "he doesn't know from the ocean. He comes from the Ural Mountains in Siberia, for goodness' sake."

Even as I defend him, I'm disappointed. I love the ocean, and I yearn to share it with my son. Instead, we spend our time on the patio of the beach house where there's a wading pool. We're joined by my mother, who was also raised in the mountains—the Blue Ridge Mountains in Virginia—and doesn't like getting sandy.

My mother gives Neal buckets to fill with water from a nearby hose. Neal fills the buckets and proudly pours the water into the wading pool. Neal sits beside my mother on the chaise lounge. He's remarkably content. She seems to understand him. Funny, I've always wanted her to understand me and never felt she did.

For instance, she never quite got why I moved to Los Angeles to study dance and acting. In those days, I supported myself by waitressing, selling flowers, or being a personal assistant—anything that gave me enough money and freedom to take dance and acting classes and pay the rent.

Every week, my mother would call to ask if I'd "gotten all that

artistic stuff out of my system," and to alert me to secretarial opportunities. As a young woman, my mother had been a secretary herself,
but that job wasn't for me, given that it's easier for me to learn to
sing an entire musical score than to figure out where to file the sheet
music.

"Honey," she would say in her sweet Southern accent, "I hear MCI
is movin' their offices to Los Angeles. You really should give them a
call. They're hirin' lots of people, ya know."

I wanted her to appreciate what I was trying to achieve, but she
never quite did. Yet, watching her now, I can see that—for reasons I
don't quite comprehend—she understands and accepts my son.

My mother always had a strong intuitive sense. She always cared
for and about those less fortunate than we were. We never had a lot
of money; my dad supported us on his modest civil servant salary,
but there was always enough food on the table to feed anyone who
needed a meal.

Across the street from our house lived Pauline Braden, a young
girl wheelchair-bound due to cerebral palsy. Encouraged by my
mom, I would go over to Pauline's house every Tuesday after school
to play with her. Pauline could barely talk and could barely feed
herself. I would talk with her, read to her, play with her, and help
her mom feed her. I looked forward to these afternoons. I especially
liked to see how calm and loving Mrs. Braden was with her daughter. It was a profoundly beautiful experience.

I still wonder why, of her three kids, my mother picked me, rather
than my sister or brother, to befriend Pauline. I believe this experience shaped my future and made me comfortable with children who
have special needs. Maybe my mom did understand me after all.

———————————————— 8. ————————————————

MY MOTHER'S UNDERSTANDING of Neal comes from her heart.
Mine does too, but it also comes from experience. As a child, I strug-

gled with my own minor disabilities. My feet turned in, so I had to wear ugly, heavy lace-up shoes. I always wanted to wear loafers, the style of the time, but I didn't own a pair until I was eleven years old. As a young child I was often sick and had to go to the hospital on several occasions. One hospital stay in particular truly shaped my inner life.

When I was two years old, I had an operation on my eyes to correct a birth defect of double vision. My parents prepared me well. They told me that when I woke up from the surgery, I would have bandages over my eyes and that I wouldn't be able to see for several days. To get me ready, we practiced by putting scarves on my eyes. It was fun, like a game.

But when I woke up from the surgery, I not only had bandages over my eyes, the doctors had put me in a body cast from head to toe. I lay there motionless and terrified. My dad said that the doctors didn't want me to move. They were afraid I'd take the bandages off my eyes. So they had trapped me in a plaster-of-paris shell. This experience was so traumatic that it seared itself into my memory, even at such a tender age. I remember feeling that the doctor should have just told me not to take the bandages off. Why didn't the doctor trust me? Why did they trick me? I was outraged!

I recall feeling trapped and isolated. That night, instead of sleeping soundly, I felt my consciousness slowly sinking down into a well. I saw myself being swallowed up by its darkness. I felt that, if I kept falling, I might fall so far that I'd disappear. Instead, a golden light displaced the darkness; the light embraced and comforted me. I knew I was safe.

This was my first experience of holiness, of connection to God, to something not only greater than myself—but to my highest self.

Even beyond that, it gave rise to my lifelong conviction that children possess an understanding and sense of self far beyond anything adults believe they have.

I've drawn on this belief repeatedly when coaching kids. It is,

I think, the reason I've worked so effectively with children that I became known as The Child Whisperer.

Today, it is an experience that continues to help me understand Neal, and teaches me to respect the nonverbal child, to listen to their inner voice as well as to my own.

9.

ALL MY LIFE, I've been fortunate to have a wonderful, loving, and playful relationship with my father. My dad is great with kids. When I was a child, neighborhood kids were always coming over to our house and asking my mom, "Can Sol come out and play?" And he did.

But that week at the beach, I see that bonding with Neal doesn't come naturally to him. This makes me sad. At heart, my dad is a big kid, a dancer, a musician, a fun-loving man who despised working in an office but did so cheerfully every day to support his family. He's always been my best friend, my dance partner, my confidant. When I was a baby, my dad would hold me and sing me to sleep. As a little girl, he taught me to foxtrot by putting my feet on his feet and dancing around the basement to Count Basie and Benny Goodman. We listened to Billie Holiday, Louis Armstrong. He even taught himself to play clarinet so he could accompany his Benny Goodman records.

In my imagination, all of these great musicians were our friends. My dad taught me to appreciate music, the arts, good food, and especially fun. He was also into "self-help" books and psychology, and he would share with me whatever he was reading. As a little girl, it was Dr. Seuss's *I Can't Get to Sleep Book*. As I grew older, it was Andrew Carnegie's *How to Win Friends and Influence People*. Then it was *Cybernetics*. As a teenager, and when I returned from college, we would stay up long hours discussing philosophy, psychology, and religion. I feel so blessed to have this amazing dad and wonderful connection to him. Even as an adult, I am Daddy's Little Girl.

I once dated a guy who asked me, early in our courtship, about my relationship with my father. I responded with, "My dad's a great man."

"Oh come on," he said. "Your dad's just a dad. Martin Luther King was a great man. John F. Kennedy was a great man."

I paused for only a second and said, "Yes, my dad is a Great Man."

That's how I see him. From the time I was small, I looked forward to the day when my own child would play with my dad. I could see them wrestling, running, tumbling together, dancing, riding bicycles, collecting seashells, all the things that he did with me and my siblings and our friends. But Neal baffles my father. My dad is not at his best when he's baffled.

MY FATHER LIKES to ruffle a kid's hair. When he ruffles Neal's hair, Neal screams. My dad is convinced that this means that Neal doesn't like him. I know that's not the case, but for my dad, it's an affront to his playful goodness.

I don't know how to convince him that he's wrong about Neal. I don't want him to feel bad and I especially don't want Neal to feel bad. So, for the first time since my rebellious teens, there's this weird space developing between my dad and me.

Neal goes around the beach house randomly opening and closing cabinet doors, spinning in circles, and withdrawing from the family. I try to laugh it off and pretend that he's just exploring new territory. But I can tell by my dad's furrowed brow that he doesn't think it's funny.

Next week, when I see Dr. Greenspan, I will learn more. I will learn that each child with autism has his own individual sensory makeup and, more often than not, they have exaggerated sensitivities. For some of these children, it can literally hurt to hear their mother's voice, or to look into her eyes. It can hurt to have their grandpa affectionately ruffle their hair.

These children may not see and hear the way you and I do. Ordinary sounds and sights become overwhelming and feel like having a tooth drilled without Novocain. That's why the sound of a workman using a jackhammer on the sidewalk can send Neal into convulsions. It's the reason that he'll walk into the kitchen, hear the dishwasher, and start screaming. It's not that he's afraid of the dishwasher. He's reacting to pain.

Imagine if connecting with another human was physically painful. What would you do? Undoubtedly, you would withdraw. The anxiety of children with autism is more than the typical anxiety that you or I might feel. Their anxiety comes from their inability to predict or control what might irritate or overwhelm their nervous system, or cause them extreme discomfort and/or pain, or result in their losing control over their body. But I can't explain all of this to my father. I don't yet have the knowledge. I don't have the words.

10.

THE WEEK AT the beach seems A LOT longer than a week. When it finally ends, we go to see Dr. Greenspan. I am excited; I feel like Dorothy going off to see the Wizard.

Dr. Greenspan's office is in the back of his house. He's wearing an old, worn sweater and moccasins. He seems kind and sweet and reminds me of Mr. Rogers. His office is a mishmash of broken toys, stacks of papers, books piled high. It's the domain of a warm, absent-minded professor, a disarming, welcoming place that is the polar opposite of the sterile testing offices we'd been to in Beverly Hills. I feel that we can make no mistakes here, that whatever we do will be okay.

Dr. Greenspan doesn't put Neal through a battery of tests. Instead, he observes how we play together. Neal and I sit on the floor. The doctor coaches me on how to relate more to Neal.

Neal picks up a toy car and stacks it on top of another car. Dr. Greenspan encourages me to play hide-and-seek with the car so that Neal will have to make me part of his play.

On the floor, there's a little doll that attracts Neal's interest. He's also interested in some cookies I brought with me.

Dr. Greenspan asks Neal, "Can you feed the dolly?"

Neal takes a cookie and gives it to the doll. Dr. Greenspan tells me to talk to Neal as if I'm the doll.

"Oh, I'm hungry," I say. "Will you feed me some more?"

I feel silly pretending to be a doll in front of this esteemed doctor. But not for long because I soon see Neal responding as he offers little pieces of the cookie.

In the past, Neal and I have wrestled and looked at books, and swung on swings. Yet we've never connected in this more "typical" creative realm of pretend play. Now we are exchanging glances, going back and forth with sounds and expressions. We are pretending that the dolly needs more food. Food is something Neal can totally relate to, so he eagerly plays along. For the first time, Neal is playing in an imaginative, rather than a merely physical, way.

Now there is a reciprocity and an actual progression to our games. As we play, something amazing happens: for the very first time Neal looks into my eyes. It's funny, but before this, I didn't even notice that Neal wasn't looking at me. Now, when he does look, it is powerful. The looks are fleeting, almost accidental, but they are there. Neal seems to be aware of me in a way he never was before.

Dr. Greenspan is the first professional to affirm my belief that Neal has innate intelligence, to agree that his development was stifled by a traumatic birth, early abandonment, and being institutionalized in infancy. I am heartened by the doctor's urging never to compare Neal's progress to that of any other child, to compare Neal only to Neal. By the time we leave that day, Dr. Greenspan has given us hope.

----------------------------- 11. -----------------------------

DR. GREENSPAN ALSO gives us a specific prescription and I'm eager to follow it. Neal is to have speech therapy three times a week to help him start forming words. When I ask if Neal will ever speak, Dr. Greenspan does not give a prognosis. He does say that for Neal to produce words he will have to develop new pathways in his brain. He explains that Neal has a condition called "apraxia," an extreme neurological difficulty that compounds—but is separate from—Neal's other challenges. Most of us learn to speak easily and effortlessly. But a person with apraxia must think out each individual sound, then learn one sound at a time by coordinating his mouth, tongue, and breath.

I can't help wondering why Neal was saddled with this additional difficulty. Maybe it's because he was isolated in a hospital for his first six months and didn't have the child/parent relationship that is so critical to developing speech; maybe it's because he had no oxygen to his brain at birth, or maybe, I muse, it's because he's so evolved that he just doesn't need words. Whatever the cause, it's a major hurdle.

Neal enjoys going to the speech therapist. She offers a playful approach, like blowing bubbles to get him to say "b" and "p" for "pop." She uses her hands to help Neal shape the sounds. Then he tries to organize these sounds into words. Hopefully these halting words will one day be organized into sentences, and the sentences will amass into paragraphs. Imagine having to take so many steps to express even the most basic thoughts and feelings!

I never considered all the steps it takes to talk. My mom and dad joked that I came out of the womb speaking full sentences. Now here I am with a child for whom every syllable he manages to utter is a hard-won triumph.

--- 12. ---

I CAN'T BELIEVE that Dr. Greenspan also prescribes three weekly sessions of occupational therapy. This sounds nuts to me. He wants my three-year-old to go to occupational therapy? What is he talking about? Does he think Neal should start preparing at the age of three to get a job?

As it turns out, Neal's occupational therapy is not at all what I assumed it would be. It's conducted in a huge room that contains a climbing structure, tunnels, and big mush balls. It looks like a Gymboree and is meant to be a place where Neal can be playful in therapeutic ways. But the room overwhelms and terrifies him. He doesn't even want to enter it.

Luckily, the owner of the clinic, Erna Blanche, takes to Neal instantly. In the past, she's worked with Romanian orphans and many kids with autism. She recognizes Neal's potential and his vulnerability too. She speaks lovingly to him, assuring him that this is a safe place; she encourages him to climb up a little ladder, to go down a slide. One small accomplishment slowly builds to others. Neal begins to climb ladders and to move through tunnels.

He does these things with great trepidation. Yet he does them. Soon, he's climbing taller slides, moving through longer tunnels, swinging on net swings, and jumping into a crash pad made of foam. When I see that they've formed their own bond, I sigh with relief. I can let go a little. I leave them alone, find a quiet area, curl up on a piece of foam padding, and instantly fall asleep.

13.

THE OCCUPATIONAL THERAPIST designs two- and three-step activities for Neal. These are called "motor planning" and "sequencing" and, in laymen's terms, refer to the ability to remember a series of steps and follow through with them. For example, most typical three-year-olds can learn to dress themselves; they can put on their underpants, then their pants, placing each foot into the requisite leg. They can make sure the tag of their shirt is in the back, and can figure out how to put their arms into the side openings. But Neal's apraxia inhibits his ability to organize his brain and then execute a task, and so Erna helps him enact this simple sequence of activity. At home, we practice sequencing, using pictures to show Neal the steps involved in every activity from picking up a fork to putting on a shirt.

Erna helps Neal learn to play with toys, and with other kids. When most children see kids chasing one another around a playground, their brain computes the activity, and they can choose to follow along. But for children with apraxia, simple play can involve so many steps in the brain that it's more agreeable to sit it out. It's not that they don't want to play with toys or with other kids. It's just very, very difficult for them to summon the huge amount of mental energy that a given activity requires. Because basic tasks are so difficult for them to learn, kids with these challenges can appear to be "stupid" or "lazy." Often, their families regard them with disappointment, or ignore their protests about playing with others, or try to bribe them into doing it, which only makes them feel bad about themselves. But what's really going on, as Erna explains, is that being in the world is a struggle for them.

Combine this with a sensory sensitivity to sounds, sights, smells, and touch, and you can see why a child with autism may choose to isolate. The desire to connect with others is often outweighed by the need to avoid being overwhelmed, to not risk the embarrassment of being incapable of doing seemingly simple things. But think about all that's required to pick up a little car, to place it on a track, rotate it around the track, stop at a pretend gas station, pretend to fill it up with gasoline, then continue around the track. This supposedly simple game is composed of hundreds of little steps that must be organized first in the brain, then put into action. This is why it's so much easier for Neal just to line up cars or stack them: Neal's way requires just a few repetitive steps that take little or no time to master.

14.

NOW I GET it! Finally, I understand why Neal does many of the things he does, among them the ritual he follows whenever we go to the park. Here's what happens: he climbs up a slide, walks two steps to the right, spins in a circle, walks around a sandbox. He repeats the entire sequence again and again. If I attempt to disrupt this ritual, he erupts in a temper tantrum of impressive scope and size. If another child attempts to go down the slide, Neal hurls himself on the ground and screams.

Whenever he gets mired in a series of movements, he's incapable of breaking out of it. It's much easier for him simply to repeat the same action over and over. Since I can't stop him, I follow the Greenspan methodology and "playfully obstruct" this ritual by providing alternatives to it.

One day, I lie down at the bottom of the slide; Neal falls on top of me. We tumble around on the ground for a few minutes before he starts to repeat his ritual. This time, as he takes his two steps to the right, I walk with him. To further disrupt his pattern, I spin with him as he spins in a circle.

Gradually, he is able to abandon his rituals, and to seek out new activities. He begins to tolerate others in his space. He even takes turns going down the slide with other kids. Despite how hard it is for him to learn an activity, once he figures it out, he executes it at a typical level.

————————— 15. —————————

THE MOST CRITICAL component of Neal's therapy is the seven daily sessions of Floortime that I do with him at home. "Floortime" is a term patented by Dr. Greenspan, and refers to the type of creative play that builds relationships and that Neal and I engaged in at his office. Each Floortime session lasts at least twenty minutes, and is time set aside solely for Neal. I follow whatever Neal is focusing on, taking my cue from his lead and his interests, even when they seem arbitrary.

One of the things Neal does almost 70 percent of his waking hours is stare at his hand. I thought he did this because his hand had been his main toy in the orphanage. Now, I realize, it's his calming mechanism, a predictable object in a world filled with unpredictable sounds, people, activity. One day, I sit beside him as he stares at his hand and I stare at mine. As I look, I discover that the hand is extraordinary. It opens, it closes, it has bumps and valleys. Then Neal and I sit looking at each other's hands in a Zenlike manner. The more that I follow Neal's lead, the more he interacts with me.

Neal likes to spin in circles. Round and round he can go like a whirling dervish, a meditative Sufi aiming, through this spinning ritual, to attain the "perfect." Now I spin with him. This becomes a game of "Ring Around the Rosie" and when "we all fall down," we laugh and laugh together. I love these twenty-minute sessions as much as Neal does. Afterward, we are both exhilarated and exhausted.

I challenge him to engage with me in back-and-forth communication. For instance, if Neal wants something to eat, he may motion to the refrigerator. Before seeing Dr. Greenspan, I would just open the refrigerator door and get something for him. But you see, this doesn't create any back-and-forth communication.

Dr. Greenspan wants me to expand these interactions to go back and forth as many times as we can. So now if Neal points to the refrigerator, I'll ask him, "You want something from there?"

Neal nods, as if to say yes.

"Oh," I'll say then, "you must be hungry."

He nods yes again.

"Do you want me to open the refrigerator door?"

Again, a nod for yes.

And so on. In this way, each interaction becomes a dialogue.

16.

I BEGIN TO see that Neal tries to tell me things that I don't always understand. For example, when I try to go on a walk with him, he insists that we stop at every single hubcap attached to every single car on every street. I used to say, "Come on, let's go." And we'd have a battle.

Now, following his lead, I stop with him, kneel down, and stare at the hubcaps. What I see is the most beautiful thing: the sun falling on a hubcap creates a starburst of brilliant, shining shards of light. They are magical, mesmeric.

"Wow," I say, "thank you so much, Neal, for showing this to me."

We get up and walk on. I have seen and appreciated the hubcaps' enchantment. Neal never stops at hubcaps again. He has accomplished his mission.

And so it goes. Neal and I spend afternoons staring at our hands or spinning in circles. In behavioral therapies, kids are told to stop spinning and sit down. But it turns out that spinning serves a purpose for the neurological system: when Neal spins in circles he's instinctively trying to activate the vestibular part of his brain.

To facilitate his spinning, the occupational therapy clinic provides a number of large net swings. The therapists wrap Neal in the net, then spin him around and around. They push him high on a swing, and have him crash into a foam pit. At home, I install a net swing in Neal's bedroom so that he can keep swinging.

Neal is slowly emerging from his shell. My longing to have him join our world is coming to pass. Not only is he is seeking to be with me more—he now wants my constant attention. (Be careful what you wish for!)

— 17. —

TWO OF MY closest friends, Vida and Rebecca, have sons the same age as Neal. We met when our kids were in strollers. Both are married to men whose work often keeps them away from home. Vida is married to a renowned bass guitarist who tours throughout Europe.

Rebecca is married to a Pulitzer Prize–winning photo journalist. They are on their own a lot, as am I.

All three of us had successful careers that we willingly gave up once we had children, Vida was an extraordinary singer/songwriter; Rebecca wrote TV movies for Lifetime and is wittier and sharper than most people. We all became mothers at a later age and, well, didn't quite "fit in" with moms in the Mommy and Me classes where I met Vida. There, young mothers were comparing their personal trainers and discussing the latest paint color chosen for their fourth bathroom in their second home while I was chasing Neal around and wondering how or if we could keep making the payments on our little town house.

Serendipity brought Rebecca and me together in the course of a rainy January. Yes, it does rain in sunny California, and we'd had rain every day for almost a month. Streets were flooded, mud slides in Malibu sent houses over cliffs, and Neal and I were caged up in our little house. On the first sunny day, I took Neal out for a stroller ride, and when we reached the street, there was Rebecca strolling Nick. Our eyes met, our stroller wheels touched, and we were soul mates from that point on. We blissfully glided down our street.

Sometimes the universe is incredibly kind. Rebecca and Nick and Vida and Leven lived within walking distance from Neal and me. We got together as much as possible. In the beginning, we had dinners together, strolled our kids to the park, debated whether it's better to use disposable diapers or to be more Earth-friendly and stick to cloth. They were there for me when I got Neal's diagnosis and support me in every way they can.

As wonderful as these friends are, as our children grow older, the differences between their sons and Neal become more apparent. In time, their kids seek to play with children who are on their developmental level. We remain close friends, but our times together have become less frequent.

Any parent raising a child with autism can tell you about the isolation. The solitary dinners. The holidays alone. Some of my other friends, who are warm and always welcoming of me, are uncomfortable around Neal. Isolation is a constant adversary that can leave me drained and dispirited, but only if I let it.

Each day, I remind myself that I am not alone, that my friends are the best friends a person could have. And they are. They support me as much as humanly possible. My task is to reconcile myself to the limits inherent in the term "humanly possible."

No matter how loving your friends and family may be, bringing a "whirling dervish" to social events isn't easy and isn't wise. A child who throws objects, jumps on tables, spins in circles is probably not destined to be the most popular kid on the block. There are so many things that Neal and I cannot do. So many places we can't go, so many invitations that I don't feel comfortable accepting. Neal gets overstimulated in many situations. He can't help it.

Simple occasions that might serve as respites end up being ordeals. One of those occasions is Neal's nightly bath. As it's been from the start, there are times when he doesn't want to get into the water and times when he's enjoying the water so much that he doesn't want to get out. There he'll be, kicking and splashing. And I'll be kneeling beside him, getting soaked, trying to protect him from slipping.

He flails around. He stands in the tub and screams. I'm terrified that he'll slip or knock his head or throw something at the mirror and get cut by flying shards. There is nothing left to do but pray, "Dear God, help me get through this bath."

"Neal," I say. "I need help and you need help. Ask your angels to help you."

I pray some more. I know that if I can calm myself, Neal will be calm. In fact, Neal can be calm only if I am calm. I take deep breaths and so does he. We get through the night. We are two facets of a single entity. He is not just my son. He is the barometer to my inner life.

———————————————— 18. ————————————————

IN SEARCH OF comfort, I attend support meetings for parents of children with special needs. I leave ten times more depressed than when I walked in. At these meetings, I find parents who are angry at their child's teachers, at their doctors, at school administrators. I wonder if this is misplaced anger: are they actually angry with God, and with autism? That's how it seems to me, but in any case, I soon realize that I can't handle "support groups" that leave me feeling hopeless. But I don't leave. Instead, I try to raise the group's energy. I become the Pollyanna reaching out to these folks, urging them to see the positive. Soon, I establish my own "uplift groups," teaching parents how to understand the sensory system, how to build a relationship with their child. Giving to others raises my mood considerably, yet I still feel bereft.

One evening, I go to a group that actually helps me. The facilitator tells us to visualize something we love about our disabled child. This is easy for me. I love Neal's heart, his mischievous nature, his honesty, the intensity of our connection. I even love Neal's will, for while it often makes things more difficult, I realize that his powerful will kept him alive in that incubator when he weighed only three pounds. It is his will that helped him overcome the loneliness of the orphanage, that made it possible for him to survive. There are so many things that I love about Neal: his spirit, his tenacity. I find myself smiling and, for the first time, enjoying a support group.

The facilitator then asks us to visualize two things that one day we would like to do with our child. This doesn't come quite as easily. So many dreams have already been shattered that I really don't want to go there. But I do. She guides us to close our eyes, let go, and see what comes to us. She tells us to dispense with the mind-set that says "it's never going to happen." Okay, I can do this.

I close my eyes, and what comes up first is sharing a day with Neal at the beach.

As you may remember from our family beach fiasco, Neal is not into beaches. But in my mind's eye, I see us playfully splashing in the waves, building sand castles, eating a healthful snack, and lying in the sun. Oh, this is heaven. Funny, when you have a child with special needs, the prospect of the simplest events takes on huge significance. We special parents are the fortunate ones because we learn to regard every typical activity with wonder and gratitude. The visualization leaves me feeling happy, joyous, serene. Although when I return to reality, I'm aware that it's about as likely to happen as it would be had I visualized us floating on Mars.

The second vision is of Neal and me going to temple together. When I was a little girl, I used to sit beside my dad in our little synagogue in Camp Springs, Maryland. As he prayed, I would play with the little fringes on his prayer shawl. I loved sitting next to him, hearing him sing, smelling his Old Spice cologne. These were times of intense closeness. While my dad was praying in Hebrew, I read the prayer book. I learned and I connected with God. I always wanted to have a similar experience with my own child.

However, like many things, this did not seem likely to happen. Still, I let the vision flow: Neal and I walking into a crowded Friday-night service at my temple. Me, smiling; Neal, peaceful. We are greeted by the rabbi and other congregants. Neal sits beside me, engaged through the entire service. Then I shake off my fantasy and recall the last time we tried to go to temple: the sounds, sights, totally overwhelmed Neal and turned him into a screeching, whirling mess. Me, apologetically carrying a flailing Neal out of the sanctuary; Neal, exhausted, shaking his head, saying "no, no, no!" I decide to toss this dream aside—along with my other discarded dreams: being in a feature film, performing on Broadway, doing something useful with the United Nations, having a happy marriage.

19.

MY DREAM OF enjoying the beach with Neal is one I cannot give up. In the summer, in Los Angeles, everyone goes to the beach, including Vida and Rebecca and their sons. I'm determined to go too, to avoid the loneliness I'd feel if I stayed home while my friends and their kids are basking in the sun and playing in the Malibu waves.

Neal knows where we're headed, so it's not easy to get him into the car. Malibu Beach is twenty miles from our house, but going twenty miles can take more than an hour depending on the day and time of travel. When I moved to Los Angeles, over thirty years ago, if you asked "how long does it take to get from Santa Monica to Malibu?" they'd say "fifteen or twenty minutes." Today, it can take fifteen to twenty minutes just to drive two miles to the start of the Pacific Coast Highway.

This is one of those bad traffic days. Vida and Rebecca drive together, but I drive alone with Neal, just in case. Good thought. Because Neal is not a happy camper. He does not like the traffic or sitting for an hour in the car. It's humid and hot. But the prospect of sitting on the beach with my friends and Neal propels me to keep edging north, until we arrive in Malibu.

Neal refuses to get out of the car. But I haven't driven this far and taken this much time simply to turn around and go home. I try to coax him to walk with me to the beach. After forty minutes of this push and pull, I finally put Neal's arms around my shoulders and, looking like a mountain mule, I carry him on my back some fifty yards along with our beach chairs, cooler, and beach bag. But it doesn't matter to me. I have a mission. When I finally reach my friends, I place Neal on their beach blanket and lie down, exhausted. For the next two hours, while Nick and Leven play, Neal doesn't move. Finally, I gird myself to carry him back to the car.

We repeat this process at least once a week, throughout the summer. Slowly, Neal begins to enjoy the beach. He even digs into the sand with a little shovel. He likes making holes in the sand that he can fill up. I bring pails of water to the blanket. He hits the water with his hands, smiling when he makes a splash.

20.

I.E.P. STANDS FOR Individualized Education Plan. Such plans are offered to every child who has special needs. Before an I.E.P. can be developed for Neal, he needs to take a battery of tests in the presence of a school psychologist, a speech therapist, an occupational therapist, a general education teacher, a special education teacher, and an assistant teacher. Later, we have a meeting to discuss the special services that Neal will need to be successful in school.

They are all open and eager to help support Neal's best interests. I learn that children like Neal are to be placed in the least restrictive environment possible, and that the government guarantees a free and appropriate education. I marvel at how far this little guy has traveled. Not long ago, in Russia, he was one of a hundred children without anyone who cared specifically for him. Now here is an entire room full of people helping to steer his education and development.

The I.E.P. team agrees with Dr. Greenspan's plan and offers Neal three sessions of speech therapy a week, and three sessions of occupational therapy. They even offer him what I've most wanted: placement in an inclusion preschool. I am stunned and moved by the efficacy and compassion of this team. I feel as if I've died and gone to academic heaven. I can't wait for the first day of school. Neal is on the path to normal. Just a few years with this diagnosis and he'll be off the charts, on the debating team, reciting Shakespeare.

21.

IN NEAL'S INCLUSION class, the majority of kids are typically developing. To help Neal be part of this class, he's paired with an aide who shadows and supports him.

Neal's teacher, Wendy Parise, guides her aides and students with stunning strength and devotion. I call her "the General." I am hesitant to leave Neal but not—for a change—because I'm concerned for him, but because I love the environment of Wendy's classroom. I love the creative "stations" in each corner: the pretend cooking station, the section with soft pillows and books; the area with dress-up clothes. This is developmental learning at its best.

As she blends the typically developing children with those who have special needs, Wendy is like the conductor of a melodic symphony. Actually, I enjoy being in her classroom so much that she has to ask me to leave. For Neal's benefit! She makes her request in the same spirit that she does everything: with humor and her signature compassion.

Neal thrives in the atmosphere that Wendy creates. He feels the love and support and responds to it. He is learning to play with the aides and the other kids. He loves going to school. He loves to climb to the top of the jungle gym, and sit atop the bars. They all are amazed at his fearlessness.

22.

I LOOK FOR ways for Neal to express himself physically. Early on, when we went to regular Mommy and Me–type gym classes, they only succeeded in making Neal's differences seem more profound. But when I discover a special gymnastics program for kids with special needs, I race to sign up.

The class is held at a gymnastics center in Santa Monica equipped with trampolines, balance bars, rings, large mats, and parallel bars. The program is run by a phenomenal, intuitive gym teacher whose expertise is children with special needs. At first, Neal won't enter the gym at all, so she rolls a four-foot-round ball to the door where he is standing. She asks him to help her push the ball into the middle of the floor. He does it with obvious reluctance. Yet, in a few months, he's jumping on the trampoline, crossing on the balance beam, and totally enjoying himself. I'm thrilled by the sheer confidence and joy that Neal exudes in gym class. By the time my dad comes to visit, Neal is truly comfortable in the gym. I can't wait for Dad to see him swinging on rings and jumping on the trampoline with panache and ease.

I suspect that my dad's visit is occasioned by the fact that my parents are worried about me. They've never questioned my decision to adopt Neal; they say that they're concerned about him in the same way that they would be concerned about any grandchild. Sometimes I misinterpret this as not loving him—or me—as much as they love my sister and her children. In my heart I know this isn't true and I'm embarrassed to think it.

I'm excited to show my father how well Neal's doing. My dad is excited too. See, sports and activity are things that my dad can really relate to. My dad is five feet three inches and his dream in life was to be a pro football player! I'm not kidding. Dad relished getting banged up playing football with his buddies. I remember how, during my childhood, Dad would break his wrist catching a baseball, or sprain his ankle playing tennis, or be knocked over in an innocent game of touch football. So often after his evenings with his buddies, my mom would have to take him to the emergency room. He loves to tell stories about being a professional featherweight boxer. He was good, but he couldn't be the best because he lacked the killer instinct. He just couldn't knock a guy out once he was down.

Now in his early seventies, he still plays tennis, swims daily, and is on the baseball team in his neighborhood. So I can't wait for him to see Neal do his gymnastics. I think Neal may be ready to show off a bit too.

When we get to the gym class, we see a guy standing on a ladder, installing a light fixture. He's got a drill in his hand. I ask him very nicely if he could finish the drilling later. He says, "I'm almost done."

I ask again, now pleading, as I know that drilling can hurt Neal's ears. He resumes the drilling. Neal falls into a convulsion. I am holding Neal down. He's crying and screaming. I am furious with the workman. His drilling is, for Neal, the most horrible sort of physical pain. He's flailing. My dad thinks he's having an epileptic fit. He wants me to grab his tongue. He wants to call an ambulance. My dad was a corps man in the Navy and, to him, this situation requires emergency action.

I know better. Neal and I go through things like this on a daily basis. If there is a sledgehammer outside, Neal can go into convulsions. If a tone from a car muffler is too deep and loud, it can send Neal over the edge. If a stupid jerk is drilling a light fixture in the middle of a children's gym class and won't stop, Neal's a goner. I try to explain to my dad that Neal will be okay once the drilling stops and he calms his body. Usually I am a centered, conscious person; however, at times like this, when someone is just not listening, I have been known to lose it. "STOP THE F . . . DRILLING!!!!!" I scream. The guy looks down from the ladder, sees Neal thrashing, me holding Neal, my frantic dad.

"I'm almost done," he says again.

He continues drilling. . . . I cannot believe his insensitivity. To this day, it blows me away. An afternoon that began with promise is ruined, for my dad, for me, and most of all, for Neal.

I get Neal home and calm him down. Finally, I can take him in my arms and tell him that I love him, that it's all right. He is worn out and I put him to bed for a nap. I try to explain to my dad what has happened. He does his best to understand. He assures me that he's not judging Neal. He simply wants to connect to him so badly.

"I just don't know what to do," he says.

The next morning my dad is in the kitchen saying his prayers. Neal slips quietly into the room and sits beside him. My dad prays in Hebrew, his head bowed. As he prays, Neal leans over and kisses his head.

23.

I WONDER IF Neal will ever say the word "Mama." Just that word. How I long to hear it. In the morning, when he runs into my bedroom and wants me to get out of bed, I tell him, "Okay, I'll get up but first say 'Mama.'" I point to my lips and model the mouth movements for Ma-ma. He tries, but nothing comes out. I applaud his effort and get out of bed. The next morning I try again. Just that one word, I keep thinking.

In November I attend a Greenspan conference in Washington, D.C. At the conference I watch endless videos of other kids being coached by Dr. Greenspan. I am away from Neal for four days. I call home several times a day. I'm not surprised by how much I miss him.

Dr. Greenspan allays my concern that Neal is not progressing faster. Until now, I've subscribed to the common belief that there is only a small amount of time in which the brain can grow and develop.

But in one of his lectures, Dr. Greenspan addresses the "window of opportunity" that is often discussed in autism circles. "The brain is constantly growing," he says. "That is why, for example, a man in his seventies can learn to play a guitar."

Later, I ask him what this means in regards to Neal. "If Neal doesn't start to speak until he's thirty years old," the doctor tells me, "he still has forty or fifty more years to speak."

Again, the doctor gives me hope. So many other people have warned me that there is only a narrow window of opportunity and that if you miss it, you're doomed. Now I understand that, although early intervention is essential, there isn't merely "a window" of opportunity; there's a veritable skyscraper of windows. It's a prospect that's immensely soothing.

——————————— 24. ———————————

MY HUSBAND BRINGS Neal to Washington, D.C., so I can take him to see Dr. Greenspan after the conference. We meet up at a restaurant. They arrive first. As I walk in, I see Neal sitting in a high chair at the table. My mom and dad, my sister, brother-in-law, and their two kids are all there. It's a fun, all-you-can-eat Italian restaurant. With Neal's love of anything pastalike, it's a perfect choice. Neal is happily seated next to his cousin Kira. Even from a distance, I can see that she's very attentive to him.

I wave. Neal sees me. He pushes to get out of his high chair and wiggles out of the release. He stands in his little chair.

As I draw near, he calls out, "Mama, Mama!"

At last Neal has spoken the word I have waited a lifetime to hear.

——————————— 25. ———————————

MY MOTHER IS rushed to the hospital. The prognosis is poor. A few months, the doctors say. No more. We keep this information from her. Later, we will learn that she knew all along. From the day of her diagnosis, each time the phone rings, I gird myself for that dreaded call.

I go to the Washington, D.C., area every few weeks to see her. (Fortunately, we have a wonderful sitter who helps my husband and Neal at home.) These trips have a terrible urgency. I need to make up for lost time. And I need to soak up every possible memory for later.

My mom, always the giver, finally has to receive. She lets me love her as she never let me before. We never were allowed even to wash dishes in her house. We didn't have chores, instead we had a "smother mother" who did everything for us. I used to go to other kids' houses and do their chores for them. My mom was extremely clean and tidy, but also a clutter maven. She kept everything, from the first Valentine I ever made her to the prom dress and corsage I wore on prom night my senior year of high school.

At home, I go through this "stuff" with her. We reminisce. Late at night, when my dad has gone to bed, we sit on the couch, watch Jay Leno, then watch our favorite Elizabeth Taylor movie, *A Place in the Sun,* or James Dean's *Rebel Without a Cause.* We snuggle together under a brightly colored afghan she crocheted. Me, a child-woman embraced in my mom's arms; she, a woman-child, fragile and needing her daughter's care.

I try to explain to Neal where I'm going. To do this, I use a six-inch-high figurine we purchased from a speech therapy clinic that looks amazingly like my mom. I lay the doll down and cover it with a little blanket.

"Grandma's sick," I say. "Mommy's going to visit her."

Neal doesn't respond. Does he understand?

26.

NEAL TAKES THREE steps forward and four steps back. To get him to all of his therapies I drive all over town, sometimes clocking a hundred miles a day. At home, we spend hours on Floortime.

It is not easy for my husband that I'm directing all of my attention to Neal. I understand his frustration. I feel for him, but I cannot stop. I read and hear about kids recovering from autism. Being cured. I am certain that I can make this happen, that Neal's diagnosis, like the malnutrition, will one day be behind us for good.

I imagine Neal talking eloquently about what it was like when he was a youngster and couldn't speak. I see him walking down our stairs, a high school teen, carrying a football, saying, "Mom, I'm off to practice. We have a big game this weekend."

I see him tall, beautiful. Normal. And it's up to me to get him that way. Like anything I have done before, I commit one hundred percent. It's my desire to respond to the need, the urgency, the immediacy, with all the heroic arrogance of a determined mother fighting for her child. Nothing matters more to me than helping Neal unlock the expressiveness that I know is within him.

TAKING NEAL PLACES is difficult. There are a lot of places that I need to take him. More often than not, when we drive in the car, Neal has a temper tantrum in his car seat. He kicks the seat in front of him, wailing for me to stop. I pull over, stop the car, and help him calm down. Sometimes I wait for more than half an hour, letting him kick the back of the passenger's seat until he is calm enough for us to continue our drive.

I take him grocery shopping. He likes to sit in the cart. I pile the groceries all around him. I've got it down to a science. When we get to the store, I help him climb into the cart. Next I purchase any and all canned goods, paper products, and things that are unbreakable. Then I surround him with the harder fruits, vegetables, and chicken. Soft fruits like grapes and bananas go on top. The eggs I place in the little space by the handles of the cart. We look like a modern-day "Ma and Pa Joad"; our cart resembles the truck packed with food and supplies in *The Grapes of Wrath*. As soon as the cart is full, I pay and we leave, whether I've got everything I need or not. Those are the good days. On bad days, Neal has a tantrum while I'm shopping. The moment it starts, I pull him out of the cart, then leave the cart—groceries and all—in the middle of an aisle while a kind and bewildered store employee helps me carry a kicking, screaming Neal to the car. I don't look back. I can't. I feel terrible that the poor guy has to put all those groceries away. I tell Neal directly, "Okay— I guess you're not ready to go to the grocery store, yet." And we wait a few days before returning. You can see why so many of our meals are takeout.

Today, when I speak at conferences and someone asks how they can help a family whose child has autism, I say, "Ask what you can pick up at the grocery store for them."

------------------------------ 27. ------------------------------

NEAL CAN HEAR an airplane long before it flies into view. Yet he has trouble responding to a human voice. To correct this imbalance, Dr. Greenspan prescribes sound and listening therapy.

He'll get treatment for this at a facility in Pasadena, a sixty-five-mile round trip from our home, and a journey that can take anywhere from forty-five minutes to three hours. Fortunately, Neal doesn't seem to mind the drives. This is surprising, since outside sounds bother him so much that it's becoming a struggle to go anywhere.

At the center, children are given headphones through which they listen to Mozart and to Gregorian chants played at different frequencies. The idea is to retrain the brain to process sounds. They also encourage practicing speech exercises while he listens to the music. I have no idea if it will work, but I'm hopeful. I'm also desperate enough to try almost anything.

I'm driving Neal home from the center, and I'm even more tired than usual. I take the wrong exit off the freeway. We land in a maze of streets smack in the middle of Koreatown on the edge of downtown Los Angeles.

Neal's in his car chair, in the backseat. I tell him, "Mama blew it."

I often talk to him during these long drives. I believe that he understands me even though he does not respond. Then I hear a blowing sound. I think I'm hearing things.

Again I say, "Mama blew it."

That blowing sound again. I look at Neal through the rearview mirror. He purses his lips together and blows, then giggles. He understands. And he's making a joke. We laugh together. It's a lovely moment. Neal is listening, hearing. He's expressing!

---------------------------------- 28. ----------------------------------

NEAL AND I prepare pretend meals together, using plastic fruits and vegetables. At dinnertime, he plays with his little basket of produce while I chop real vegetables. I marvel at this, for it's the first "normal" experience we share. After dinner, we do piggyback rides and I try to draw out sounds from him. Our back-and-forth circles of communication have increased to over twenty exchanges. All of this connotes real progress. But the rest of the time he's in a place that's private and isolated, and cannot be breached.

I am desperate to keep Neal connected, to have his every interaction be purposeful and engaging so that he will stay in the world. When Neal spaces out and wants to open and close the cabinets or repeat a single activity, I don't try to make him stop. Instead of trying to control his behavior, I focus on building my relationship with him. If he's banging cabinet doors open and shut, I bang on the doors too, and make it a game. I try to sense what's attracting him to a particular activity: if it's sound that he's after, I take pots and pans and make noises with him; if it's the movement of the cabinets that's intriguing him, I play peekaboo or hide-and-seek.

With the help of our sitter, I begin using PECS, a picture exchange system, to help Neal communicate. I make hundreds of little pictures that Neal can use to express his wants. There are pictures of every person he comes in contact with; there are pictures of apples, bananas, and sandwiches, of beds and blankets, toilets and towels.

Now Neal can convey not only that he's hungry, but what he wants to eat. He loves to communicate in this way. He loves to be able to tell me where he wants to go, who he wants to go with, and what he wants to do there. A huge door has been opened.

I am hopeful, determined, and exhausted. Often I feel like someone trying to keep a fire going in the wild so that I and my loved ones will not freeze. And Neal isn't freezing. He's moving forward bit by bit. His affect is no longer entirely flat. At times, I see emotions on his face. Different emotions: happy, sad, excited, scared. I never knew these expressions were absent until I see them emerge.

------------------------------- 29. -------------------------------

ARE WE SLOUCHING toward normal? Sometimes it seems that way. Neal now rides the school bus. He's learning to play with other kids. Although he can easily become overstimulated, Wendy directs her aides to comfort him, giving him big bear hugs when needed, and playfully following his lead. He's so eager to learn that everyone loves having him in class. He plays at the plastic kitchen set, he climbs up on the monkey bars, and, though he can't cross over them, he loves the feeling of being high up and the sensation of being on top of the world. At the little closing ceremony that Wendy arranges for the end of the year, Neal is given an award for "Best Climber." We all joke that he will one day be the first Russian-born American Olympic Gold Medal gymnast.

------------------------------- 30. -------------------------------

THE FUTURE GOLD medalist is determined to master crossing the monkey bars. Although he can climb up the monkey bars' ladder, when he gets to the top he tries to do what he's seen other kids do: move across the bars using hand over hand movements with arms stretched, legs and body hanging. But he keeps falling down. He gets up and tries again and again. Another testament to his will. Every day throughout the summer we go to the monkey bars in the park. I start with Neal on my shoulders and we "motor plan" the activity. One arm at a time, hand grasping the bar, switching to the other hand, letting go, then doing it again and again until we get to the other side.

Once he understands the sequence, I let him hang on by himself and see how far he can cross on his own. At first, he can do only two bars before he falls, picks himself up off the ground, and begins again. He does this until he's exhausted. But he's relentless. He practices every day until it's mission accomplished! I watch as he crosses triumphantly from one side to the other. A magnificent achievement. Or, as I like to say, "What is one small step for a typical kid, is one giant leap for my special child."

–––––––––––––––––––––––––––– 31. ––––––––––––––––––––––––––––

WHAT A DIFFERENCE a teacher makes. For better or for worse. Unfortunately for Neal, his wonderful teacher from the previous year, Wendy Parise, has left the school district to teach special education courses at a local college. As much as Neal bloomed in her classroom, he's wilting in the preschool classroom of his new teacher.

She isn't the least bit interested in understanding him. She only wants to control him. She won't allow his aides to hold him or hug him, even though he's only four years old and can only feel safe in this inclusion class if he knows that he can be held by an adult if he needs comfort. When I come to class, I find his aide crying because she's been reprimanded for allowing Neal to climb in her lap. The teacher told her that she's merely indulging him.

In the absence of necessary support and guidance, Neal is lost. He's taken out of the inclusion class and placed in a behavioral-based classroom with the most developmentally challenged and severely autistic children in the district. In this classroom there are rigid rules and repetitive activities that alarm every aspect of Neal's being. What Neal craves and responds to is relationships. This behavioral approach may be ideal for other kids, but it doesn't work for Neal. It's a method reliant on coercing children to comply by breaking their will, and to break Neal's will is to destroy the part of him that accounts for his very survival. Being forced to sit in a chair, or to do rote behaviors in exchange for rewards, is the exact opposite of what he needs. Sometimes the reward is M&Ms, but for Neal, who never had enough food as a baby, the withholding or rewarding of food simply brings up his early hunger, hoarding, and helplessness. Other rewards are star-shaped stickers. Neal could care less about stickers.

Before Neal goes to school each day, he's overcome with panic and tears. At school, he manages to keep himself together, but the moment he comes home he loses it completely. He bursts out in tantrums. He throws objects at Luckie, hurls plates, glasses, anything within reach. We can't keep any pictures on the walls, or have anything out in the open or on shelves. Everything that we don't put away can be thrown or eaten or destroyed.

At home, we continue the Floortime sessions, during which Neal can become engaged and present, if only for moments. Yet, as his anxiety increases, even those sessions become compromised. Neal no longer wants to play with me. He is sullen, angry. I have let him down. As Neal retreats into his own world, I try to press on with our Floortime. Before, we set up little play mealtimes, complete with plastic replicas of food and a doll for Neal to feed. Now Neal pulls the head off the doll, tosses it, screams, and throws himself into walls. I stare at him, speechless. I, too, am lost.

The irony is that, as Neal regresses, I am asked by other parents to speak to their parent groups and to educators about my positive approach and to share what I've learned and accomplished with Neal. I start teaching a course that I call "Let's Be Autistic."

I create games to help parents understand sensory integration from the inside out; I design movement and drama activities in which I ask the parents to move their bodies in the same ways their children do. For example, if their child flaps his hands, I encourage the parents to do this too. They leave the group with a far deeper understanding of their child and of how to help them.

Parents thank me for my insights, but I'm living a lie. In the outside world, I'm touting the benefits of Floortime while my own son is suffering in a behavioral-based environment and I'm looking on helplessly as he regresses. As I watch Neal, my friends and family

watch me. Their looks betray grave concern. As for my husband—
he just stops looking.

───────────────────── 32. ─────────────────────

THE WORSE NEAL gets, the more my friends and relatives tell me
that I could still have the normalcy I crave if I would just give up
and put Neal in a home and adopt a typically developing child. I am
urged to do this by many well-meaning people.

"That could never happen," I tell them, "he's my son."

At the same time, I am secretly terrified by the prospect that Neal
will be in his own world forever. I do not mention this to anyone and
am barely able to admit it to myself. How strong is he? I wonder.
How strong am I? Am I strong enough to combat the growing pressure to place him in an institution? You just brought him out of an
institution, I tell myself. You can never send him back.

───────────────────── 33. ─────────────────────

MY MOTHER IS dying. My marriage is dying. Neal is slipping away.
His gaze is increasingly inward. If he goes, I fear that I will never
find him again.

I take Neal out of school. The school authorities do not protest.
They do not know what to do with him, and recognize that they
aren't helping him at all. Though I am not the professional, I know
enough to recognize that until Neal can regulate and calm his own
body, he will not be able to be in a school environment or anywhere
else.

The one thing that helps him is our seven daily sessions of Floortime. During each twenty-minute session, he is more engaged than
at any other time in the day. Floortime is the only way that I know
to bring him out of his shell, if only temporarily. It is his lifeline. I
need to press on with it.

** **

I GO TO see my mother. I return wiped out emotionally and physically drained with a fever of 104. I lie on the floor, barely keeping
my head up, knowing that I still must do the Floortime. I want to
but I barely can. I need to find people to help me. I cannot continue
this way.

"Dear God, please help Neal," I pray that night. "Please help us."

———————————————— 34. ————————————————

THROUGH A PARENT network, I learn of DanaKae Bonahoom, a
Floortime specialist who is one of the few practitioners on the West
Coast trained by Dr. Greenspan. DanaKae goes to the homes of
children throughout Los Angeles and conducts extensive Floortime
sessions with each of them. She's had tremendous success connecting
with kids.

DanaKae is an impressive presence who conveys a strong sense of
purpose. I see immediately why she's in demand. The first time she
comes to the house, she and her associate swing Neal in a hammock
that they hold on each side. And they don't simply swing him. They
get him to say words like "more" and "up."

After an hour with DanaKae, Neal is more engaged than I've ever
seen him. I beg her to work with him more. She's already working
sixty hours a week and hasn't the time. So I talk her into coming to
my house once a month to train me and several graduate students
who are getting a master's degree in family therapy. To pay for this
training I take a job coaching teenagers on the set of a Nickelodeon
show called *The Journey of Allen Strange*. We find a lovely sitter to
watch Neal while I work. Curiously, it's a show about a young alien
who has to learn all the nuances of this world. Kind of reminds me
of Neal.

DanaKae gives us an intensive course in a brand-new philosophy. I
feel that I am part of an avant-garde movement, like the Bloomsbury

group in the 1920s. Soon, word gets out about what we're doing, and our group expands to include certified therapists interested in this new mode of treatment.

Unfortunately, many of these students and therapists have preconceived notions about autism and about what is appropriate and nonappropriate behavior for the child and for them. To them, it's not appropriate for a child to bang things. To DanaKae and me, the only thing that matters is why he wants to bang.

To unearth those "why's," DanaKae doesn't simply follow a child's lead, she also follows their need. For example, Neal bangs because he needs to be in control of the noises in his environment. When he bangs, he's the one making the noise. She encourages us to find creative ways to make those noises with him. I get a tambourine and drums, and Neal and I make terrible music together, with Neal as the bandleader. He soon stops the random banging. To me, this is a clear rebuke to therapists who regard Neal's behavior as disruptive and random. The truth is that everything he does is occasioned by his own imperatives.

I learn that this is the case even when Neal pushes other children to the ground. The children's parents tell me he's violent. They don't want their kids around him. I don't blame them. Still, I don't believe that Neal is "violent." Webster's dictionary states that violence includes the intent to cause harm to another. I don't understand why Neal is pushing, but I know that he doesn't intend to cause pain to any child.

DanaKae explains that Neal is going through the early developmental stage in which children learn about cause and effect. Having never had a chance to explore it, he's intrigued to discover that when he pushes someone, they fall down.

I get Neal toys that have little buttons for him to push. He loves the way pushing the button causes a duck to pop up. I also get him big rubber toys that he can knock over. They pop up too. He knocks them down again and again. Neal has found a way to satisfy his curiosity and to enact his need. He stops pushing other kids, and I'm thinking that maybe—just maybe—things are looking up.

————————————— 35. —————————————

MY MOTHER IS in the hospital. She can no longer wash herself. I wash her feet. I rub them with lotion that I warm in my hands. This is a privilege, like a sacred rite. Whenever I am with her, I feel blessed that I have this chance to give. I sneak the cappuccinos she asks for into her hospital room. I brush her hair. I marvel that she never complains. She asks the same two questions she has always asked: "How are you" and "What did you eat?"

Inevitably, her condition deteriorates. Is she afraid of dying? I don't know. The subject is never raised.

She weighs ninety pounds. When she comes home, she lies on her couch, curled in the fetal position, blanketed in her multicolored afghan.

My husband calls. He's in Los Angeles, trying his best to take care of Neal with the help of our sitter. He's having a tough time. "You need to get home," he says.

I leave immediately. "Be strong," I tell my mom, "be strong." I wonder if these will be the last words I ever say to her.

I don't want her to leave us. It's selfish, I know. Yet I also know that her illness has provided a healing, that it has brought me as close to her as I always longed to be. In the past, I wanted her to understand me. Yet her illness has taught me the wisdom of the St. Francis prayer: " . . . that we may seek not to be consoled as to console, to be understood as to understand, to be loved as to love. For it is in giving that we receive, it is in pardoning that we are pardoned, and it is in dying that we are born to eternal life."

Two weeks later, the dreaded call comes. The pain in my chest feels as if an anvil has been dropped on my bones. I wonder, how does anyone survive a mother's death? How can someone be here one minute and disappear the next? How can it be that every molecule that was my mom has disappeared into the unknown?

When I was a child, I knew that my mother was the confidante of all our neighbors. Even in the supermarket, people would stop her to unburden themselves of their woes. My mom was not a religious woman (although she did go to our temple every Thursday—to play Bingo), yet she led a spiritual life because she was always of service to others. Every Christmas, we would visit one of our neighbors, Mrs. Hartley, a single mother with five kids. Mrs. Hartley's house was always a mess; dirty clothes all over the place, filthy floor with cockroaches crawling up the walls. My mom and I would bring all the kids presents, a holiday dinner, and clothes. Amazingly, my mother managed to overlook the state of the house. Mom was a clean freak. Most of all she hated bugs! She was a ninja with a flyswatter and a can of Raid. When we visited Mrs. Hartley, though, she set all that aside. Instead, she would compliment Mrs. Hartley on how nice her hair looked, or how pretty her daughter was. She focused on everything positive.

Three hundred people attend her funeral. I am amazed by how many of them tell me, "I couldn't have gotten through my surgery . . . my divorce . . . my husband's illness . . . if it hadn't been for your mom."

She had helped all these people. Yes, I knew she was a helper, but the extent of what she did is a revelation. All I knew before was that people came over all the time and talked for hours and that she always showed them her Avon books and served them a cup of instant Yuban coffee with condensed milk and a slice of Sara Lee cake. She was not just feeding their bellies, she was feeding their souls. Now I make a conscious decision to be like my mom, to be of service, as she was.

My mother's funeral is the most difficult day of my life. To see her coffin loaded into the ground—well, it is surreal. I am infinitely grateful for our final year together. I am glad for the gratitude I was able to show her; I am glad that I thanked her for teaching me how to love, to mother, to give. Most of all, I am grateful that she let me take care of her, that she allowed us to forge a connection, at the last, that will remain with me forever.

At my home in Santa Monica we sit shiva, the Jewish rite of mourning, in which friends and family gather every evening for a week after burial. Neal seems oblivious to my sorrow. I notice but I don't mind.

But then Neal finds the little figurine that resembles my mother and brings it to me. He puts his finger to his eye and motions down, as if wiping away a tear. This has become his sign language for "sad."

He holds the figurine to his heart. I love him so much I can hardly breathe.

"Yes, we're sad," I say finally. "We're going to miss grandma very much."

36.

USUALLY I'VE BEEN the one to supply the positivity and joy to our marriage. But in my grief, I cannot supply it. My husband is having trouble parenting Neal and I can't say I blame him. Considering the dishes Neal breaks, the doors he slams, the pictures he pulls off walls, and the general chaos of our home life, I wonder if it seems to my husband that we're living in a war zone. Many things that don't bother me bother him a lot. We cannot agree on anything, especially on how to parent Neal. Our fights are unbearable. We've grown so far apart that it's hard to remember why we're together.

My heart says, "Your marriage is over."

I am not ready to accept this. I do not want Neal to be without a father in the house. I think about the wonderful love and support I received from my own father. I know how important it is for a child to grow up with both parents. At his best, my husband can have a lot of fun with Neal. At his worst, well, it's the worst. But I'm not ready to take action. I can't deal with the pains of a divorce when I'm still trying to come to terms with my mother's passing.

I feel for Neal. Just because a child doesn't speak does not mean that he doesn't hear. Neal hears and feels everything. He hears me yelling at my husband to stop yelling at me. Hearing us fight sends Neal further into his shell. He sits in corners, stacking cars, spinning in circles, banging his head. He can't focus or sit still for as much as a minute. He connects when I engage him during Floortime, but as soon as the session is over he retreats once again.

Neal can't take the fighting. One night, he goes to the fireplace, pushes aside the wire-mesh screen, grabs two handfuls of ash from the grate, and eats them. I race over to him, but not before my little fair-haired boy has black soot all over his beautiful features. He looks like a forlorn chimney sweep.

Communication has many forms. Neal is communicating his misery in the best way he knows how. What are we doing to this poor little boy? It's got to stop. Now!

MY HUSBAND AND I separate that night. He wants us to go to marriage therapy. Would it help? I'm not sure. Yet there are so many reasons to try again: for Neal's sake, for my sake, and because once I make a commitment I stick to it.

I wonder a lot about this thing called commitment. My parents taught me about it at an early age. We didn't have a lot of money when I was growing up; we lived on my dad's modest government salary and my parents sacrificed their own dreams to make certain that my brother, sister, and I were able to follow our passions. My brother got drum lessons; my sister got lessons in gymnastics; I was given all things artistic. They insisted that we commit to these activities. If I asked for piano lessons and then decided, halfway through the year, that I wanted dance lessons instead, my parents would make me finish the year of piano lessons and start dance the following year. Dad gave us long lectures. "You need to follow a path to the end," he would say, "before you start off on another."

I learned to stick with things even when my desire drifted. So as an adult, commitment came easily to me, even when what I was committing to wasn't in my best interest.

I also witnessed the terrible marriages of many of my mother's friends. This was the 1960s when women didn't leave their husbands. They stayed, they suffered, they endured. And then some of them came to my mom for Yuban and Sara Lee.

There was the neighbor whose husband was having an affair with his tennis partner. Everyone knew it. She stayed with him, but they slept in separate bedrooms. I remember going to their house and peeking around corners to see what it looked like when a husband and wife had their own rooms.

When I was older, we moved to a military neighborhood near Andrews Air Force Base. We were surrounded by generals and colonels whose wives learned early on to be dutiful. The week we moved in, one of them, whose husband was a raging alcoholic, called my mom and dad in the middle of the night from a roadside telephone booth, begging them to rescue her from being berated by her husband. He had pushed her out of the car and she was stuck in the heart of Washington, D.C. Yet they stayed together.

Then there was my mom and dad. Blissfully in love with each other until the day my mom passed and, I believe, beyond. If there was a couch in a room, my mom and dad would sit side by side, leaving space for three more people whether there were others in the room or not. They always walked hand in hand and gazed into each other's starry eyes like young lovers.

My mom thought my dad was the handsomest, smartest, and most talented guy on the planet. My dad knew how lucky he was to have my mom. He called her his angel. In fact, their "song" was the 1950s classic "I Married an Angel." My dad's nickname for my mom was "Tink" because that's the sound made by an angel's bell.

I grew up with this vision of marriage, romance, commitment, love. It's what I longed for and it's what I don't have. My marriage, always difficult, is a battleground, like the dreadful marriages of my parents' neighbors.

You can be a contemporary woman, and still believe in "'til death do us part." I take seriously the pledge I made after walking down the aisle on my wedding day: to be committed to my marriage for better or for worse.

My husband stuck beside me during my miscarriages; now I need to stick by him. I try to remember the good times. I remind myself that my husband has a wonderful sense of humor, playfulness, and sense of adventure, but when it comes to good times . . . well, I can't remember the last time we experienced one. Still, if I am honest with myself, I know that I'm staying mostly because I'm afraid to be alone, afraid that no one else would ever want a forty-something woman who has a child with autism. So when my husband asks me to give it one more go, I agree, but on the condition that we live separately while we go to marriage therapy.

37.

NEAL AND I don't go to soccer games or Little League like my friends and their kids do. When I try to do something "normal" with him, it often takes a strange turn. How I wish there were more things we could do together.

One day my girlfriend Ida and I take Neal on a hike at Will Rogers State Park. We convince him to walk with us up a small hill that leads to the highest point in the park and an expansive view of the ocean in the far distance. At first, he doesn't want to go, but once we get him going, he actually starts to enjoy himself. It's a short trek of about half a mile. What we don't know is that, deep in the canyon, there's a tractor making a humming sound.

Ida and I barely hear that sound, but it sends Neal into panic and convulsions. We are high on the hill now and cannot get him down. He freezes and will not move. He screams and yells. He's too heavy and too upset for us to carry him. Suddenly, a tall man approaches us and asks if he can help.

"Yes, please," I say.

Neal allows himself to be carried down the hill by this kind stranger.

"I knew there must be a reason," the man tells me, "for why I was just standing here."

When he saw us, he realized that he had been "waiting" for Neal. To me, this is a miracle. Such gentle miracles happen all the time. I just need to be open to them.

38.

NEAL LOVES BUGS. He loves to look at books about bugs. He loves to dig for bugs, catch bugs, befriend bugs, smash bugs. Neal is an equal-opportunity bug lover: rolly-pollys, ladybugs, ants, spiders, bees. You name it: if it crawls, or bites, or flies, Neal is digging it.

Most of all, Neal loves butterflies. He can look at pictures of butterflies for hours. I bring him butterfly books. He is rapturous as I turn page after page. When we get to the end, he mimes to indicate "more, more, more." If by chance a real butterfly flitters past us on an outing, Neal shrieks with excitement. I often think of Neal as my little butterfly.

There's a story about a man so eager to "help" a butterfly into the world that he opens its chrysalis too soon. The result is tragic: the wings never develop properly, the butterfly cannot fly, and it dies. I tell this story to parents and educators who seek to force kids to be something they are not, who pressure them into compliance or try to coerce them to be part of this world before they are ready. My experience with Neal has taught me that we must yield to slow yet natural progress: caterpillar, to chrysalis, to beautiful creatures that can soar on their own.

Because Neal loves butterflies, I am overjoyed to hear about a butterfly exhibit that will be coming to the Los Angeles Natural History Museum. It sounds extraordinary. There is a "Pavilion of Wings" and the brochure reads, "Stroll through a beautifully landscaped exhibit, see Monarch butterflies, giant swallow tail butterflies, and more." I can't wait.

I prepare Neal with butterfly books and manuals. We act out the life cycle of a butterfly. We pretend to crawl like caterpillars, munch on leaves, and roll ourselves into a cocoon and wait, wait, wait, until we develop wings. Then we fly around our house in a rainbow of laughter. I have often used this kind of creative play in my coaching career. Now I get to do it with my boy. We have so much fun.

We read the book *The Very Hungry Caterpillar* so often that its cardboard edges fray. Neal, who can eat all day long without getting full—apples, bananas, broccoli, string cheese, you name it—can totally relate to a caterpillar with insatiable hunger.

Finally, the exhibit opens. We want to be among the first to go. We are excited. I get Neal into the car effortlessly, and we head downtown to the museum. Neal is a little reluctant to walk across the large parking lot, but once he nears the exhibit, his eyes widen.

We enter the Pavilion. Neal is in awe. He is in heaven. Neal loves the butterflies.

He loves them too much. When he sees these familiar, angel-like creatures, he wants to get close to them, to smell them, to touch them. He starts reaching out ecstatically to touch each butterfly. Like King Kong snatching airplanes from atop the Empire State Building, Neal grabs for butterflies.

"He's killing the butterflies!" shouts a little boy.

"Butterfly killer," screams a tiny girl.

Now all the kids and adults are yelling, "Stop him! Get him! He's killing the butterflies!!!"

"Murderer!"

This terrifies Neal. He grabs a plant. He pulls it out of its pot.

He knocks over other pots. The butterflies are flapping. A security guard swoops in.

"I am so sorry," I keep saying, "I am so sorry. He has autism. He loves butterflies. He didn't mean to harm them."

"Get that kid out of here!" someone shouts, loudly enough to be heard over the others who are still screaming at Neal.

But Neal doesn't want to leave. He is actually quite amused by the commotion he's causing. I can't get him out of there. Finally, I see some fake, made-to-look-real butterflies at the counter. I rush in front of the line. People glare at me for cutting in. I beg to buy one of the $2.00 Monarchs. I can't wait for change, so I place a $10.00 bill on the counter, grab a fake butterfly, and race back to Neal.

I use this insect amulet to coax Neal out of the Pavilion, through the long parking lot, and back to the car. There, Neal and I stare blankly out the front window. I look at Neal. I see the puzzled look in his eyes give way to sadness. I start to cry. Neal stares back at me. He gets teary-eyed. He's ashamed of what happened.

We look long at each other. The tears give way to smiles. The smiles become laughter. It's one of those situations in which everything is so terrible that it's ultimately absurd.

But that night I pray, "Dear God, I need help. We need help. It's just not working."

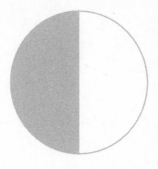

phase three: connecting

No pessimist ever discovered the secret of the stars or sailed an

uncharted land, or opened a new doorway for the human spirit.

HELEN KELLER

SON-RISE IS THE title of a book that I find at precisely the right time. It was written by Barry Neil Kaufman, and tells of how he and his wife cured their son of autism through the gentle process of joining his world. I understand what he means by "joining" as it's quite similar to the Greenspan concept of following a child's lead. I start reading *Son-Rise* late one night, and can't put the book down. I learn that the Kaufmans kept their son isolated from the real world until he was ready to enter it. Thirstily, I drink the book in. I read all night. I need to absorb everything that he's written.

It turns out that the Kaufmans have established The Autism Treatment Center of America at The Option Institute, in Massachusetts, where they help parents whose children are like their son. Both my husband and I are eager to go there and learn from them. We decide that he should go first.

When my husband calls me from The Option Institute, he says that he feels reborn. He has learned so much in a week about himself, about autism, and about parenting. When he returns, he feels, and seems, like a new man. He's recommitted to our marriage and has a deepened appreciation of Neal.

We've been separated for five months. Now we reconcile. We rent out our town house and lease a five-bedroom house on one of the prettiest streets in Santa Monica, a mile and a half north of where we've been. To disrupt Neal as little as possible, I instruct the movers to pack his room last and unpack it first, and to set it up in the new house exactly as it was before.

I hope that Neal is glad that his parents are back together. I can't tell if he is. I'm prepared to give the marriage all I have, but it's been so long since my husband and I have been together that I feel as if I'm moving in with a stranger.

——————————————— 2. ———————————————

THE SON-RISE PROGRAM educates and encourages parents to take control of their child's education program and general well-being. It helps parents view their child and their own situation in a more positive manner. They emphasize something that I've already come to believe: that the seemingly bizarre behaviors of autism have meaning and purpose.

They also believe, as I do, that you can maintain a positive attitude even if your child is banging on cabinets or tearing things off walls. They believe that it's up to the parent to set the right tone. It's a message similar to the one I offered when I taught parent workshops and "let's be autistic" games. Still, when I finally go to Son-Rise, I find that it's truly a godsend to take part in a program that packages these ideas in a systematic, attainable form.

I'm interested to see how many of the principles at the Son-Rise Program are similar to Dr. Greenspan's Floortime approach. In both programs, the parent is essential in reaching the child and developing their relationship. Both programs encourage the parent to follow the child's lead, and both believe in a developmental approach. Not only is the Son-Rise Program a great adjunct to the Greenspan program, but, perhaps more important, it gives me support that I desperately need. It's a huge relief to be surrounded by other parents who are as desperate and committed as I am. The beauty of the Berkshire Mountains that surround us is as calming and inspiring. I can't think of anything that could be more restorative.

——————————————— 3. ———————————————

I AM STILL not able to admit that Neal has autism. I can say, "My child has special needs." Or, "My son has 'autisticlike behaviors.'" But for me, embracing the "A word" means admitting defeat, opening the door to institutionalized life, dismal existence. Son-Rise takes the stigma out of the diagnosis. In one of the first workshops, parents are taught to regard that diagnosis as meaningless. The diagnosis, we're told, is merely words and letters: PDD, ASD, ADHD, ABC's. No matter what he or she is called or dubbed, your child is a child, first and foremost. So let go of the diagnosis and see the child. Oh, this feels good right away.

The facilitators at the training reinforce my strong belief that my attitude has an impact on all of Neal's development. They help me with my fears. My greatest fear is that Neal is going to be in his own world forever.

The staff at the Son-Rise Program help me see that Neal is content in his own little world. He is happy staring into space, stacking cars, endlessly gazing at his hand. What makes him discontented is when I try to get him to do other things. In other words, the one who's discontented isn't Neal, it's me. They help me see that what causes distress is not his need to be in my world; it's my need for Neal to be in this world with me.

At the Son-Rise Program, I learn to examine my fear, to confront the worst thing that could happen. The worst thing would be that Neal lives happily in his own little world, where he is fed and cared for by me or even, in the worst case of all, in a home where he is cared for by loving, understanding people. Could I live with that? I suppose I could. Although I would never want this for Neal—if that was the worst, I could live with it, if I absolutely had to.

This may seem ironic, but by accepting my worst fear, I find that I am able to let it go. This keeps me in the moment, where I am safe and Neal is safe and which is, in reality, all we have. I've heard it said that yesterday is the past, tomorrow is the future, today is a gift—that's why it's called "the present."

The coaching at the Son-Rise Program has many facets. I learn how to rally friends, neighbors, and community to help me with Neal; I learn how to create my own inner circle of people who "totally get" Neal. I'm told it's okay if my family has trouble accepting

Neal or being with him. If that's the case, I need to find other people with whom I can create a second family for him that will accept him for exactly who he is.

To my surprise, they recommend NOT driving Neal to his various and sundry therapies. They help me see that all the driving requires Neal to constantly adjust his sensory system, forcing him to change, transition, put up his guard. They suggest that I conduct all of Neal's interventions in a playroom at home.

The week is a catharsis for all the parents. At the workshops, we break down in tears. We share challenges, worries, hopes, and dreams. The topics range from how to set up a proper therapeutic playroom, to inspirational stories of people who overcame phenomenal obstacles to achieve extraordinary results, like Wilma Rudolf, who was born premature and couldn't walk without braces on her legs until she was twelve years old and went on to be the first American woman to win three Olympic gold medals. Stories like this shore up my conviction that anything is possible.

FINALLY, I AM talking to other parents with whom I can reason, laugh, and cry. We support each other as we take turns sharing the weight of our burdens. Soon we are enjoying mealtimes together, midday walks, and late-night talks. We laugh into dusk and sometimes till dawn. I haven't felt this freedom and this kind of cathartic laughter since my years touring the country with *Sesame Street Live*!

Yes, one of my claims to fame is that, before my marriage, I played Oscar the Grouch as a dancer for the Live Tour Arena Show of *Sesame Street*. I was also the featured warm-up dancer —a "Keystone Cop" dressed in an overstuffed uniform with clown shoes a foot and a half long. Every day for over six months, I would dress up in this garb and play to an audience of as many as five hundred three- and four-year-olds. I'd get them clapping and stomping and then I'd quickly change backstage and step into a plastic trash can with a three-foot green puppet on my arm. To be Oscar, I held my arm high—I developed a muscular right arm that year—and used my thumb to manipulate his mouth and my peace-sign fingers to move his eyes.

After that aerobic performance, my two roommates in the tour group and I stayed up late, laughing and playing. Now here I am, almost twenty years later, laughing and playing with these strangers with the same sense of joy and freedom that I felt in my late twenties. I am not only learning how to heal Neal. I am beginning to heal myself.

I return from freezing cold Massachusetts to sunny California armed with a mission. I, too, am going to "cure" my son of autism. If these parents could do it, so can I.

I will do everything in my power to "cure" my son and, in the process, live a normal life.

In the coming months, people will comment on my "sacrifice." And, sure, it looks like I am doing this for Neal, but I'm also doing it for me.

My need to have a so-called normal son will prompt me to put the rest of my life on hold, and focus on autism. In actuality, this is self-interest. What I could not have known then is that, in the coming months and years, my sense of what is in my interest will be entirely changed. In any case, I've become fascinated by autism. I'm an autism nerd.

4.

THE PLAYROOM IS to be a room absent of "no's." In this room, Neal can pretty much do whatever he wants. Anything goes: if he wants to spin, he can spin; if he wants to take off his clothes and run around screaming, he can; if he needs to throw things, we provide safe plushy objects for him to throw.

In the rest of the house, there are rules. Clothes can't be thrown off, objects cannot be thrown, pictures must stay on walls. "If you want to be in our world," we tell Neal, "this is how we do things.

But in the playroom you are welcome to throw and take things off walls."

It's all about giving Neal a choice. What we are doing is literally creating new pathways to Neal's brain through the choices we give him and through constant, purposeful play. We work on eye contact constantly, and on back-and-forth interaction.

We build the playroom in our converted garage, which has wood floors, high beamed ceilings, a bathroom, and a private entrance. It's perfect for the program. But even if we'd lived in only one room, we still could have set up a playroom. After all, the playroom in which the Son-Rise founders "cured" their son was constructed in their bathroom.

We hire a handyman to build a mini–occupational therapy clinic, complete with a hanging net swing. He installs a two-way mirror so that we can observe what Neal is doing in the room without disrupting him. Another feature of this playroom is the location of shelves, which are placed high up so that Neal cannot reach his toys on his own and will have to ask someone in the playroom for help in getting them down. This is important because it helps the child learn to connect with other people and to perceive them as helpful. We also put up a big, beautiful redwood climbing structure in the backyard.

I'm convinced that if I could work with Neal all the time, it would benefit him tremendously. I'm relieved and gratified when my husband encourages me to stay home with Neal and give up my work as an acting coach. I now commit a hundred percent to overseeing Neal's program and to training others.

Try as I may, I can't seem to get the graduate students and therapists to understand following Neal's lead. Perhaps they feel it's a waste of time or a lapse of dignity to spin in circles with him or stare at their hands. They're still more concerned with getting Neal to do what they want him to do, with controlling the interactions. They were having a tough enough time understanding the Floortime approach, as it is counter to what has been taught in the traditional autism schools. Now I am asking them to embrace the Son-Rise Program, which is even more drastic.

Really, when it comes right down to it, they don't seem to understand autism. They don't understand, for example, that when Neal seems to be afraid of going outdoors what he's really afraid of are the unpredictable sounds that he may hear. To me, it is simple: the outside world overwhelms Neal, because he has sensitivities to sights and sounds that so-called normal people don't possess. Sometimes it's hard for me to grasp why these students and therapists don't get this.

When I let them know that I want to keep Neal indoors until he is able to regulate himself and process his senses, this puts them over the edge. Gradually, one by one, they give notice.

I cannot say that I blame them. I just know that I have to find people who do not have preconceived ideas of what autism is—so that they can learn to join Neal's world. The Son-Rise Program staff encourage me to find volunteers to keep Neal continuously engaged. I want to find people to work with him seven days a week, ten hours a day. I decide to look for people like me, who don't have preconceived notions of what autism is. I need to find actors, artists, writers, and other creative types who are open-minded and willing to learn: those who can "think outside the box." I place an ad on an Internet job-search website: "Special Coaches Wanted for a Special Boy."

———————————————— 5. ————————————————

BRIDGET IS BARELY twenty years old, though she's clearly street-wise. She's petite, with short-cropped honey-brown hair, and looks like a kid herself, kind of a Jodie Foster, all-American girl, but with a modern edge. She is the first person to respond to my online request and does so with a letter. "I am the eldest of five girls and the eldest of twenty-seven cousins," it reads. "I have been babysitting since I was 8 years old. I aspire to be a writer and an actress and I know nothing about autism, have not read any of the books, but I know this is what I want and need to do. I know that I can help you and help your son."

When Bridget meets Neal, she picks up a Hula Hoop and starts to spin. Then she tosses it to Neal. Neal instinctively tosses it back. There is instant reciprocity, a two-way back-and-forth communication.

What I don't know is that by bringing people into Neal's world, I am asking them for something superhuman. Neal can be a real soul-twister: how can I expect anyone to be saintly, calm, and patient when they're smacked in the face or utterly ignored? Being with Neal requires more than patience; it requires a degree of fortitude that I can't expect from everyone.

Knowing Neal is not just an experience, it's a journey down a path interspersed with sudden turns. As Bridget quickly discovers, when Neal meets new people he has a "honeymoon" period with them, where he listens to them, engages with them, and plays with them. Then in a few weeks, when he begins to feel close to them, his abandonment issues rear their ugly heads and, like Dr. Jekyll and Mr. Hyde, he becomes a totally different person, pushing his new friend away and not allowing for closeness. It's one of those "I'm going to reject you before you have a chance to reject me" kinds of things.

When this happens, the person with whom he was playing happily is in for a big surprise. Now Neal head-butts them or throws things at them. He seems hopelessly hostile, but really he's testing. His inner dialogue is: "Okay, you say you want to connect with me. But if I show you my most unlovable side, my worst side, will you really stay?" Only the strong survive.

"I go home every day, crying and drained," Bridget tells me. "Neal pushes all my buttons, during every session."

I understand how difficult it is to work with a child who is uncontrollable. The answer, to the degree that there is an answer at all, is to join Neal, to let him lead you. But for Bridget to understand this at depth, she needs to come to this realization herself, and I need to give her the time and space to do so.

In the meantime, she battles with Neal, and nicknames him "Taz," explaining that he's her "little Tasmanian devil." She tries to get him to sit and draw, to toss a ball, to skip, holding her hand. Neal isn't having any of it. If she tells him to sit, he stands. "I want to quit," she says one night. "Give up, go back to waiting tables or something that requires no emotional investment. It's too hard. I can't do it. Neal hates me."

Finally, after weeks of this, Bridget is fed up and completely discouraged. Neal can see that he's gotten to her and one afternoon, when she tells him to help her clean up the playroom, he does the opposite, tearing every toy off the shelf, hurling blocks, crayons, pens, balls, and whatever else he can get his hands on. Bridget yells at Neal to calm down, all the while running around the room as she tries to clean up. She's frantic, desperate, trying not to cry. "Why are you doing this to me, Neal?" she says.

Neal looks her directly in the eye, and smirks. He pees all over her, laughing hysterically the whole time. Bridget stands there stunned, about to flip out. Instead, she takes a deep breath. Rather than take Neal's measure, she takes her own and realizes what's become obvious: that she hasn't been trying to join Neal, she's been trying to control him.

Relieved and exhausted, Bridget laughs. Neal laughs too, and soon both of them are laughing hysterically. "Okay, Neal," Bridget says, "you don't need to act out. Now I understand what you've been telling me all along."

With that, everything changes. Neal emerges. He bonds. Sometimes he'll let Bridget push him on a swing for hours. At other times, he just wants to sit and listen as Bridget strums a guitar. It is a time of what Bridget calls "beautiful simplicity." At first, he offers two seconds of eye contact, then five. In time, Neal looks Bridget square in the face and right into her eyes for up to ten seconds.

————————————— 6. —————————————

NEAL LIKES TO hang things on hooks. And I don't mean little things. He hangs chairs on the hooks in the playroom to see if they can balance. He then hangs another chair on the edge of that chair, creating cantilevers in the best modernist architectural mode. A traditional therapist might caution that "chairs should not be hung on walls." But his various coaches and I follow Neal's lead. We find many things to hang and many ways to hang them. We put different-size hooks all over the playroom and join Neal's fascination with balance and symmetry. I love this creative exploration. I am proud of my budding engineer. Once again, I am grateful for what he's showing me.

After weeks of random hanging, we make mobiles. We gather tree branches and hang pinecones from them, or we pick up driftwood at the beach and tie on seashells. For some undisclosed reason, Neal loves Tupperware, so we hang all different sizes of lids and containers. The playroom looks like a whacked-out exhibit of contemporary art.

We next take hangers from Neal's closet and teach Neal how to hang his clothes. We spend another six weeks hanging things, at which point Neal doesn't feel the need to hang any more. When he's done, he's done. But he's learned how to hang up his clothes.

————————————— 7. —————————————

NEAL LOVES TO rip up magazines, including ones I've just bought and have yet to read. So I collect about-to-be-discarded magazines from friends and neighbors, and place huge stacks of them in the playroom.

"If you want to rip magazines," I tell Neal, "you need to go to the playroom and rip."

The coaches and I rip with him. For hour upon hour. Soon we're making beautiful collages out of the pages we've mangled.

This is when I begin wondering whether there is a fine line between autism and certain kinds of genius, which I call "Artism." I mean, think about it: anyone who excels at something has to have spent countless hours each day perfecting their craft or art or gift.

For instance, if the mother of a young would-be juggler were to say, "It's inappropriate to toss little balls up and down," no one would ever have the joy of watching an accomplished juggler. Or, think of scientists who spend hours in their laboratories developing cures for all sorts of ills. Clearly, the world has repeatedly benefited from people who've been free to explore and enact their obsessions. It's in this spirit that we encourage Neal to explore his "isms," as obsessions are termed in the Son-Rise Program. I like to call them "preferred interests," but in any case we let Neal explore these interests, and let him abandon them in his own time, not ours.

Of all of Neal's preferred interests, my favorite—and the most magical—are his bubbles. He blows one bubble inside another inside another inside another. They float through the playroom, transparent, shimmering with color. They are breathtaking spheres of magical light. Sometimes I think that if Neal had words, this is exactly how he would describe them.

8.

NEAL STILL LOVES matchbox cars. He still spends hours stacking them. These cars become the basis of his relationship with Tom, who loves matchbox cars almost as much as Neal does.

Tom is in his late forties; his wife, Beth, is one of my best friends. He's well over six feet tall, has white hair, and a long white beard. I've known Tom for over fifteen years, and he's always had white hair and a white beard. I actually picture him as a toddler with white hair and beard, a two-year-old Tom with his signature wisdom and playful, childlike spirit.

Tom is a truly exceptional human being. He's a lighting designer and a theater professional, and a volunteer who taught blind adults how to ski. He's a "kid magnet": children readily jump in Tom's lap and climb all over him. I knew he would do well with Neal. I some-times think that I "tricked" him into working with Neal by asking him to house-sit for me when I had to go back East for another train-ing session in Massachusetts. Tom agreed to oversee Neal's program while I was away, and the two of them bonded as I knew they would. By the time I returned, Tom was ready to sign up to be one of Neal's coaches.

Neal stacks his cars as Tom sits beside him, stacking his own cars and identifying each one of them. "Here's a Corvette," he'll say, "and this one's a Thunderbird, and here's a Camaro and a Volkswagen."

Tom builds intricate roads out of plastic pieces and races his cars, while Neal, seemingly in his own world, makes no eye contact and appears disinterested. For weeks, Neal stacks and stares and does his best to ignore Tom. One day, Tom tells him, "That 1956 red Ford pickup is mine."

Each time Tom sees that car, he takes it from the pile of cars and claims it. Neal doesn't like that, but Tom won't give it back. This continues for a couple of weeks. Then one day, as Neal starts taking cars out of their boxes, Tom asks him for "my car." Without hesi-tation, Neal digs through the box, finds the little red pickup, and hands it to Tom. He doesn't look at Tom when he does this, but Tom rightly takes it as a sign that he's "in." Neal is understanding.

This is the beginning of Neal forming a relationship with Tom. Each time they play with the cars, Neal hands Tom the red pickup. For Neal, the cars—which have previously been a substitute for connection—have now become the basis of connection. It's a huge, significant difference.

I've always been convinced that as long as Neal played with cars, the cars would be a block between him and other people. But then the miracle happens: Neal begins abandoning the cars. Whenever it's time to leave the house, Neal makes sure his pockets are filled with cars. When we go to the grocery store he leaves two or three cars on the counter. When we take a walk, he drops cars along the way, like Hansel and Gretel, but unlike in the fairy tale, the purpose is not to find his way home. Neal is leaving cars to find a new way for himself. He is readying himself for more connections. Each time he lets go of a car, he is becoming more willing to let people in. He doesn't need words to express what the tossed-away cars are telling us: "I don't need to hide behind them anymore."

9.

TOM TAKES NEAL outside. Neal is afraid to leave the house, afraid of the startling sounds he may hear in this uncontrolled environment. They start with Neal balanced on Tom's shoulders. They stay in the yard, but eventually go "outside the fence." Tom always tells Neal how far they are going to go. He never goes farther. This builds trust. Since Neal refuses to get off Tom's shoulders, Tom starts to kneel down so that Neal's feet can touch the ground. After a while, Neal is willing to stand there for a few moments before getting up on Tom's shoulders again for the walk back.

Tom takes Neal to Will Rogers State Park, the place where Neal was terrified by the sound of the tractor. The moment Tom turns onto the street that leads to the park, he can see that Neal is anxious. But he's recognized the street, which is pretty amazing. As Tom drives on, he asks Neal if this is the place that scared him. Neal hums "mmm," for yes. Tom tells him, "If you get scared again, you can stand close to me." They walk. When they near the tractor, Neal stands very close to Tom. Then, taking small, careful steps, he walks right up to the tractor. Neal stands there proudly, his devil vanquished. Tom gives Neal a hug. He tells him, "What a spirit you have!"

The next week, Tom takes Neal to Temescal Canyon Park, a beautiful spot in the hills above the Pacific Palisades. Neal is afraid to walk, so Tom carries him into the park on his shoulders. For over a mile, they make their way through the tall oaks and pastures and eucalyptus trees. Then Tom, with Neal still perched above him, carries him the whole way back. Slowly, in the weeks to come, Neal begins to walk through the park. He goes a little further each time. Soon, he's able to identify the various trees. He picks wildflowers. He rejoices in the feeling of the sun on his face. He's a hiker now.

———————————————— 10. ————————————————

NEAL SITS IN a corner of the playroom, looking up, staring into the middle distance, babbling and motioning with his hands. His first coach enters the playroom for a two-hour session. When the coach leaves the playroom, he says, "Neal stayed in the same spot the entire time. I think he was talking to an angel."

The next coach enters the playroom to work with Neal. He emerges two hours later, saying, "I know this is going to sound really strange but I think Neal was talking to angels."

This continues throughout the day. "I'm telling you," says another coach, "there's an angel in that room and Neal's talking to it."

Was he or wasn't he? I've wondered about that ever since. All I can say for sure is that kids with autism seem to live on a plane where anything is possible.

One day, I'm about to walk in the front door when I see, through the window, a cup of coffee that Bridget left on the floor. She'd set it there an hour and a half ago and it had remained undisturbed throughout her entire session with Neal. When I see it I think, "Why would she leave that coffee on the floor? Neal is bound to knock it over."

The moment this thought crosses my mind, Neal marches over to the coffee cup and kicks it as hard as he can. I truly believe that he was saying, "You don't trust me, Mom? Then take this!"

Another time, a friend gives me a photograph of me with my tap-dance partner from years ago, the only picture of us that I'd ever seen. On the way home, I manage to lose it. When I get home, Neal, who has no way of knowing about the photograph, hands me a videotape he's extracted from a box of tapes that I'd randomly stored. It turns out to be a tape of me dancing with my tap partner. In time, I learn from other parents whose children have autism that their kids also do things that require superhuman perception.

11.

THE COACHES AND I listen to Neal, and usually we understand him. In some situations, we're able to say the words that we're certain he would say himself, if he could. This voicing helps him to feel "heard," and goes a long way toward showing our empathy and our connection to him. Still, there are times when he is angry, very angry, and we don't know precisely why.

Instead of trying to shut down this anger, we create a safe environment where Neal can work it out of his system. In the safety of the playroom, we give Neal things he can destroy. He's not allowed to leave the playroom, but he is allowed to scream, kick, and throw things for as long as he needs to do so. We find safe objects for Neal to throw, old chairs for him to break, telephone books for him to rip through. We protect ourselves with big pillows. And we do not stop the rages. Sometimes they go on for hours at a time. As long as I know that Neal is safe in the playroom, that he's not going to hurt anyone or himself, I don't let these rages affect me. I just love him. I love him through them. The more upset he becomes, the more love I feel. Calmly, I tell him, "I'm here when you are done."

The theory behind this type of intervention is that, through expressing his emotions, Neal will experience a sense of relief and, soothed by that feeling, he can learn to calm himself. This calming—which is also called "self-regulating"—is very difficult for the vast majority of children with autism to master. But it's vital, for their quality of life depends in great measure on their learning this skill of self-regulation.

In time, Neal's tantrums become fewer and less intense. We are all moved when we watch him restore himself to a state of calm after his rage is spent.

Neal has a profound impact on everyone who takes the time to truly know him. He is changing, and so are we. All of us who work with Neal are finding reserves of love and acceptance that we did not know we had. You know how they say it takes a village to raise a child? I have learned that it takes a child with special needs to raise the consciousness of a village.

12.

THE PROGRESSION WE'VE adhered to has three specific stages:

First stage: Neal's in his own world.

Second stage: we join his world.

Third stage: we help morph Neal's world into our world—as when we guided him from hanging up guitars to hanging up his clothes.

For the fourth stage, we stop following Neal's lead all the time and introduce him to what are called "adult-directed activities."

"Before you do what you want to do," we tell him, "we're going to do something that I want to do."

This "something" could be building with blocks, or blowing up a balloon, or throwing a beanbag through a hole. We ask him to do this with us, in as playful and engaging a manner as possible. If he does the activity that we suggest for one minute, he then gets to do whatever he wants for the next hour. Then we pick another activity.

This would be easy were it not for the fact that Neal hates doing what anyone else wants to do, no matter how much fun it might be. Simply, if it's not his idea, he's not gonna do it. So we sit patiently during his tantrums as he screams, flails, or throws himself on the floor, until he accepts the fact that these "persuasions" will not work. This is a battle of wills. And the parent absolutely cannot give in. What I've learned is that if you don't give in 99 out of 100 times, and then you give in just once, you're teaching the child that eventually you will cave, if they just wait you out.

Neal knows that I won't cave. Finally, he spends one minute doing what I want to do. These minutes grow to two, to five, to ten.

All the coaches have success with this—with the exception of Kenny.

13.

KENNY IS ONE of Bridget's oldest friends. He's an actor, fresh from the Midwest, who, like so many young, good-looking, talented kids, has come to Los Angeles to be a star. At first, he's hesitant to commit to Neal because he's afraid that it will take away from pursuing his ambitions. Yet, like all the coaches who work with Neal, he'll come to see that the freedom that comes from joining Neal's world has positive consequences that spill over into the rest of your life. By the time Kenny is finished working with Neal, he'll have appeared in several commercials.

Energetic and playful, Kenny is a natural to work with Neal. He can get lost in Neal's world for hours at a time, playing hide-and-seek in the playroom, playing on the net swing, crashing onto the crash pad. They play big, physical, rowdy games. But when it comes time for Kenny to introduce his own agenda, the love affair is over. Neal vehemently refuses to do anything different from the hide-and-seek game that he and Kenny so enjoy.

At our weekly team meetings, each coach boasts about how well they are doing with adult-directed activity: one coach is teaching Neal to finger paint, another is directing him to help mix the ingredients to make brownies. Kenny is still not able to get Neal to do anything he wants him to do. We encourage Kenny to reflect on why this is happening. Kenny says that it upsets him so much when Neal protests that he simply gives in.

Now, Neal knows that if he protests enough, he'll never have to do what Kenny wants him to do. We challenge Kenny to let Neal protest, even if the protest lasts the full two hours of their session. We help Kenny find the activity that he will present to Neal. We decide that Kenny will ask Neal to take some large cardboard building blocks and put one block on top of another.

Naturally, Neal resists. He tries to get Kenny to play the hide-and-seek game instead. Kenny holds his ground. "Neal, all you gotta do is put this one block on top of the other block and we will play hide-and-seek the rest of our time."

Nothing doing. Neal throws one of his tantrums. Usually, this would cause Kenny to give in. We all watch through the two-way mirror to see what will happen. Will today be the day? Kenny knows that we are watching and I think, more than anything, that he doesn't want to show up at the next feedback session knowing that he has once again failed to get Neal to do his task.

"Neal, come on, buddy, just one block on top of the other," Kenny cajoles.

"Ahhhhh!" Neal throws himself on the floor. He bangs his head on the gymnastics mat. We discover that the head banging doesn't really bother Neal; but it bothers all of us, so we've taught him that if he wants to bang his head, he has to do it on something soft like a gymnastics mat. After banging his head, he flails on the floor. He whines, he protests. Kenny will not give in. This goes on for an hour and fifty-five minutes, with Kenny cajoling and Neal tantrumming. Finally, five minutes before the session will end, both Neal and Kenny are exhausted, like two boxers in the fifteenth round. Kenny makes one last plea.

"Neal, dude, I've gotta go in five minutes. If you want to play hide-and-seek with me, you're gonna have to put the brick block on top of the other block, now. Just one block, man."

Neal doesn't respond.

Kenny goes to the closet, puts on his cap and backpack. Neal looks at him, then slowly picks up a red cardboard brick and places it on top of a blue brick.

"Neal, man, you did it!" says Kenny. "You did it! How amazing! Quick, let's play that game of hide-and-seek."

And they do. From that day on, Neal and Kenny build cardboard brick houses, towers, hospitals, and fortresses. They stack bricks together as high as they can go and throw cushy balls to knock them down. Neal learns to take turns, to take direction, to be reciprocal, to not always get his own way. Little by little, Neal is entering our world.

14.

NEAL AND I cook together. We make soup, cookies, and applesauce. He helps me with day-to-day cooking chores: he puts spices in the pan for me; he helps pour water into the pot; he puts vegetables into the skillet. It's wonderful. When he takes a pan out of the cupboard and gestures for me to cook—making a simple dinner becomes an experience.

The cooking is another one of those times when I realize anew that one of the many great rewards about having a special child is that things that most parents take for granted with their typical children are miracles for us. When Neal asks to go to the "little toy store," I rush there because he's communicating his desires and I want to respond to them.

Four and a half years have passed since Neal left the orphanage, and our journey has just begun. I am grateful for all that I've learned and hopeful that within a year or so, Neal will experience enough of a recovery that he can go to school.

When I look back at this time with Neal, I can honestly tell you that it contained many moments that are among the most extraordinary of my life. To see my little hungry caterpillar, protected in the chrysalis of his playroom, emerge as a new butterfly . . . well, although I have never physically given birth, this is as close to creation as I ever need to get.

<hr> 15. <hr>

NEAL REFERS TO himself and Bridget as "Didget and Zeal." He hasn't simply bonded with her; he's in love.

"One of the things I adore about Neal," Bridget tells me, "is the way he reduces everything to its basic roots. His eye contact speaks volumes. We have entire conversations with a glance."

One day Neal bumps Bridget's head with his. He's just playing, but he hurts her. He rubs her forehead and touches a finger to his eye, his way of saying, I'm sorry.

Then suddenly, too quickly, Bridget's year and a half commitment to Neal comes to an end. She's moving back East. She assures Neal that she will always be in his life, that she will see him again. I want to believe her, but she's barely twenty years old and that's a big promise for a young girl to make.

In her final month with Neal, Bridget begins her withdrawal according to the plan we've agreed on together. She shortens her hours; then begins training the coaches who will take her place. But in Neal's heart, no one can take Bridget's place. Her wonderful success with him exacts a steep price: try as she might to soften the blow of her departure, she leaves him with a broken heart.

He goes into a tailspin, tearing up his room, banging his head. I sit with him in the playroom as he cries, rages, destroys. Bridget's exit has brought to the surface all of Neal's pent-up feelings of abandonment, of low self-worth, of anxiety, of rage. I am helpless in the wake of his tidal wave of emotion. And I am absolutely terrified that he will never recover.

I wonder if I've made a mistake by bringing into his life people who will inevitably have to go. Yet what other option do I have? The answer: none. I have to accept that I am destined to be the only constant in his life.

I watch quietly as he tears the playroom apart. I hold him tight as he melts down. When he is done, I calmly say, "Darling, Bridget loves you too. Just because she is no longer working with you, does not mean she doesn't love you. You can carry Bridget with you in your heart, forever."

And then, one more time, he slowly puts the room back together.

16.

NEAL LOVES TO learn. With some financial help from the school district, we start with a kindergarten home-school program. My friend Rebecca brings us her son's General Education curriculum, which includes helpful notes, guides, and a complete syllabus.

Neal's coaches teach him the alphabet. We choose what we call "a letter of the week" and pick activities to go with that letter. For example, when the letter is "A," we draw an A, then make an A out of Play-Doh. We teach him words that begin with A and then cook something that starts with an A—like applesauce. Slowly, he learns to read words, to write and to draw. Everybody pitches in, including Neal's favorite babysitter, Ruth, and her twelve-year-old daughter Maria, who puts butcher-block paper on the walls and, with long sweeping strokes, guides Neal to draw giant-size letters.

We want Neal to love learning, so we make everything into a game. We use beanbags for games like "toss the red beanbag onto the letter A." Learning becomes an exciting adventure for Neal, for me, for all of us. It makes me wonder why all kids aren't taught academics in a playful, engaging way.

We incorporate science and history into his curriculum. Like most seven-year-old boys, he loves science and science books. One of his new playroom coaches, Jami, teaches Neal his body parts through creative movement exercises and art. She traces Neal's body with a marker onto butcher-block paper, then cuts out the words and pictures of "ankle," "foot," "toes," from magazines. Neal pins the appropriate name onto the paper body, as if he's playing pin the tail on the donkey. Jami then creates dances focusing on each body part.

The school district sends an assessor to the playroom to determine Neal's progress. She's armed with a notepad and scrutinizing eyes. It's obvious that she disapproves of our methods and wants to show the pointless absurdity of what we are doing.

I believe she's determined to write up a report that states that Neal is indeed severely mentally impaired, that school district money and time are being wasted on this crazy developmental type of education. I'm sure she'll insist that Neal be placed in a severe special education class, and that he and I both accept that his destiny is to do menial labor.

One of the first things she tests is Neal's knowledge of his body parts. I am permitted to be in the playroom during the assessment, but I am not allowed to help Neal. I listen attentively as she calls out body parts to Neal.

"Neal," I instruct him, before I'm silenced, "listen to the teacher and point to the body part when she calls it out."

"Neal, where is your elbow?" the woman asks.

Neal immediately points to his elbow.

"And where's your shoulder?"

And so on, until Neal has identified almost every body part.

I can tell that this does not make the assessor happy.

"I have one more," she says.

Okay, I think, Neal's doing great. He's on a roll.

"Neal, where is your calf?"

I can see that she's trying to trip him up. Neal looks at me. He's bewildered. In all of our teaching, we have forgotten to teach him the calf. If she had shown him a picture of a baby cow, he would have pointed to that. I see that Neal is confused. I also see the woman smile and start to jot something down on her notepad.

"Neal," I blurt out, disobeying the mandate to keep quiet, "it's between your ankle and your knee!"

Neal immediately points to his calf.

The woman erases what she wrote. Her eyebrows go up and her eyes widen. She's obviously impressed. Not only has Neal successfully pointed out this body part, he has also shown an ability to handle more complex thought and to problem-solve.

Neal passes the test glowingly, knowing pretty much everything he is supposed to know in order to go to first grade. The woman from the school district is not pleased. But we are. Really, it's amazing progress when you consider that only two years before, Neal was identified as severely mentally retarded and spent the majority of his time staring at his hand and spinning in circles. I am ecstatic and happy for Neal, and for all of us who've participated in his learning. We've taken time, we've taken risks, and now we are seeing the fruits of our labors.

17.

THE PLAYROOM IS where we rehearse for life, where we ready Neal to enter the world beyond it. For example, before going to the dentist, we spend two weeks in the playroom "acting out" going to the dentist. With pretend dental kit in hand, we pretend to be the dentist, then the hygienist, then we let Neal pretend to be the dentist.

Through a parent network I hear of a pediatric dentist who is totally in tune with this type of approach. For Neal's first session with the dentist, we simply go into the waiting room. Dr. Gross meets us there and playfully asks Neal if he has teeth. Neal shows him his teeth. Dr. Gross gives him a toy ball from a treasure chest, and we go home.

The next time, we go in and explore the dentist's office. It has a fish tank! Fun! We sit in the dental chair, and then go home. We make two or three more "practice" visits before having our first real appointment, which goes so smoothly I can't believe it. Dr. Gross is a gem.

——————————————— 18. ———————————————

WE USE THIS same, gradual process to help Neal adjust to other situations. Like the beach. Neal's not the only stubborn one: I still haven't given up hope of enjoying the beach with him.

Yes, I've dragged him to the beach with some success, but I wonder if he could really enjoy being there. I turn to Shelley Cox, a friend, confidante, and special needs advocate who helped craft Neal's first I.E.P.

For a week, Neal and Shelley and I go to the beach and park ourselves on a step near the ocean. Shelley takes a bucket of sand and actually brings the ocean to Neal. First, she puts sand on his feet, rubbing it gently into his skin.

Seeing this, I realize that the hot, scratchy sand must have been irritating to his sensitive tactile system. This must be why he wanted to be carried to the beach blanket and did not want to walk on the sand. As usual, Neal's fierce preferences are not random.

Each day Neal walks a few steps closer to the beach. Shelley continues to bring ocean water to him. He smells it; she pours the water over his legs. This goes on for seven days, until finally Neal walks on the sand to the ocean. For the rest of the summer, Neal is able to walk to the ocean with me. No more carrying him while he tantrums on my back.

He still won't go in the water, but he is becoming what he looks like: a California boy.

———————————————— 19. ————————————————

OF THE MANY things we practice in the playroom, the most sensitive is when we practice for the electroencephalogram (EEG) that Neal's doctors want him to undergo in order to determine whether he is prone to seizures. An EEG can be a very scary experience for any child, especially one prone to sensory overload.

To ready him, several of his coaches and I put him through a number of brand-new scenarios: we get a bathing cap and work at having him put it on; we glue curled-up papers to the bathing cap; we practice putting little things on his head like barrettes and bobby pins. Whatever we do to him, we also do to ourselves. Finally, the day comes to take him to the hospital. There, we find a big toy wagon. Neal sits in it happily as we cart him through the halls until we locate the EEG room. Neal enters the room, all smiles. The nurses are not kid friendly. They want to hold Neal down and sedate him.

I ask if I can talk with Neal instead. He's totally attentive and reasonable. He doesn't want to take the bad tasting medicine before they glue the electrodes to his head. So I give him a choice: take the medicine which will put you to sleep, or lie down real still while they put the electrodes on. He chooses to lie down without sedation as they glue nineteen electrodes onto his scalp. He helps count to twenty as they put the glue on his head. They then wrap his head in a gauze turban and tell him not to touch. I also have them wrap my head. Throughout the entire experience, which lasts more than an hour and a half, Neal is calm and patient. He's amazing.

Neal keeps the turban on all night long. All and all, it is an incredibly positive experience, especially when you consider all that might have gone wrong. Happily, his brain showed no seizure activity.

Neal's awareness level has increased exponentially. I trust that he will continue to progress. There is still a long way to go.

phase four:
never give up

Hope begins in the dark, the stubborn hope that if you just

show up and try to do the right thing, the dawn will come.

You wait and watch and work: you don't give up.

ANNE LAMOTT

AS NEAL PROGRESSES, I begin to wear down. It isn't Neal that's depleting me. It's my marriage. From the outside, we have it all—a lovely house, wonderful friends, and an amazing support system.

Still, I am fading inside. My husband is rarely home, and when he is, his criticisms of me, of Neal's program, and of everyone around me tear at my core. The truth is that most nights my husband sleeps at his office. We barely speak, and when we do, it isn't good. I lose weight, and much of the time I'm mired in unshakable sadness.

My family is convinced that the problem is Neal. "He's too much for you," they say. "You're spending too much time with his program. You can't handle this anymore. You need to send him away. You've done enough, Elaine."

We go to San Diego for a July Fourth vacation with my sister, brother, and their families. I know that I look terrible. My family is frantic. I wish my family would accept what is causing my breakdown. I wish they would understand that Neal is my lifeblood. My work with him, my focus on him, and my love for him are the things that comprise my salvation.

Yet what I must accept is that Neal will never get well in a home so riddled with tension. I can no longer ignore the elephant in the room: my marriage is a mess.

In addition to losing a marriage, I'm losing all vestiges of self-esteem. Now no matter what I do for Neal, I am convinced that it's not enough. A friend encourages me to write down everything I do for Neal each day. And then, beside it, to write the words "I did it." She also tells me to write down three positive things that I do for myself each day, and three positive things that others say about me. I have long neglected to think of myself or to think anything positive about myself. I do what my friend tells me to do and slowly I begin to feel better.

When I made the decision, after my mother's death, to focus all of my energy on others, I had not learned the value of self-care. I did not know then that taking care of myself was essential not just for my well-being but for Neal's. It is critical that children see that their parents value themselves. In the end, it's all about setting an example.

———————————————— 2. ————————————————

I NEED SLEEP. For me to sleep, Neal has to sleep. He has not slept through the night—ever. This is typical of kids with autism, so much so that entire conferences are dedicated to the issue of their insomnia. If Neal doesn't sleep, neither do I. Actually, I've never been much of a sleeper. When I was a little girl, my dad read me Dr. Seuss's *I Can't Get to Sleep Book* every night. I didn't seem to require a lot of sleep, but five years of never sleeping through the night is taking a terrible toll.

Over the years I tried many things to help Neal sleep: melatonin, a natural hormone that helps regulate the sleep/wake cycle; high-protein foods before bed; back rubs, head rubs. These things helped a little but not enough.

Neal could fall asleep, but he couldn't stay asleep. I would tuck him into bed, rub his head, sing a lullaby, and within an hour he'd fall asleep in my arms. Some evenings, I would fall asleep too. But Neal's body could not rest. In sleep, he tossed and turned, flailing his little arms and legs, which would knock me awake.

If I put Neal to bed and he woke up and I wasn't there, he got scared. So I put a pillow and blanket beside his bed and slept on the floor. Gradually, inch by inch, I slept farther from him, moving closer to my own room each night.

Once I got all the way to my bed, he would wake up and call out

"Mama! Mama!" I would come back into his bed and the entire ritual would start again.

Some nights, he didn't go back to sleep. I didn't want to miss any opportunity to connect with Neal, so on many nights I would entertain him until the sun came up. Once Neal's morning coach arrived, I would shuffle into my own bed to steal a few hours' sleep.

Now I take a multipronged approach that makes me feel as if I'm on one of those mythical journeys in which the seeker embarks on a quest:

I go to an occupational therapist who recommends lots of exercise early in the day for Neal, followed by calming activities starting at 5:30 P.M. I go to a nutritionist who recommends a gluten-free, dairy-free diet. No carbohydrates. No sugar. This helps Neal be calmer immediately.

I go to a homeopathic doctor who suggests a remedy geared to Neal's particular body chemistry that alleviates his nighttime fears. I go to a cranial osteopath, Dr. Eric Dolgin, who helps Neal calm his agitated neurological state. At first, Neal resists the gentle manipulation of his cranium. He hits the doctor, and pushes him away. But the doctor's motto is "I like to treat problems no one else can help," and he comes through.

I learn about a bedtime prayer that invites angels to surround Neal at night. I play gentle meditation music on a cassette player. When Neal wakes in the middle of the night, I say, "Neal, you are a big boy now. You can go to sleep all by yourself. You have your angels to protect you."

Neal sleeps through one night, then another. Soon, he is in bed and asleep every night from 8:15 P.M. until 6:00 A.M.

To this day, Neal is one of the best sleepers I've ever known. We still recite the bedtime angel prayer. If he wakes up, he may take a shower or calm himself by paging through a magazine. He then sleeps soundly until morning. Once we completed our quest, it wasn't Neal who was keeping me from sleep. It was me.

—————————————————— 3. ——————————————————

DR. MARGARET PAUL, the therapist my husband and I were seeing, is leading a five-day intensive retreat. I need to go, to take some action on my own behalf. It's the first time in over two years that I've spent an extended time away from Neal, except to go to an autism workshop, or to be with my mom. Before I leave, I schedule Neal's days and nights with full support from all of his coaches.

The retreat is held at a center in the high desert about three hours east of Los Angeles. For five days, I am surrounded by so much love and acceptance that I am finally able to break down, to cry, to fully grieve my mother's passing and my difficult marriage. I'm swaddled in the love and support of Margaret, her assistants, my friend Ida, and eleven other participants.

Margaret tells me to take a padded plastic bat and hit a pillow, as if it is someone I am angry with. I calmly respond that I am not angry with anyone. She directs me just to swing anyway, to hit the pillow, and see what comes up.

At first, I hit it delicately. After several swings, I begin to feel rage well up in me and I express the anger that I've buried. I am angry at my marriage, BAM! at God, BAM! Above all, I'm angry, at myself. BAM, BAM, BAM! I hit, I vent, I wail. I collapse into the loving support of this group. Margaret helps me see that I am enraged at me because I've abandoned myself. She guides me to be as loving to myself as I am with Neal, to imagine that I have another child who needs my attention as much as Neal does, and that child is me. She calls this process "Inner Bonding." This lends me a sense of peace and calm. It is as if I am connecting to something in me that is true and deep, something that I've lost and that I need.

So often, those of us who have kids with special needs feel that we must put our own needs aside. But I am becoming aware that only when I am healthy physically, emotionally, and spiritually, am I able to be fully available to Neal. It's like what flight attendants tell you on an airplane: in case of emergency, place your own oxygen mask on first before placing one on your child. I also learn at the retreat that when we do what is in our highest good, it is ultimately in the highest good for others—even if they are unable to see it at the time.

When I return home, I find that it is impossible for me to exist in such an unloving atmosphere. Am I still afraid of being alone? Perhaps. But fear no longer holds me. I am reminded of the Anaïs Nin quote "And the day came when the risk it took to remain closed in a bud became more painful than the risk it took to blossom."

I stop fighting. I live my life. I disengage from my husband. I refuse to be pulled into negativity. Soon, my husband leaves. There's nothing unique about my situation: 80 percent of the couples who have a child with autism get divorced. Congratulations, I tell myself, you've become a statistic.

4.

WHEN I WAS married, I used to think that we just needed to get through these difficult years, that when we were old we'd look back on this time and laugh at the troubles we'd had and be glad we'd gotten through them. For fourteen years, my husband and I tried. We tried therapies, support groups, personal inventories. Some of these remedies worked for a while, and some just didn't work, but eventually they were revealed as nothing more than Band-Aids on a wound that required a suture.

Our marriage was a roller coaster that I boarded at age thirty-one. Now, after a dizzying ride, I'm worn out, I'm middle-aged, and I'm disembarking.

We called it a marriage, but really it was a system of "giving to get." The doomed bargain I struck with my husband was: I will be there for you if you will become who I want you to be. How ironic that even as I was totally accepting Neal, I was working tirelessly to get my husband to turn into someone he wasn't.

Had I accepted him for who he was, I might have left years before. But I stayed, charmed by potential and clinging to the fancy that this union could work. Now, at last, I see through the magician's smoke and mirrors: the illusion was just that—an illusion.

Finally, freedom. I should be happy. I'm surprised that I'm so sad. I'm mourning the little girl's dream of living "happily ever after," or at least the part about "ever after."

Now, suddenly, everywhere I go, I'm confronted with divorce. The bank teller reveals that she's a single mother raising three kids and that she and her kids were sleeping in her car before she got her current job. My hairdresser tells me that she was raised by a single mother, my attorney says she's become single after her second marriage failed. Divorcees here, single moms there. Divorce is nothing to be ashamed of, I tell myself: it's everywhere. Divorce is rampant. It's the new pink.

———————————— 5. ————————————

ON SOME MORNINGS, I want to pull the covers over my head. At other times, I want to leap out of bed and begin my new life. Like any grief, this one comes and goes in waves.

I run into my friend Jodi Seidler, who started a singles website called "Making Lemonade." Jodi encourages me to get up, make my bed, and dress nicely no matter what. "If you look good, you'll start to feel good," she says. I meet some of her friends—other divorcees. They're getting through, getting on. They're getting out of bed.

I need to learn about this brave new world of divorce. Like Woody Allen in *Annie Hall,* I become the relationships inquisitor, the difference being that Allen's character was asking couples how they stay together. Me, I'm Alvy Singer asking everyone I encounter how to navigate a divorce. How do you handle the court battles, the loss of financial security; how do you recover from low self-esteem, how do you get through weekends, what do I do with this ring?

———————————— 6. ————————————

TODAY IS ONE of those days. You know, the kind when you just don't want to do anything. While Neal works with one of his coaches, I'm in my bedroom, spacing out over a game of computer solitaire. Naturally, I'm losing. Just as I'm about to win for the first time all day, I'm jolted back into the world by the sound of the front door opening.

"Who's there?" I say, quickly clicking a jack of hearts over a queen of spades, then racing into the foyer where I find a woman of about sixty who's wearing an Armani suit and a stern look on her face.

"I manage this property," she says.

Oh no. I'm two months behind in the rent. She's come to evict us.

"I'm going through a divorce," I say. "I have a child with autism." I try to hold it together, but I can't stop crying. I'm mortified. "I have nowhere to go right now," I say "In two months we can move back to our town house—but for now it's rented out. I need the money. If I have to leave before then, Neal and I will be homeless."

The woman's face softens. "I was in your shoes fifteen years ago," she says. "My husband left me for his secretary. Men did the leaving in those days. Now that women have their own money, they're doing the leaving."

She takes a picture out of her Gucci wallet and shows me her handsome, grown-up sons.

"I raised my two boys by myself," she says. "And this is me with my second husband. He's ten years younger than I am. I've never been happier. You'll be okay," she comforts.

She pauses a moment. "Look," she says, "I'll forget what's past due. Stay until you can move back to your town house. The owner's out of the country. I won't tell him if you don't. Deal?"

I've been dealing cyber cards all day. This deal's real. I'll take it.

——————————————— 7. ———————————————

NEAL IS ACTING out. He feels the stress of all this change. One day, he defecates on his bed. At other times, he throws objects at Luckie and torments her. It's the kick-the-dog syndrome. Literally. Poor Neal. His life has been blown apart. But I can't let him take his frustrations out on our sweet dog. I don't want to give Luckie away. But I need to. My brother, who lives on a ranch, offers to take her. Losing Luckie is one more bit of collateral damage from the divorce.

It's a three-hour drive to my brother's place. Going there, I think of the twelve years I had with Luckie, my "first child," who came into my life one year after I was married. I think of how I delighted in her being the "butler dog," of how she climbed up the slide in the park and slid down! The ride to my brother's is okay because I can look through the rearview mirror and see Luckie's adorable, familiar face. It's the ride back alone that's the hardest part. I cry the whole drive home, thinking about the day that Luckie and I met, and of how she endeared herself to me by licking my hand.

——————————————— 8. ———————————————

THERE'S A PARABLE about a cruise ship passenger who falls overboard. The captain throws him a life raft. "No thanks," the man says, "I'm waiting for God to rescue me."

The captain sends a lifeboat. "Nope," says the man, "not getting on. I'm waiting for God to come." Then a Coast Guard helicopter hovers above, and extends a ladder. "Don't want it," says the man, "I'm waiting for God." And he drowns. When he gets to heaven he's mad at God. He says, "Why didn't you save me?" God says, "I threw you a life raft, a lifeboat, a helicopter. I was there all the time."

I'm determined not to drown. I am moved and humbled by the unexpected kindnesses that are offered to me. On a day when I'm especially rattled, I lose my wallet. I go to a support group, and share.

I am fixated on loss, I tell the group: loss of my marriage, my dog, and now, that wallet. A person I do not know slips me a hundred-dollar bill. I try to give it back. She won't take no for an answer.

Good people are everywhere. This is something that I'm reminded of every day as I reach out for help more than ever before, because I need to. When the time comes to pack up the big house, a woman from the support group whom I barely know offers to help pack my kitchen. I gratefully accept this life raft. She stays for hours at my house, gently wrapping each glass in newspaper and placing it in a box. This vision of kindness stays with me. It is something that my mom would have done.

------------------------------ 9. ------------------------------

SINCE MY MOM'S passing, my former mother-in-law, Neal's Grandma Dorothy, has taken over the role of my mother. I call her my mother-in-love. She constantly checks in on Neal and me, and loves us through this transition time with an open heart and open spirit.

When Dorothy and I met, we were worlds apart. She, a sophisticated, elegant lady and me, well, I was a professional dancer—a gypsy. As well dressed and perfectly manicured as Dorothy was, I was equally bohemian. When her son and I became seriously involved, she took it on herself to "spiff me up." Her first gift to me was yards of black wool fabric and the name of her seamstress with instructions to get a formal suit made so I could join them at the "Club" in style.

Throughout the years, we've become as close as if she had borne me. She's been by my side, sweeping up debris in our house after an earthquake, holding my hand after surgeries, taking me to plays and movies to brighten my spirit. I draw strength from her caring.

Now Dorothy comes to the house and helps me pack up my clothes, including the lovely black suit she had made for me some fourteen years ago.

——————————————— 10. ———————————————

I AM FRIGHTENED and fragile as the move approaches. I need a day to rest, to sort things out. One of Neal's coaches offers to stay with him overnight so that I can go to a little hotel by the beach where my ex and I sometimes went for a quick nearby getaway. There, I give the desk clerk my one joint credit card. It's declined. Embarrassed, I retreat to my car, and head home, stopping at a Starbucks to drown my sorrows in a decaf cappuccino, nonfat milk, please. As I rain chocolate sprinkles down on the foam peaks, in walks Paloma, an Argentine woman I met at the dog park in Brentwood.

Paloma is about fifty. She's beautiful, with masses of dark hair and deep dark eyes. She brings her equally gorgeous Irish setter with her wherever she goes. When Paloma says hello, I try to hide my despair but I find myself telling her about the canceled card.

"Come stay with me," she says.

"Oh, thank you, but I can't," I say. She doesn't listen. She writes out directions to her place in the Malibu hills. "There's a key hidden in a flowerpot by the front door. Go in, make yourself at home."

I can't do this. I barely know this woman. She insists. Another kindness.

Paloma's house is spacious with hand-painted china, gauzy curtains, and linen sheets. In the near distance, I see the surf crashing onto the sand. I am at peace. I lie down on the pale pink bed in the guest room, and fall asleep. When I awake, it's morning. I find Paloma in the kitchen, pouring fresh coffee. I am so curious about this glowing woman who seems so strong, yet so gentle. I ask about her life. She tells me her story.

"I married a man in the construction business. He was rich and controlling. When I wouldn't put up with him, he left me penniless. I moved to a shelter for homeless women. Then I read in the newspaper about land that was for sale. I had no money to purchase the land, but I still had nice clothes, so I dressed in my finest suit, and found investors. People laughed at the thought of a woman contractor. But I knew I could do it. Since then I've developed many projects in Malibu."

Paloma's dark eyes beam into mine. Her dog's head rests in her lap. "Never give up," Paloma says as she strokes her dog's red mane. "No matter what happens, NEVER give up."

11.

I COME FROM a long line of women who did not give up, among them my aunt Pearl. She was born with a hole in her heart. Her hands always shook, yet throughout her life she knitted many beautiful items despite the tremors. They never got in the way of her doing things.

All the Goldenberg children were given middle names, except for Pearl. This was because, at her birth, the doctors told my grandparents that she was about to die. The birth certificate had to be filled out so quickly that they had no time to settle on a middle name.

Though Pearl survived, she wasn't expected to live beyond her twelfth year. In school, she could only attend classes held on the first floor, since she needed to avoid even the slight exertion posed by a single flight of stairs.

In the Orthodox Jewish tradition in which she was raised, the sole reason to marry was to have children. Because of her condition, Aunt Pearl couldn't have children, so instead she took care of my grandfather as he aged and was always regarded—though not by me—as a "spinster." Aunt Pearl fascinated me. She smelled of rose toilet water, which stung my nose. Brown hairs grew out of the moles on her face. I liked to stare at them, wondering how they got there, and how long they would grow.

Every Sunday, when we visited my grandfather, my dad would arrive at their five-story brick house, toolbox in hand, prepared to fix whatever was broken: old plumbing, stopped-up garbage disposals, a light switch—my dad would repair them all. What he couldn't repair was his sister's loneliness.

Every Sunday, as we entered the house, Aunt Pearl would grab my father and hug him. Then she would cry, pounding on his back as if trying to beat out her own emotional pain, "Sollie, Sollie, Sollie. I can't do this anymore! I am so alone."

Every Sunday, my dad would hold her, calm her down, and then we would eat dinner. On the drive home across the Fourteenth Street Bridge, my dad would tell us stories about his three older sisters, Pearl, Shirley, and Bella.

"They spoiled him," my mom would tease.

"Yes, they did." He'd smile with sweet guilt. "My mother was busy sewing, so my sisters raised me and spoiled me. Pearlie is the smartest of all of us: a writing genius. She wrote for the local Jewish papers. And she worked for the government in the State Department. You have to be really bright to work there—especially if you are a woman, and a Jewish woman at that."

Whenever we needed any information, we went to Aunt Pearl. She was the original Google.

My brother and I confided in Pearl about things that we would never talk about to our parents—especially if it concerned something we wanted. Aunt Pearl was logical. If she took our side, my parents couldn't refuse. My brother, at age fourteen, wanted his own phone. My parents said no, so he went to Aunt Pearl.

After a three-minute conversation, she convinced my parents that getting him a phone was in their best interest, if they didn't want their own phone to be busy all the time. Her reasoning was so basic and simple that you could never question it.

I took her the BIG questions. "My Hebrew teachers say that God is up there," I told her, pointing to the sky. "They say that only our forefathers spoke with God. But I feel God is in here," I said, indicating my heart. "And I talk to God all the time!"

"Yes, of course, Lainie. God is everywhere," said Aunt Pearl.

I went back to Hebrew school and rebuffed my teachers. "See? I'm right! I know I am, because my aunt Pearl said so!"

My dad loved to tell stories about his beloved family. I loved to listen to them, even when he told them again and again. I modeled myself on his sisters: when I learned that Aunt Pearl kept diaries as a young child, I kept a diary. I wanted to be a writer just like my aunt Pearl.

I also wanted to be a dancer like my aunt Bella, who gave up a promising career to get married, though I vowed never to give up my dance career for a man. And I wanted to be as kind and loving as my aunt Shirley, who always called me "darling" and whose hugs were delicious. You know that feeling when someone hugs you with all their heart? I would wonder, how can anyone be so warm, so loving, so bubbly, so positive ALL the time?

After my grandpa passed away, Aunt Pearl got her own apartment. She worked into her mid-sixties. In her seventies, she had open-heart surgery, which finally repaired the hole that had become the size of a silver dollar.

While she was on the operating table, Aunt Pearl "died" for several seconds. She left her body and saw herself on the operating table as the doctors and nurses were resuscitating her. She distinctly remembers being brought back to life. And the life she led after that was joyful: she always kept up with her nieces, nephews, cousins, and extended family. She even got a boyfriend. Her heart was made whole by science and by love. Aunt Pearl, who was supposed to die at birth, did not give up, and died peacefully in her eighties.

-------------------- 12. --------------------

NEAL CAN'T ADJUST to his new surroundings. Who can blame him? The small living room is filled with boxes on top of boxes. I can't see how I will ever unpack. My girlfriend Ida tells me to do just one box a day. Okay, I tell her, I can handle that. But it still feels overwhelming.

I try to ease the transition for Neal. I do my best to make his new room replicate his room at the big house. Taking the small amount of cash I have left, I hire a handyman to convert the downstairs garage into a playroom.

I'm actually pretty proud of myself for sketching out precisely how I want the room. I have him build a solid wooden beam so that we can safely hang a swing. I like seeing my vision take shape. Yet, once it's complete, it's just not like the spacious playroom at the old house. Neal doesn't want to use it.

"Waah waah," Neal mouths one night. I press my finger on his neck to help him finish the word. Waah . . . K. It's his sound for "walk."

He takes my arm and leads me out the door, moving west toward the ocean. He walks swiftly, nearly dragging me along, face solemn, eyes cast at some point in the middle distance. I have no idea where he's headed. I only know that he's determined to get there. Then he heads north on Eleventh Street and crosses Montana Avenue, and I realize that he's leading me back to our old neighborhood.

As it comes into view, his face brightens. He touches the tree that Tom carried him to when he was still afraid to walk out the front door. He asks to be pushed in the tire swing that one of our old neighbors always welcomed Neal to play on. Then he asks to go inside the old house.

"No, darling, we can't go in there," I say, "someone else lives there now."

Still, for years to come, Neal will lead me back to that house. There's some security he gets from knowing that it's there and that he can find it. So many things happened to him at that house. I think he perceives this house as the cocoon in which he began to become a butterfly. It touches my heart that this house has such totemic power for him. Yet I always remind him that our new house is a special place too. I always tell him that God dwells in him wherever he lives.

—————————————————— 13. ——————————————————

MY SAVINGS ARE depleted. I'm living entirely on my 0 percent credit cards. Thank God I kept all of those promotional offers in a file. One day, I'll be able to pay them off. Just not now. To raise money, I sell my furniture and jewelry. My brother, cousin, sister, and dad send me money. I can't believe I'm in this situation. I've been on my own since I was seventeen. I've been working since I was a kid.

Even at age seven, I knew I needed my own stash of cash. My mother had taken my little sister and me to see the movie *Babes in Toyland*. It was enchanting. I could have stayed in that imaginary world forever. After the show, we went to a gift shop that sold a picturebook about the movie. I wanted it.

"You need that like you need a hole in your head," my mother said.

"But it's a book!" I reasoned. "Books are good for you!"

"No. You saw the movie. That's enough."

Now I wanted the book more than ever. "Mommy, I have to have that book!"

"Absolutely not!" she said.

Okay, I thought, I'll buy it myself. I looked in my pocket for money, but all that was there were two dirty lemon drops; a flattened, dried-out Junior Mint; plus two dimes and a penny. That incident taught me how bad it feels to be dependent for money on anyone but myself. I will always have my own money, I vowed. And for most of my life I did.

As a kid, I made anything that I thought I could sell: lemonade, sand terrariums, beaded jewelry, rose perfume produced by crushing summer roses from our backyard.

My best customer was Mrs. Rich, who lived across the street. She was French. Even as a kid, I loved anything French: the Eiffel Tower, Edith Piaf, French toast.

Mrs. Rich had the most beautiful accent. Her house was always in order, and when she traveled to France to see her mother, she took just one small suitcase. How did she manage that? What perfect things does she put in there? I wondered. Or did her suitcase expand like Mary Poppins's magical bag?

Mrs. Rich never said no to me, no matter what I was selling. The one exception was my hand-squished rose perfume.

"No, I am sorry." She apologized in her thick, beautiful French accent. "I can't buy that!"

Of course she couldn't. The perfume was made in America. Mrs. Rich bought perfume made in France. This made me adore her even more.

All year long, I sold my handicrafts throughout the neighborhood, door to door, using the proceeds to buy my mom earrings on her birthday, to buy Old Spice aftershave for my dad, and, of course, to purchase lemon drops and Junior Mints for me at the local drugstore.

In the summers, I held dance classes and summer camp in my basement for the neighborhood children, asking each of their parents for twenty-five cents a day. I saved a significant portion of my earnings, hiding the money in jars and boxes.

My first "real" job was selling popcorn at a movie theater near my house. I was fourteen. It was a great job, because you could see all the movies for free and because I had a crush on the projectionist. During films, we'd make out, pausing while he changed the reel. Then we'd start up again.

By my second year in college, I was teaching dance classes like my aunt Bella. I was good at it, and it was what stuck. I was making a lot of money then. My boyfriend at the time would "borrow" my cash and never return it. This was the first time that I allowed my security to be undermined. It wasn't the last.

In my marriage, though I made a good living as an acting coach, I let my husband take charge of the finances. We agreed that I should quit work after Neal was diagnosed. In doing this, I fell into one of the oldest traps: I became dependent on a man for my survival.

Now the man is gone, I have no job, and debt engulfs me like an avalanche.

———————————— 14. ————————————

"WHAT HAVE YOU done for fun today?" my dad asks in a spirited voice.

"Nothing much, Daddy," I answer, holding back tears.

My dad loves to have fun. He found ways to be playful even when he was recovering from quadruple bypass surgery and a massive stroke and had to learn to speak again, and to walk after being told that he would never walk again. He had fun even as he learned again to eat with a fork, and to see out of eyes that render him legally blind. "For a man in my condition," he likes to say, "I'm in great condition."

When I ask my dad if he ever feels down, he says, "The thoughts come to me, but I decide not to think them."

I want to think like my dad.

My cousin tells me that in our religious tradition, we are to thank God at least a hundred times a day. Whenever we voice something positive, we are to follow it with *Baruch Hashem.* "Thank you, God." Whenever we can, we are to focus on the positive, on beauty, on gratitude. "What a great discipline," I muse. I try it on. It's easier than you might imagine.

"I am grateful that I have eyes to see," I say aloud. "Thank you, God. I am grateful that I have ears to hear. Thank you, God. I am grateful for the hum of the hummingbird. Thank you, God. I am grateful that my eyes can see the bird and my ears can hear the hum. Thank you . . ." That's four "thank you, God's" and it's still only 7:30 A.M. I have the rest of the day to find the other ninety-six. I'm liking this.

I DETERMINE TO make a conscious decision every day to see the bright and the light in my world. I discipline my mind the way I would exert a muscle. It is a conscious mental workout to choose to

see the good rather than the bad, to feel gratitude rather than enti-
tlement, to perceive autism as extraordinary rather than horrible. I
liken it to when I first started yoga and couldn't touch my toes. Then
every day I got closer—first to my knees, then to my shins, then I
touched the baby toe. Today, I am Gumby, bending so effortlessly
that people assume I've always been this flexible.

So it is with this happiness "muscle." Sure, there are many sad
things in the world. But there's a difference between justified sorrow
and voluntary suffering. I choose to see the gift in simple things like
sunlight and flowers, in friends and family who love me, in miracles
that occur unbidden. I choose to find the silver lining, to locate the
positive in a given situation. Thank you, Dad.

15.

IT'S NEAL'S EIGHTH birthday. All of his birthdays since the diagnosis have been difficult for me. Each year, they remind me that
there's one more milestone we haven't reached: three years old and
he's not talking . . . five years old and he's still spinning in circles
and banging his head . . . six years old and he still prefers being
alone to being with people.

Now I realize that while Neal has come far, he has not left the
autism world. Perhaps, I think for the very first time, he may never.

What if Neal has autism for the rest of his life? What if there is no
way out of this maze and we are stuck in it forever? Can I live with
that? Can he live with that? I believe that he can, provided that I can
accept it. If there was ever a time I needed to exercise my happiness
muscle it is now. The maze is not an obstacle to our life. It IS our life.
Instead of trying to "cure" Neal of his autism, the time has come for
me to accept the autism that is in Neal. No longer will I attempt to
cure him. Instead, I see my mission as helping him to live the happiest, most fulfilled, and independent life that he can.

I realize that it's not about me having a "normal" life, or a "normal" kid. It's about happiness. And for me, happiness begins with acceptance. Truly accepting what I cannot change: Neal's neurological makeup. Finally, I am the beneficiary of all the efforts that I have made, of all the experts whose help I've sought, of all the books I've read, the prayers I've uttered, and those hundred "thank you, God's" a day. Now I not only embrace Neal's loving, beautiful, courageous soul. I embrace the possibility that one reason Neal and others like him were put on this Earth is to teach the meaning of unconditional love. I love Neal for who he is, without revision. On Neal's eighth birthday, I am reborn.

phase five:
a teenager again

Once we believe in ourselves, we can risk curiosity, wonder, spontaneous delight, or any experience that reveals the human spirit.

—— 1. ——

NEAL ADORES FIREWORKS. For the Fourth of July, I splurge. I figure, I'm already so maxed out on credit cards anyway, what's one more charge? I take Neal to a small hotel on Malibu beach, where the fireworks displays are spectacular. The loud, crackling sounds they make can be difficult for him, but the visuals trump the sound.

It's been a great summer. Neal has lost his fear of the outdoors and loves to be anywhere there is sun, fresh air, and a breeze. We head out to Malibu, driving twenty-five minutes up the winding coast to get there. You can see the ocean the entire way, stretching out infinitely beneath the robin's-egg-blue sky.

Neal and I play by the water. We climb rocks, we build sand castles, we eat gluten-free crackers and apple slices. Our favorite thing is watching the kite surfers, who thrill and amaze us with their daring and grace. The young men who kite surf are, to us, magical creatures: they glide across the surface of the ocean, until the wind lifts them, sending them high into the air, where they float until they land with grace on the water again. The first time I saw them I thought I was seeing things. They seemed like the brave, bold figures that populate Greek myths: half-man, half-gods, equally at home in the heavens and on Earth.

That evening, we share a meal at an outdoor restaurant and wait for the fireworks to start. The sun sets late on summer evenings, so we sit side by side, eyes on the darkening ocean and sky. Neal loves sunsets. He's mesmerized by the way the sky deepens from blue to dramatic shades of mauve and purple. I love seeing him so happy.

Neal is patient, and excited when he sees the fireworks barge move across the horizon, then in toward shore. In Malibu, residents pitch in to pay for the barge. They hold huge parties at which they watch the amazing pyrotechnic display. One summer, I went to one of these beachhouse parties. Next door, Tom Cruise, Danny DeVito, and many other Hollywood stars were celebrating. Tonight, from our humble lookout, the only stars we see are the ones in the Malibu sky. To Neal and to me, this is heaven.

Finally, the sky turns the color of dark blue ink. The fireworks are launched from the barge and splay out against the backdrop of darkness, setting the sky ablaze with brilliant washes of fiery color. Neal is riveted; his eyes are as wide as saucers. He's as awed by the sight of the fireworks as I am awed by the sight of his rapt, joyous face.

It's a two-night minimum at the hotel, so we stay the next day and play at the beach again. That night, we share dinner at the same outdoor restaurant. Afterward, Neal insists that there will be fireworks again. I tell him that fireworks come on July 4 and that this is July 5, a different day altogether. He will not listen. He refuses to go to bed. He sits again for three hours, watching the sunset, waiting for the first star to appear, all in the fervent belief that the barge will again sail in and the fireworks will start.

8:00 P.M.—no barge; 9:00—no fireworks. He still will not leave. Neal is convinced that any night he stays at the beach is a fireworks night. I am touched by his unwavering belief and sense of purpose.

Oh, how I wish I could magically make a fireworks barge appear. Or wiggle my nose like Samantha in *Bewitched* to send us to Disneyland where there are fireworks every night. But I have no way of satisfying his ardent wish, no way to bring him fireworks. Finally, at 10:00 P.M., he accepts that they won't appear. We make our way back to the hotel. As we walk, Neal's head droops low with disappointment. He wraps his hand around my wrist, and clutches it tight.

The next day, on our drive home, I purchase a Nova fireworks video so that Neal can watch fireworks whenever he wants. He wears that video out.

————————————— 2. —————————————

MY SISTER-IN-LAW, JULIA, and her husband, Gary, have a great marriage, a true partnership. I was struck by the respect and care they showed each other from the time they met. If I asked them a question, they would turn to look at each other, as if tacitly determining who would speak first. Then one of them would respond. Their conversations—like all their actions—were like two people dancing. They moved together, never stepping on each other's feet. Twenty years later, they are still deeply in love. They still look toward each other when asked a question. Julia believes in love. I do not. She has proof. I have my experience.

"You know, Elaine," Julia says one day as we walk on the beach, "I think you're going to meet a man and begin a new life."

"No," I say as I kick at the sand. "I'm pretty happy with my life just as it is."

For the most part, this is true. I have great friends, a deep spiritual life. Neal is more and more content. Why would I mess this up with a new man and another relationship?

The truth is, my relationship history has never been that positive, except when I was young. In high school, I had wonderful, nurturing boyfriends. Nice guys. They wanted to marry me, but I, like many women, sought out bad boys who were more exciting—or seemed to be. Now I believe that I would choose differently. But I have no desire to enter into another relationship.

When I was married, I marveled at how certain couples were truly partners. I'd note how they manifested that unity. Julia and Gary had their "look to." My yoga instructor, Paul, and his wife, Susie, were playfully physical, like two puppies romping around. They taught yoga classes, seamlessly working together, demonstrating postures, spotting each other for handstands. My friend Elaine and her husband, Curtis, check in with each another several times a day, telling jokes, sharing the minutiae of their daily existence.

When I was married, I longed for companionship of this sort. Now I am content not to be in battle. It's not what I dreamed of, that's for sure. But I'll settle for it.

In any case, I don't think anyone would want a forty-something woman who can't give birth, and has a child with severe special needs. I feel too old, too damaged, and I'm carrying enough baggage to make a Skycap's eyes bug out. It makes me sad to think of spending the rest of my life alone, but I have come to accept my life for what it is.

"My world is just the way I like it," I tell Julia as I pick up a seashell and toss it into the waves. "No drama. I want to keep it this way."

"No," Julia insists. "I definitely see someone in your future."

Though I'm prepared to be without a relationship, it amazes me that all my friends are convinced that I need one.

"But what about passion?" says my friend Colin. "You can't live a life without passion."

What is he, crazy? I want to tell him: "Be in a difficult marriage. You'll live without passion for years."

Sure, sometimes I think about having a companion. Especially at mealtimes when it's just Nealie and me at home, eating takeout, or something bland that I've thrown together for its nutritional value. It would be nice to have someone to share my day with. And holidays are hard. But I don't believe that partnership is in the cards for me. And for the most part, I don't mind.

I'm alone, but sometimes, when I watch the sunset or see the kite surfers skimming across the ocean, I feel as if someone is embracing me. At these moments, I feel that I am being held and comforted by a nurturing spirit. Perhaps it's God's presence. In this partnership I trust.

3.

I'M GOING OUT for the evening. My friend Ida has invited me to join her and some friends at *The Sound of Music* sing-along at the

Hollywood Bowl. I can't resist. It's my first night out in ages. I pull on some fun jeans that I got at a yard sale, a black V-neck long-sleeved T-shirt, a sparkly belt, and a short black boa that a friend crocheted for me. I've been running on the beach all day with Neal, so my calves are sore. I should wear tennis shoes—but they don't go with the "look." I put on black high-heeled boots. For a middle-aged mom, I look pretty good!

I muster the courage to drive myself through gnarly traffic to the Hollywood Bowl, an open-air theater set in lush, hilly woodlands where people enjoy concerts and good food in the fresh night air. *The Sound of Music* sing-along is a fun occasion. The entire movie is shown on a giant screen, and—you got it—we all sing along! Many participants come dressed as characters from the film and parade across the stage before the screening starts. Imagine sitting next to someone dressed as a Von Trapp family singer, or a nun, or my favorite, a man dressed as the curtains from which Maria made play clothes for the Von Trapp children—a costume that includes a pulley and a curtain rod above his head!

I happen to sit next to a guy who's dressed in blue jeans and a black Patagonia fleece jacket. He's a friend of Ida's who's recently gone back to graduate school to become a play therapist, a method of psychotherapy that uses play to connect with children. Jeff has peaceful dark eyes, strong features, and an angular build. He's a few years younger than me and cute, fun, and charming. He's also a good cook, as I discover when he offers me some homemade ceviche that he made to share with the group.

I like that we're sitting together. I'm thinking that, as a play therapist, he might be a good person to come play with Neal. What can I tell you? I'm always on the lookout for a caring coach.

Throughout the movie, we laugh and sing. At one point I think, "What a cute guy." By then, I'm singing so loudly and being so "out there" that I wonder if I ought to be a bit more "ladylike" and tone myself down. But instead of harking to my inner critic, I heed a voice within me that shouts, "You must never hold yourself back. You can never, ever again make yourself less than you are to please a man." So I stay big and loud, and we laugh and joke. Later I'll learn that Jeff is attracted to me precisely because I'm so out there, and uninhibited. (And I think he liked the boa!)

4.

"WOULD YOU LIKE to go out for coffee or something?" reads the e-mail.

Who is this from? He's asking for my phone number and makes a reference to the Hollywood Bowl.

Oh, it's from Jeff! I wonder if he's contacting me because he's interested in working with Neal or if he's asking me for a date. I haven't been on a date in fifteen years. Since I'm not interested in dating, I dismiss the notion that he might want to take me out. But I send him my phone number in case he'd like to do play therapy with Neal. Turns out he does want to play—but with me!

When he calls, we connect instantly; we have so much in common. I studied developmental play therapy; he's studying to be a play therapist. I worked in film and TV; he's worked with special effects and sound effects. I danced professionally; he had a brief stint as a stand-up comic. We go on and on.

I also find out that his family is from France. What could be better? I love when he speaks French to me.

He calls several times a week. We talk, often for hours, laughing, connecting. I tell no one about our calls. It's my own private diversion. One day he phones while my girlfriend Alice is visiting. We speak for a few minutes.

"Hmmmm," Alice says when I hang up. "That was a bit of a flirty phone call."

I'm busted.

Although I enjoy these conversations, I'm in no hurry actually to have a date. In any case, he's traveling a lot, so getting together isn't an option. That's fine with me. The phone calls are completely satisfying. I could keep them up indefinitely.

----- 5. -----

TO BRING IN some money, I coach typical teens for professional jobs in the entertainment industry. I use theater games and improvisation—simple acting exercises that bolster people in many areas of their lives. Our sessions explore everything from how to deal with auditions to difficulties with parents, to peer pressure, and general teen angst.

One afternoon, one of my students talks to me about guys. She's always chosen not-so-nice ones, and now there's a really nice guy who she likes a lot, but she's anxious about letting him know she likes him. As I encourage her to take a risk, my phone rings.

"Hey, Elaine, how you doin'?" I hear Jeff say. "Would you like to get together for dinner tomorrow night?"

Quickly, I reach for the answering machine and turn the volume down. My student looks at me and smiles. When her session ends, I sit on the couch, staring at the phone for two hours. I ruminate. Okay: I obsess.

He's asking me out for tomorrow night. Shouldn't he give me proper notice, and ask me out for later in the week? If I accept will I look too eager?

"Elaine," I tell myself. "Stop trying to control EVERYTHING!" I call one of Neal's coaches to see if she can stay late and babysit for Neal. If I can't get a sitter at the last minute, it will give me the perfect out. Uh-oh. She's available. I call him back. He answers. I accept. We're going to dinner tomorrow night. I start to sweat.

THE NEXT MORNING, I panic. I call a dozen friends. "I have not been on a date in fifteen years," I tell them. "I don't know how to behave!" As soon as I get guidance from one, I call another and repeat my mantra.

"You've gone out to business dinners in the past twenty years, right?" asks Jodi.

"Sure," I say.

"Well, pretend it's a business dinner."

This calms me for a few minutes. Then I panic again and call another friend.

"What are the rules?" I ask. "Do I let him pay? What if he wants to kiss me?"

My friends are amused. I'm a mess.

"It's like riding a bicycle," says Tami. "Once you start, it all comes back to you."

6.

WHAT TO WEAR? I haven't bought anything for myself in years. I put on nice jeans, a magenta long-sleeved T-shirt, and my black leather jacket. I ask Neal's coach to come early to take Neal to the park. I don't want him to see Mom going out on a date.

I am on the phone getting one last smidgen of advice when Jeff walks into my house, wearing the warmest, biggest smile I've ever seen. We hug. We laugh at how long it took us to actually go on a date. And here we are.

There is not a single moment of awkwardness. Jeff steers his little green Honda Civic—"Greeny" he calls it—up the winding Pacific Coast Highway. The sun is setting; all around us, everything is bright and golden. As he drives, Jeff tells me about his recent adventures at Burning Man, an artists' gathering in the desert. His excitement is contagious.

At a Thai restaurant, we order pad thai and a tangy, crispy rice salad. We talk. It's so natural, so easy, so effortless. I don't want the evening to end. When the bill comes, Jeff casually picks it up. (Phew!

I don't have to worry about that one!) He asks if I'd like to walk on the beach. He doesn't want to end the evening, either.

At the beach, we walk along the edge of the ocean that glows with the reflection of the crescent moon. After a while, we sit on the sand. Our conversation hits a lull, but not from lack of interest. We just enjoy the quiet together. Jeff shivers. I offer to share my jacket with him. He huddles into it. I'm overwhelmed by the night air, the ocean breeze, the nice, cute guy still shivering beside me.

"I need to hug you," I blurt out.

I put my arms around him. He leans in and gently kisses me on the lips. I kiss him back. We sit there, hugging, listening to the crashing waves, and gazing at the moon, my old friend.

"I didn't mean for this night to be romantic," Jeff says. He leans in to kiss me again. Wow! So natural, so easy. Like riding a bicycle. Only better.

7.

JEFF CALLS THE next day, and the next. I'm steeped in the afterglow of our wonderful evening, though I can't help wondering what engendered the magic. Was it Jeff? Or was it the beach and the moonlight?

For our second date, we join a group of my friends in Hollywood for an outdoor concert. On the way there, we shop for food to share. Like kids, we play peekaboo from opposite ends of the snack-food aisle. Jeff holds my hand in the car as we drive to the theater.

In the parking lot, he swings me around, "Fred Astaire and Ginger Rogers" style. He kisses me. With this one kiss, years of loneliness, despair, isolation fade away. The magic returns, and this time there's no moon, no beach—just me, Jeff, and a mundane parking lot. I am blissful. I feel as if I've been caressed by an angel.

"I thought the magic might have come from the moon, but it came from you," I say.

That night, huddled under the stars, listening to Sephardic music, we "make out." Afterward, we drive along Mulholland Drive. Taking our cue from teenyboppers, we park on a hill overlooking the ever-flickering lights of the San Fernando Valley, a lovely perch far from everything and everyone.

I arrive home speechless, dazed. I have not felt like this in years. Years! I comb my ruffled hair, pull myself together, and try to look like a mom. The babysitter, a girl in her twenties, smiles knowingly.

Jeff and I spend as much time together as possible. Sometimes, during the day while Neal is with his coaches, we sneak out to movies. Our first is *My Big Fat Greek Wedding*. We leave holding hands, racing to the car. Like the lovers in the film, we remain in the car, kissing, embracing, steaming up the windows.

One day, we take the entire afternoon and evening off to go to Disneyland. We go on all the rides. I am terrified of roller coasters. Jeff assures me that there's nothing to be afraid of. He tells me to let go of my fear and enjoy. This simple directive becomes a template for our relationship. I go on all the roller coasters—Space Mountain, Thunder Mountain, and finally Splash Mountain, the one I come to love most. My screams of terror soon become screams of joy.

At the end of the day, we sail into It's a Small World, my childhood favorite. Even as an adult, this space of worldwide love and acceptance, of voices joining together as one, brings tears to my eyes. As we meander down the waterway and circle around toward the Tahitian dancers, Jeff leans into me.

He whispers, "I love you."

I smile, entranced. But I don't respond.

8.

JEFF MAKES A commitment of sorts: he buys us both a year-round pass to Disneyland! The next time we go, his entire family is there: his brother, Dave; Dave's wife, Bella; and their seven-year-old son,

Eitan, who has cerebral palsy and is traversing Disneyland on his walker. I meet his sister, Evette; her husband, Mark; and their two kids. I meet his mom and dad, his aunts, uncles, cousins, and his ninety-four-year-old grandpa.

Grandpa John does not look or act a day over eighty. He's handsome and charming, kind of like Maurice Chevalier crossed with Tony Curtis. He walks briskly and goes on many rides. A Holocaust survivor, he is now a thriver. Ever since Jeff's grandmother passed away a year ago, Grandpa John has been looking for his next bride.

I love this colorful family. Throughout the day, into the evening, they disperse throughout the park, staying connected by cell phones and meeting up at various locations. Later that night, we gather at Downtown Disney for an Italian meal. This family is close. Very close. There's lots of love and lots of laughter. Jeff's sister sits on her husband's lap; his parents walk arm in arm. Everyone is in each other's space. I feel that I have come home.

9.

"I LOVE YOU," Jeff insists at every opportunity. I cannot answer him back. I don't know if I am afraid of my feelings, or if I just don't feel that way about him.

"It's too soon for you to really love me," I say. "You're infatuated, maybe, but this isn't true love."

He answers, "Just as you have a knowingness of God, I know I love you. And I pray that you will feel the same about me."

One evening, Jeff tells me, "I don't make a lot of money. I will never be able to support you financially as you were supported in your marriage. But I will hold you, I will love you, I will cook for you, and I will be there for you, always. I will never hurt you. Let me help you heal."

As we slow dance in my living room to Ben Harper's "Forever," I feel like the Meryl Streep character in *The Bridges of Madison County,* whose brief encounter with a man fills her lonely heart forever. Still, I don't expect this relationship with Jeff to last, but this night of soulful connection brings me so much of what I've always longed for. The feelings are so profound and true that I believe they will carry me through a lifetime.

Jeff's love washes over me like summer rain, nourishing all that was parched. For the first time in my adult life, I experience true intimacy. We laugh, we play, we watch movies, we cry. We share our deepest fears, our dreams. In our first months together, we share more intimate moments than I experienced in fourteen years of marriage. We're like one of those slow, sappy montages in a million movies as we watch sunsets and pick flowers and take long walks around my neighborhood. These small, sweet occurrences are truly healing for me. When I'm with Jeff, time is suspended.

Then time resumes and I need to be back with Neal, tending to his daily challenges. I'd like to introduce Jeff to Neal, but I don't because I can't bring Neal into a relationship that is merely temporary. Once Jeff sees the craziness of my life, he will run like the wind. I just know it. So I avoid talk of our future even as Jeff insists that we'll be together forever.

Finally, my divorce is settled. I'm awarded full custody of Neal and enough money for us to be comfortable. Amen! What a relief! My friends take me out to lunch to rejoice. Later that night, after Neal has gone to bed, Jeff comes over with a celebratory bottle of wine. I am so happy to see him, to see his kind eyes.

He says, "Now, you may kiss the boyfriend."

I do.

10.

JEFF AND I are growing closer, despite my fears. He keeps saying he's here with me forever. He keeps asking to meet Neal. Finally, I agree. It will be a major litmus test: if Jeff is comfortable around

Neal, we really might have a future; if he's not, that would end any future possibilities for me, and, no doubt, for him. I'm concerned for Jeff and me but, most important, for Neal. I don't want him to become attached to Jeff, only to go through another wrenching separation.

"Sweetheart, we're going to meet a really good friend of Mommy's," I say one afternoon.

Neal seems fine about it. We meet up at Back on the Beach, our café on the sand, yards from the ocean. Jeff is a kid magnet. He and Neal instantly bond. Jeff is open, playful, and loving. Neal senses this immediately. We sit down at our table and within minutes, Neal grabs Jeff's wrist and leads him across the bike path out onto the sand. Still holding Jeff's arm, Neal leans back. Jeff picks up on the cue and slowly begins to swing Neal in a circle. Around and around they go until they laugh themselves dizzy. Neal could spin for hours. Fortunately for Jeff, the food arrives just as he's turning a light shade of green.

They seem so natural together. The smile I feel begins in my heart. We stay and watch the sunset. As Neal gets into the back of our car, Jeff gives me a gentle kiss good night. Neal observes us out of the corner of his eye through the tinted car window. He giggles gleefully. We take his joy as his blessing on our relationship.

11.

"THE WIND IS blowin' 20 knots," Jeff e-mails me one day, "gusting to 28. I'm going out for a sesh. Should be good. Any interest in coming out?"

To add to my sense of wonder about Jeff, it turns out that he is a kite surfer, one of those spiritual daredevils that Neal and I watched and adored throughout the summer. How amazing, I think, that he's one of those men who sail over the ocean, into the sky, making a playground of wind and waves. When Neal and I were admiring the kite surfers floating high above the ocean, we were probably admiring Jeff! I can't wait to see him fly.

Funny, we never get over our early fantasies, but it's so rare that we actually get to live them out. Yet here I am putting on my red-and-white polka-dot bikini (with a coverup these days) to go off to Malibu and watch Jeff surf. I'm about to experience the "Gidget and Moondoggie" fantasy of my childhood.

JEFF GREETS ME with a kiss. He's wearing his wet suit and looks really good. I am giddy with teenage excitement. He readies his garb and gear: wet suit, harness, bar and lines, board, and kite. With the assistance of a fellow sailor, Jeff launches his kite into the air and heads toward the surf line, board in hand. I gaze at him as he sails, so beautifully, gliding over the ocean, riding the waves until the wind lifts him off the water, into the air where he floats, suspended, then gently reunites with the water's surface. He rises into the air again, embodiment of "poetry in motion."

Jeff returns from the water. He lands his kite back on the sand. He heads toward me, face glowing with exuberance from his "sesh" with wind and waves. As he comes closer, I am taken by his body, wet from the ocean, smelling of salt water. He leans in to kiss me. A feeling stirs deep within me, and wells up into my chest. The words I have been unable to speak push up from my soul.

"I love you," I whisper.

Those words have overwhelmed me. Even if I wanted to, I could not hold back.

—————————————————— 12. ——————————————————

EACH MONTH THAT we're together, Jeff and I celebrate our "month-iversary." I can't believe I'm falling in love in my late forties! I joke that we're still together because of Jeff's investment in those year-round Disneyland passes.

"We've used up three months," I tease.

Neal, Jeff, and I are happy together. We build a cocoon around us.

For the first time in years, I feel safe. We are not ready to butterfly out into the world, but then the holidays arrive, and with them come family celebrations. The families invite us. Like it or not, we must accept. No wonder holidays are the most stressful time of the year even for "normies."

I have kept my interactions with Jeff's family very brief. They know about Neal but have not yet met him. But now we agree to bring Neal to a Hanukah dinner at the home of Jeff's brother, Dave.

Jeff's family is casual about time. They call dinner for 5:00, which means that everyone gets there at 5:30, or maybe even 6:30. When Neal and I arrive promptly at 5:00, they are just walking in the door with the groceries. At 6:00, they start preparing food, which they do in the kitchen as one big family. I am anxious, but try not to show it. I introduce Neal. Everyone is warm and welcoming.

Neal charms Jeff's mom immediately. He takes her arm and guides her to the refrigerator, pointing to string cheese. He's a smart one, already knowing that the way to any Jewish mother's heart is to let her feed you. Things are going well. I'm relieved. Neal is delightful and calm and sweet, especially with Eitan, who cannot walk without his walker (yet). Eitan crawls around the house. Neal crawls with him. They bond.

"Neal's doing Floortime," I think. "He's joining Eitan's world!"

But soon Neal gets restless. Its past 7:00 and we haven't eaten. I'm nervous, afraid that Neal has "spent" his goodness. Finally, at 7:30 dinner is served. A beautiful holiday feast: the food, the presentation, everything homemade. It's amazing. Neal is hungry, antsy, and tired. He digs into his food with his hands. He gobbles down potato latkes, he spills applesauce all over the floor. He doesn't sit well. He tries. It's awkward. Jeff tries to help by cleaning up Neal's mess and letting him and me know that everything is okay.

I know it's not. I know that Neal wanted to show his best, but it's late and it's just not working. I take Neal from the table and walk him around the block. When we return, the family has been talking.

They fall silent as we approach the table. I get it. It's time for us to go. I want to leave before there are any more problems.

But we haven't celebrated the holiday yet. There are presents. Tons of presents, presents for me, presents for Neal. They are such a generous family. Neal is given trucks and airplanes. "Vroom! Vroom!" He and Eitan drive the trucks across the floor and "fly" the planes. This is so exciting to Neal that he starts running around the room. It's 8:45 and past his bedtime. I say thank you to everyone for the fabulous feast and gifts and nudge Neal toward the door. Neal doesn't want to leave. He's having too much fun. He's overtired and overstimulated. He loves the "Vroom."

"Neal, I'm counting to three. It's time to go," I say sternly.

Neal throws down one of the trucks and kicks the toys. Jeff and his brother, Dave, grab Neal's feet, which sets him screaming and kicking and tantrumming, so much so that both Dave and Jeff have to carry him shrieking out of the house, into the car as I say an apologetic good night and race out the door. Jeff pulls the seat belt over a crying, kicking Neal.

"I'll call you later," he says solemnly. He's not following us home. Not a good sign.

How I wish I had known then what I know now: that an evening such as this can work if we time things right by arriving just as the salad is being passed and by leaving long before bedtime. Though we'd miss the lovely family time of preparing food together, we'd avoid the chaos likely to ensue if Neal has to wait too long.

But on that night, Neal and I are silent throughout the drive home. He wakes up as we pull into our street. His sad, sweet face reveals that he feels bad about what happened. I feel terrible. I set him up for failure. I didn't mean to. We all wanted it work out. It just got too late.

That night, Jeff's family will stay at the table trying to talk Jeff out of continuing his relationship with me. Jeff calls me on his drive home and says he'll see me in a few days. He is distant. I'm afraid.

When I see him, Jeff tells me what his family said: "Neal's only going to get bigger"; "You won't be able to control him"; "He's aggressive. He's violent. He needs to be socialized . . ." And then the kicker: "Why would you want to bring this into our family?"

I understand how his family feels. I don't blame them at all. I am ready to break up with Jeff, so that he can move on to have his own children and a more traditional wife. I thank the stars for bringing me this beautiful man who showed me that I can love again. Instead, what seemed to be the end of our relationship only brings us closer.

We decide not to bring Neal around for a while. In time, this loving family will open their hearts and home and embrace us all, but for now, we will let them get to know me, to see how and why we are so good as a couple. We want them to understand that together we can face anything.

13.

WHEN I BECAME a parent, I made a pact with myself: I will never do something that I know I might regret later. I never leave Neal alone in the car or in the bath, and never leave him alone in the house without supervision. In these situations if, God forbid, something happened to him, I could not forgive myself. I am aware, of course, that accidents happen. I know that there are many variables that you can't control. For me, controlling things that I truly can control has always been essential.

Now we're about to go back East for Passover to see my dad, my sister's family, and my cousins. I want to control everything I can. It will be a time of many "firsts": the first time that Jeff is meeting my family, the first time we take a trip with Neal, the first time Neal is staying at my cousin's house. If our relationship can survive this, it can survive anything.

Weeks before leaving on this trip, Jeff and I go into "what I can control" mode, rehearsing Neal in everything that flying on an airplane entails. Trouble is, things come up that you just don't think to rehearse.

Neal is just shy of nine years old. He's four feet seven inches, almost my height. To outward appearances, he looks like a "typical" or "normal" kid. In some ways, this is to his advantage; in other ways, it's not. For most people, it's easier to feel compassion for a child in a wheelchair, or for a teen with a Seeing Eye dog. But autism is an "invisible disability." Most kids with autism look like other kids—but tend to exhibit "bad" behavior.

At the airport, as we wait to board, Neal stares excitedly out the window at the huge planes. I turn my head for a second. I hear the sound of an alarm. Neal has raced to the exit door and tried to open it so that he can go outside and be with the airplanes. Now the loud alarm has set Neal off. He's freaking out. People glare at him. Security races over.

"It's okay, sweetheart," I tell Neal, then I call out to the panicky crowd, "It's okay everyone! He has autism! He just likes airplanes! He didn't mean any harm!"

We are seated in coach, about eight rows back from first class. Neal puts his backpack under his chair and snaps on his seat belt. He covers his ears with his hands before takeoff just as we rehearsed.

Soon, the flight attendant comes over and asks if we want anything to drink. We practiced this too, and Neal knows to ask for water. He does. Success. But then Neal wants to go to the bathroom. He needs to go, NOW. The flight attendant's cart is blocking the aisle. This is not something we rehearsed.

He can't wait the thirty minutes it could take for the attendant to get to the back of the plane, so Neal and I get up from our seats and I ask one of the flight attendants if Neal can use the bathroom that's right in front of us. As I ask, a man from first class, clearly able to overhear me, heads into the bathroom, pushing ahead of Neal.

"No," the flight attendant tells me curtly. "That restroom is for first-class passengers only."

"We know this," I say, calmly but determined. "But my son has autism and he really needs to go to the bathroom."

"Well," she answers, "he's going to have to wait like everyone else."

Neal sees an opening. He darts toward the bathroom door. Another man jumps in front of the door and glares at him with the cocky condescension of a first-class citizen. Neal tantrums.

"Return to your seats," demands the flight attendant.

Neal grabs her eyeglasses off her face. She panics and calls for security.

All this happens within twenty seconds. I'm losing it. Jeff steps in. He calms me, then calms Neal enough to get him to wait behind the cart as it passes each seat. He then takes Neal to the bathroom. I go back to my seat, fuming: if that stupid flight attendant hadn't been so stuck on her rules, if that guy in first class hadn't been so arrogant, none of this would have happened. Today, I know that I need to call the airline in advance and let them know I'm traveling with a child who has special needs. When I do this, they are more than accommodating, especially on smaller airlines. At the time, all I could think was Oh boy, we've just started out, and already, chaos.

14.

EVER SINCE WE gave our dog, Luckie, away, Neal has become terrified of dogs. The minute we walk in my cousin's front door, one of her three dogs jumps on Neal. He runs and lands on the kitchen table, grabs the glass chandelier, causing dishes and food to come crashing down.

My cousin screams at me. "Get him off of there!" she cries. Neal is panicked and won't move. Jeff picks him up and takes him outside. Neal climbs on the picnic table and refuses to get down.

My cousin is a wonderful housekeeper. Much better than I am. She runs a house in which everything has its place. She has really mellowed out over the years, but she was anything but mellow then. She has white carpet in her basement playroom. Back then, if someone spilled water, it would conjure up an "Oh my God," as if it were a crisis.

Now imagine Neal, who spills, drops, and breaks things on an hourly basis. Add to this his extreme fear of dogs and you have disaster in the making. My cousin is well-meaning. She's fond of Neal. She just doesn't know what to do with him. She tries so hard. I feel bad for her. My nephew, Max, takes it as his task to constantly clean up after Neal, while my niece, Kira, comforts Neal. I try not to get drawn into drama.

Initially, because of the dogs, I had planned to stay in a hotel. My cousin insisted that we stay with her. I knew it was the wrong decision the moment I agreed to it.

15.

A SEDER IS an annual ritual with religious significance. My cousin prepares the seder dinner over a number of days, and creates a fabulous feast. Before the meal is eaten, her husband leads a short service that tells the Passover story of the Jews and their Exodus from Egypt. This is always a meaningful time for me.

Passover was one of my favorite holidays as a child. We would sit around the table while my dad led the service in Hebrew. Even as small children we got to drink real wine and sing our hearts out. It was over the Passover holiday that I brought Neal home from Russia, which makes the notion of the Exodus even more special.

I love sharing this holiday with my family. I love that Jeff and Neal are here. My cousin agrees to keep the dogs behind locked doors, and Neal sits on a chair in the dining room, instead of climbing onto the table. Throughout the service and the meal, Neal sits close to Jeff and eats matzoh. A lot of matzoh. For the most part, I've kept Neal wheat free, as he's calmer when he doesn't consume wheat products. However, it's Passover, so I go with the flow. What a shame that I didn't know about spelt matzoh then.

Express Check #2

Items that you checked out

Title: Portugal, Madeira, the Azores
ID: 31221117086529
Due: June-22-17

Title: The tea planter's wife
ID: 31221117055462
Due: June-22-17

Title: Fodor's 2016 Hawaii
ID: 31221118016171
Due: June-22-17

Title: Blueprints
ID: 31221114823243
Due: June-22-17

Title:
Now I see the moon : a mother, a son, a
miracle
ID: 31221095161323
Due: June-22-17

Total items: 5
Account balance: $1.50
June-01-17
Checked out: 5
Overdue: 0
Hold requests: 0
Ready for pickup: 0

Thank you for visiting the Edmonton
Public Library

www.epl.ca

Edmonton Public Library
Woodcroft (Westmount)
Express Check #2

Customer ID: **********0063

Items that you checked out

Title: Portugal, Madeira, the Azores
ID: 31221111708629
Due: June-22-17

Title: The tea planter's wife
ID: 31221117055462
Due: June-22-17

Title: Fodor's 2016 Hawaii
ID: 31221111801671
Due: June-22-17

Title: Blueprints
ID: 31221114823243
Due: June-22-17

Title:
 Now I see the moon : a mother, a son, a
 miracle
ID: 31221096161323
Due: June-22-17

Total items: 5
Account balance: $1.50
June-01-17
Checked out: 5
Overdue: 0
Hold requests: 0
Ready for pickup: 0

Thank you for visiting the Edmonton
Public Library

www.epl.ca

When it gets close to Neal's bedtime, I take him downstairs and get him settled into a room that is both guest room and exercise studio. I wait until he is fully asleep before going upstairs, where we finish the service and eat dessert. All I can think is, We got through the seder! What a relief!

Then: Crash! Bang! The sounds are coming from Neal's room. Everyone races downstairs, where we find a terrified Neal, standing naked in the middle of the room. Broken glass is everywhere. Little red toeprints lead a trail to a cut on Neal's foot that's dripping blood across the white carpet. My cousin races to get carpet cleaner. Jeff embraces Neal. I run for my dad. Everyone's frantic.

Jeff carries Neal into the bathroom. Neal screams as my dad calmly takes glass shards out of his toes. We bandage him up. We clean up the carpet and finally get Neal calm enough to sleep.

What happened? How I wish I knew. But Neal does not have the words to tell me. Of all of my frustrations and his, this inability to express himself clearly is the one that troubles us most. As long as he cannot tell me what disturbed him, I cannot comfort him adequately.

So I am left to conjecture and to conduct an amateur forensic examination. Most likely, Neal fell asleep and was awakened by loud foot- and paw-steps above. Alone downstairs, with no words to call for us, he must have become frightened. Perhaps he saw himself in the mirror and got scared and threw the hand weights, readily accessible in the workout room, at what appeared to be a menacing image. Perhaps he just wanted our attention. Perhaps the wheat in all that matzoh put his system into overload.

All I know for sure is that this is my worst nightmare. Neal is upset, my family's upset. They're all afraid of Neal and pitying me. Into the small hours, I ponder how I will do things better "next time." If there ever is a next time. Here's what I know: I should have heeded my intuition and not stayed at my cousin's.

Around 3:00 A.M., Jeff and I walk out the back door of my cousin's house, take a deep breath, and look up at the stars. I am distant and afraid. This, I tell myself, will be our last night together.

"I'm not going anywhere," he says.

16.

JUST WHEN WE think it's safe to go back into the water . . . comes the weekly holy day of Shabbat. It is a time when the rigors of the week are set aside for twenty-four hours, when the pace slows down and the most important thing is being with family and friends, eating and sharing together.

A few days after returning from my cousin's, Neal and I go to Shabbat dinner at the home of my friend Norma, who has also invited a number of other people we know. Neal and I have been to Norma's house many times. Although she has two dogs, they have never bothered Neal in the past.

As soon as we arrive, Neal recoils from the dogs and jumps onto a chair. It seems that he's reenacting what happened at my cousin's where, by breaking the mirror and seeing everyone react to it, he got a powerful and stimulating sense of cause and effect.

"Neal, you can't do that," I tell him. "Chairs are for sitting."

I take him outside and give him a choice of staying for dinner and sitting on the chair, or leaving and going home. He chooses to sit on the chair and stay for dinner.

Throughout the meal, he watches the dogs out of the corners of his almond eyes. He is acutely aware of them. When he isn't feeling terrified of them, he plays with them a bit, feeding them under the table when I'm not looking. One of the dogs licks Neal's hand. Before we know it, he takes a glass from the table and hurls it, sending it crashing onto the floor. Norma's husband and two other men carry a kicking and screaming Neal out of the house. Everyone is terrified. Neal is out of control . . . again.

I get Neal into the car, calm him down, and drive home. Once he's in bed, we reflect on what happened. He is aware that he cannot behave as he just did if he wants to go to people's homes. He seems embarrassed and ashamed that he could not control his impulses.

Long ago, I learned that you cannot "punish" autism out of children. But you can discipline them. The word "discipline" actually means "to disciple," which means to teach. As Neal's mom, it is my job to disciple him in this and all other instances, and to turn any upsetting event into an opportunity to learn.

The next day, with my help, Neal writes apology letters to everyone he harmed—to Norma, her kids, and the dogs. It is not easy for Neal to write and this takes about two hours. I tell him that we cannot go back to Norma's, or to anyone else's house, until he is certain that he can sit appropriately and not throw things.

I give Neal a choice of three "consequences" for his behavior from the previous night. The choices are: for the next week, he cannot buy cookies, candy, or pasta; he cannot go to the park; he cannot go to the "little store." Neal chooses to go without cookies, candy, and pasta.

I am calm with Neal, but when I think about what happened, I feel shaken. People could have gotten hurt, the dogs could have gotten hurt. It was scary.

----------------------- 17. -----------------------

NORMA CALLS. I have never heard her so upset. Norma is one of my closest friends and one of the most well-adjusted people I know. Life, living life, being on planet Earth, come easily to her. She has the quality my dad calls "solid." She's been there through my divorce, my financial troubles, my early dating queries. What she's not good at is people with disabilities. I've never judged Norma for this. She doesn't pretend to be anything that she isn't. She's just not comfortable with Neal. I understand. I love her regardless.

But even knowing who Norma is, I am stunned by what she tells me in a quivering voice as we take a walk down California Avenue toward the beach.

"After you left, we all talked about what happened. What Neal did. He could have really hurt someone. The glass could have broken and he could have killed my dog or hurt my kids. This is serious."

"I know, Norma. I'm so sorry it happened . . ."

"Elaine, this is really hard for me: I think you are in denial. Neal is only getting bigger. I'm afraid for you. He's not safe. We all think it's time that you find a home for him to stay in."

I am numb. Neal and I have spent many holidays with Norma and her family. We've often eaten dinner at her house, and it's a place where, despite Norma's unease with Neal, we've been made to feel safe and welcome. Now, it seems, we are not welcome. As Norma talks, I try to be open and listen. She gives me three examples of "loved ones" that had to be sent away: the first was a dog that three professionals said was unsafe; the second was a cat who needed to be put to sleep; the third was a child with special needs who repeatedly destroyed the family home and caused bruises to the mother. I can't believe that she is saying this to me.

Does she really think that Neal is that bad? Yes, there were times in the past when he was not able to function. But he has come so far. Can't she see this?

She continues. "I just don't want you to put your new relationship in jeopardy. You've been through enough . . . you deserve to be happy."

We stop at the cliffs overlooking the beach. I gaze out over the ocean, holding back tears. We walk back to my house in silence.

When she leaves and I'm alone again, I feel betrayed, unwanted. I wonder now when we felt embraced at Norma's, was it only because Neal had been on "good" behavior? Are we not to be embraced when he is "bad"?

I could understand if Norma had said, "Please do not bring Neal here again until he works out his anger issues. As things are now, having him with us isn't safe for me, the dogs or my children." But that isn't what happened.

I don't see Neal's behavior as Norma does. To me, what happened at her house was difficult and regrettable, but also constitutes a form of progress.

Events like that used to be everyday occurrences. Now they happen only once in a great while. Neal used to tantrum for hours at a time. This time, in a few minutes, he pulled himself together. At the same time, we've now had two such episodes in less than a week. Clearly, measures need to be taken—but not measures as extreme as Norma and my friends are suggesting.

As for Neal destroying my relationship with Jeff, that's impossible. I would never choose a man over my son.

And yet. Norma's words linger. I need a reality check. "Is Neal dangerous?" I ask a therapist.

"Neal has a good arm," he says. "If he wanted to he could have thrown the glass at someone. He didn't. He was more in control than you think."

"Am I in denial?"

"Of course you are in denial. You chose to see the glass half full. You choose to see the beauty and growth in Neal. Sure, there are ugly things: the tantrums, the rages. But they are not who Neal is."

That night, as I put Neal to bed, I sing the Shema, the bedtime prayer that I sing to him each evening, the prayer that has helped him sleep through the night. I take in the fresh scent of shampoo in his hair. I gaze at his beautiful face. I turn back the covers, he climbs into bed, and we "recite" the bedtime prayers, me, in Hebrew, Neal nodding his head.

We talk about the great things he did today, how he helped mama in the store and found the vitamins, cereal, and string cheese all on his own; we talk about how gentle he was and how he helped carry in the groceries.

We reflect on how well he is taking his "consequences" for his behavior at Norma's. We also talk about how he can do better to-morrow. I kiss him gently, and leave the room. I think how awful it would be not to have him in my life.

I am blessed to be entrusted with the care of this child's soul.

Although I appreciate my friend's good intentions, I do not believe that I am in denial. I believe that I am guided by divine purpose. My son's disabilities have taught me greater patience, compassion, and understanding than I have ever known. I believe that he is perfect in the eyes of God, and that has brought me closer to the God of my understanding.

One day, I may choose to have someone else wash my son's hair, say prayers with him, and tuck him in at night. One night, I may choose to have someone else care for his soul—because it is best for him and best for me. Tonight is not that night.

18.

I AM AT peace with Neal, but Neal is not at peace with the world. His lack of control escalates. Calming himself is no longer an option. At home, he throws glasses across the kitchen. He is wild and will not listen. I watch with dismay and alarm as he regresses into behavior that he hasn't evinced in years.

My family calls constantly to make sure that I am safe. Friends continue to urge me to send Neal away and send e-mails about "homes" for kids with autism. Before I would even consider such a drastic decision, I must do everything in my power to avoid it.

This is not the first time that I've felt like Sisyphus, pushing a boulder up the hill, only to see it roll down again. This time, I can only hope that the boulder won't pick up speed as it heads down-ward, overwhelming and crushing us all.

In recent months, I've given Neal a great deal of freedom. He's been out in the world a lot. Now I can see that he's been out in the world too much. Until Neal can make the right choices again, I need to confine his activities to the playroom. It's a radical move, but he seems to experience this confinement as a relief.

In the playroom, Neal is free to express his anger. Once again, his coaches sit with protective pillows over their heads while Neal hurls cushy toys and balls. I'm certain he's reacting to the changes in our lives: the divorce, moving, sharing Mom with Jeff, sharing Jeff with Mom. It's been a rock-strewn path, that's for sure.

Watching him flail, I can only wish that he could communicate in ways that aren't purely physical. Though his rage is a form of communication, I can only surmise what he's experiencing. How different things might be if Neal could say what he feels, or have a more precise way to convey his feelings. In any case, one thing is clear: Neal has a lot of anger.

I GIVE NEAL boundaries and establish rules that he must follow. If he trashes his room, I wait—however long it takes—for him to regain his calm, at which point he is required to clean up the room and put it back together. In this way, each of his actions has a logical and meaningful consequence.

This work is painstaking and difficult. I don't mind. It's the right path and, really, there's no alternative. Either Neal becomes socialized, calm, and able to be part of this world, or he doesn't, in which case I'll have no choice but to send him away. I give this last-ditch effort everything I've got. If it doesn't work, I will have to accept that Neal is too much for me.

I focus on the positive whenever possible. I praise Neal when he makes good choices, controls his impulses, helps out. The more I do this, the more Neal makes better choices.

I've always believed in the power of positive energy; I'm convinced that it's a key element in helping people grow. Think of a garden: if you give lots of energy to the weeds, feeding them, emphasizing them, they will eventually take over. But if you focus on the seeds, prepare the soil, plant a rosebush and tend it, it will bloom in time.

So it has been with Neal. That's why, when he was small, I didn't give him negative instruction. I never said, "Don't use your hands when you eat."

Instead, I would say, "Look how beautifully you picked up the fork." Now, years later, we are pointing out the positive again, applauding Neal not only for his ability to calm himself and control his impulses, but also for his willingness to do so.

By autumn, Neal is centered again, and ready to be back in the world.

Everyone remarks on how much calmer he is. This brings me solace and justifies the extreme measures I've taken.

----- 19. -----

AT NINE AND a half years old, Neal would ordinarily be in the fourth grade, but instead, he's enrolled in the same, severely challenged class where his "education" consists of identifying primary colors and putting square pegs in square holes.

At home, with his coaches, we challenge him academically. Because he loves Earth science, we construct a papier-mâché volcano that spews forth a bubbling mixture of dish soap, baking soda, and vinegar. He loves it when we read him age-appropriate books like the Anansi the Spider series. He seems to understand everything that we tell him. But I cannot convince anyone at the school of this. I know that Neal comprehends the world around him. Because he cannot speak, I have no way to prove it.

At school, where nothing is expected of him, Neal is bored, and doesn't respond to the restricted environment or the simple tasks. He becomes disruptive. Here we go again.

I take Neal to see Dr. Ricki Robinson, a West Coast pediatrician trained in Dr. Greenspan's relationship approach. She has become Neal's primary doctor; having him under the wing of someone who is both brilliant and nearby is as much a blessing as it is a relief.

Dr. Ricki, as she is affectionately called by her many patients, is beautiful, with the essence of an angel. She's been instrumental in overseeing our home programming and with the school system. Each time we see her, she marvels at how well Neal is doing.

Now I tell her, "I just can't convince the school district that Neal is capable of much more than they give him credit for."

Dr. Ricki suggests that we seek help from Darlene Hanson, a very special speech pathologist. She always guides us in the right direction.

DARLENE HANSON IS an expert in communication with nonverbal kids like Neal. She has been a speech pathologist for more than twenty years. Her credo is "Everyone communicates. You just have to listen."

As soon as Darlene meets Neal, she speaks to him in her down-to-earth, matter-of-fact manner. "Hey there, Neal," she says, "what do you want to tell me today?"

Neal looks over at her with a sly smile, then quickly looks away.

The first thing Darlene does is draw a grid with a black marker on a dry erase board, creating four squares. In the top left square, she writes, "Bush," in the top right, "Clinton," in the bottom left, "Vote," and in the bottom right, "Washington, D.C." She calls this a choice board.

While she composes the board, Neal is distracted and wiggly. Darlene just smiles at him. "Come on, Neal," she says. "Let me see what you know."

"Who is the president of the United States?" she asks.

Neal points to the top left: "Bush."

"Who was president before him?"

Neal quickly points to the word "Clinton."

"Where do they live?"

Neal points to "Washington, D.C."

"What did your mom do so they could get there?"

Neal immediately points to "Vote."

For Neal, these are much more than "correct answers." They're proof of what I've always, always believed: that Neal comprehends the world around him and views it with interest. Still, I'm astonished. I knew he was smart, but I had no idea that he possessed this read-it-in-the-paper kind of information.

When I tell people about Neal and the choice board, they ask, how does he know these things? And guess what? I don't know how he knows them. I think of all the times I've seen him thumb through newspapers and magazines when he seemed to be just enjoying the feel of the paper on his fingers. I think of times I've watched or listened to newscasts and assumed he wasn't paying attention. Neal is proving what I've sensed all along: that the world he inhabits is richer than any of us imagine.

The choice board allows us to read books to him, and ask him multiple-choice questions about their content. Neal answers correctly. He takes it all in stride, as if to say, "Of course I knew these things."

Because of the choice board we are able to move Neal out of his special ed class and into a typical third-grade classroom, where he will be helped by his wonderful one-on-one aide, Randy.

The more Neal is able to display his knowledge, the fewer tantrums and frustrations he has. The more he's able to convey his emotions, the more confident and independent he becomes.

Until we found the choice board, I didn't acknowledge Neal in certain ways. I'm embarrassed to say that I didn't consult him to see how he felt, or what he wanted. I assumed that I knew what he wanted and my assumptions were often accurate. Yet at other times I misinterpreted his gestures or attitudes, and this would cause him to fling his body around or bang his head. Now we can probe Neal's feelings. We can ask if he is scared or happy or just fine. We offer him multiple choices so that he can indicate what is troubling him.

The choice board is a revelation. How I wish we had had one this past summer when he began to go wild, or when he tantrummed at

Norma's house, or on the night that he threw those hand weights into my cousin's mirror. This communication device transforms our relationship. For the first time ever, I have real, back-and-forth dialogues with Neal on any topic, at any time, for any duration. I'll write a question at the top of a page and then offer choices that I read to him or let him read for himself:

Neal, what would you like to do this morning?

Go to the park.

Go to Starbucks.

Go to the "little store" (his name for The Farms—his favorite small grocery store).

Go somewhere else.

If he chooses "somewhere else," I offer still more choices.

If Neal throws something or is inappropriate in any way, we explore his reasons for the action. "Neal, why did you throw that apple on the floor?"

Because I thought it was funny.

Because I was angry.

To get a reaction from Mom.

Or something else.

I go through this process until I understand the "why" behind Neal's actions. For the first time in his life, Neal is able to tell me not simply that he feels but what he is feeling. Soon, Darlene will teach Neal to type with one finger on a keyboard. The keyboard will have voice output. Neal will have a voice.

Neal is not simply growing. The seeds that we've planted and tended and nurtured have taken root. Like the beautiful rosebush, he's in bloom.

phase six:
the miracle project

Start by doing what's necessary; then do what's possible,

and suddenly you are doing the impossible.

ST. FRANCIS OF ASSISI

1

"DO YOU EVER feel sadness because you don't have biological children?" I ask my friend Alice.

We're sharing some delicious baked polenta at one of our favorite restaurants, Hugo's, in the Valley. We've known each other since we both began the adoption process that led to my finding Neal and to her adopting two beautiful girls from China.

"I never feel lonely," Alice replies. "I feel complete—as if I gave birth to my girls myself."

I'm not surprised by her answer. Alice and I often say that we birthed our kids from our hearts rather than from our bellies.

"I couldn't love Neal more if he came from my own womb," I tell her. "It's just that I feel this loneliness sometimes. I dunno."

"Elaine, what you are missing is not a biological child," she says. "You're missing a group, a community of other families who have special needs. You're missing a place where you can share experiences."

This makes total sense to me. The fact is, I've homeschooled Neal for so long, and been so burdened with the divorce, that I haven't had time or energy to socialize in any meaningful way. Sure, I have wonderful, supportive, loving friends whose typical kids play with Neal on Shabbat. But to a great extent, I've worn these friends out with my trials and tribulations. And, as their kids grow older, the gaps between Neal and them grow larger as they go off to dances and join sports teams. Over time, the sense of community that Neal and I once had with these families has slowly evaporated.

I do see parents who have kids with special needs. I see them in the waiting rooms of doctors' offices and therapy clinics. They, like me, are focused on their child. We share new therapies we are trying, or reveal our latest "war" stories with the school systems. At times, we have controlled, facilitated playdates—but these occasions are more therapeutic than social. There is nothing really "normal" about any of these interactions.

The one wonderfully normal-seeming day is an annual event for families of children with special needs at the Zimmer Children's Museum, a Jewish Family Service event.

It's a great occasion, during which parents get to watch their kids do things that range from exploring a real airplane cockpit, to climbing into a real ambulance, to putting on a firefighter's work boots, to fashioning art projects, to placing prayers in a mock Wailing Wall modeled after the Wall in Jerusalem. Though it takes place only once a year, each time we get together at this event it's like being with family members.

I seem to be yearning for more of this sort of interaction, for Neal and for myself. We need a sense of community now, more than ever.

—————————— 2. ——————————

AT THE ZIMMER Children's Museum, I run into my friend Michelle. whose son, Danny, has cerebral palsy. Her typically developing daughter, Rachel, was a member of Kids on Stage, a musical theater program I founded several years ago that is still thriving under other leadership.

Kids on Stage is based on the premise that the creative arts play a tremendous part in fostering self-expression, social consciousness, personal growth, and joy. The participants create their own musical but with a twist. For example, instead of doing *Annie*, we made our own irreverent version: our Annie was a homeless girl in East Los Angeles with a gang of homeless sidekicks. She had dreadlocks and we changed the music to reggae.

Another time, we wrote a play in which traditional fairy-tale "villains" defend themselves to the audience, which takes on the role of a jury. The Big Bad Wolf came out dressed like Hannibal Lecter. His defense was that he had an eating disorder, but the audience found him guilty. We even had Prince Charming on trial for polygamy.

These inventive plays were derived from the kids' improvisations. Initially, the parents worried when their kids weren't given traditional scripts and lines to learn. But after they witnessed the finished production, Kids on Stage was a huge hit and attracted the children of many celebrities, among them Dustin Hoffman and Ted Danson.

"You know, Elaine," Michelle says, "you should start a program like Kids on Stage for kids with special needs."

"Uh-huh," I answer.

I'm only half listening as I watch Neal dart into the pretend grocery store and then race to stop him from eating the plastic grapes.

"There may be some grant money available," she continues. "I'll help you."

"Maybe one day," I say, "but not now. I've got too much on my plate."

I give no thought to Michelle's suggestion. Sure, it would be a meaningful project, but I've found my meaningful work through Neal. Thanks to the financial settlement I received when my divorce was finalized, I am one of the lucky mothers who has been able to dedicate herself exclusively to her child. Nothing I have ever done— or can imagine doing—could bring me more joy.

We proceed to lunch, where our kids eat pizza while we clean up spilled apple juice and wipe the dripping tomato sauce from their happy faces.

———————————— 3. ————————————

MY EX-HUSBAND HAS returned to Los Angeles after being out of the country a year. He wants to reverse the original judgment through which Neal and I were granted financial security. He also wants joint custody of Neal. Can you believe it?

The judge reaffirms my full custody. That's the good news. The bad news is that he reduces my financial support to a sum significantly below the poverty level. I feel as if a piano has been dropped on my chest. As of tomorrow, the money I receive will barely be enough to buy food for Neal and me.

To take care of Neal, I will have to get a full-time job and I can't work full time because I need to monitor Neal's home program and his school program, not to mention the fact that he needs me to be at home, caring for him. All of the medical professionals have agreed that my intense involvement with Neal is essential to his well-being and that if I take on a full-time job Neal's progress will be negatively affected.

My attorney appeals to the judge, telling him that it would be a catastrophe for us to be without income. But the court does not understand autism. They look at our situation as if it were any other divorce and custody situation: child in school, mother should work.

I shouldn't be surprised, given that early in our divorce proceedings the court ordered that Neal engage in "daily, hour-long phone calls with his father." It would have been funny if it weren't so sad. Obviously—since Neal can't talk—he couldn't do this. Still, I was charged with disregarding the court's order! I had to hire doctors to assert that Neal does not speak. What part of "nonverbal, autistic child" did the court not understand?

Now another judge, another absurd order, at another critical time. Neal is just learning to communicate; he's becoming socialized at school, and his homeschooling remains the key to his growth and education. The judge has put all this at risk. Other than the day of my mother's funeral, this is the worst day that I've ever experienced.

———————————— 4. ————————————

I AM A mess. I don't want Neal to see me like this. Luckily, when I get home, he's with one of his coaches working on the computer. Now that he's learning to type, he loves to Google. As I walk in the door, he's typed some random letters into the Google box. He wants me to see what came up. I can't be with Neal now. I don't know what to say.

"Mommy has a tummy ache," I tell him. "I'll look at it later."

I go upstairs. I'm in shock. How can I take care of Neal and his intense needs and work at the same time? I sob. I wail. I don't call anyone or seek support because nothing and no one can comfort me. I don't want to burden Jeff with this. He's a full-time student with his own financial woes. I'm determined not to drag him down into my rabbit hole. Our relationship has been stressed so many times. This could put the nail in the coffin.

The one call I make is to my attorney. "Can we reverse this?" I ask.

"We could try," he says nonchalantly. "We could go back to court. But it could cost more than $20,000 and there are no guarantees."

Like so many women, I am now too poor to fight being poor. I fall to my knees and call out, "Dear God, what am I supposed to do? How am I supposed to support us? How can I help Neal if I cannot be available to him?"

I HAVE TO pull myself together. Neal's coach is about to go home, I have to put Neal to bed. I stand up, throw cold water on my face. I try to seem calm, but Neal senses my distress. I don't give him specifics, but I tell him, "Mama had a bad day. Don't worry. We're going to be okay, darling."

I try hard to convince him. If I can convince him, it will help me to convince myself.

"Mama is going to take care of Mama," I say. "And I will take care of you. I promise."

But Neal can feel that something is seriously wrong. He looks at me with sad, frightened eyes.

Later, I go downstairs and look at the computer that Neal was using. His random Googling has produced something amazing: a passage from Isaiah 30:19: " . . . thou shalt weep no more: He will be very gracious unto thee at the voice of thy cry; when He shall hear it, He will answer thee."

———————— 5. ————————

THE NEXT MORNING, I awake with a new sense of peace to a curious, inner conversation. A thought comes to me with irrefutable force: "Teach children with special needs. Teach them acting, singing, and dance."

I dismiss this, thinking, I have no degree, no formal education about children with special needs.

But this force or voice or whatever it may be is insistent, telling me, "Do this for me and I will make sure that you and Neal are taken care of."

I know this sounds very "woo-woo" and weird. But you should know me well enough by now to know that my inner voice has always been my best and most reliable guide. It's a voice that comes to me—loud and true and clear—when I need it most.

"Teach children with special needs to act, sing, and dance."

All morning long, those words nag at me. I think about Michelle and that grant.

I call her. "Is it still available?" I ask, hoping that I'm masking my desperation.

"Is what available?" Michelle asks.

"That grant."

"Yes," she says.

"Okay. I'll give it a go."

I read the grant-proposal form. It's for what is called a New and Innovative Grant from The Jewish Community Foundation.

Sure, I can be new and innovative—but then DARN IT! The deadline for submission is Friday at 3:00 P.M. It's Thursday, at noon! I can't do this. I can't.

That voice comes again. It says, "You can."

_____ 6. _____

EARLY IN NEAL'S diagnosis, before I stopped working altogether, I taught a group of eleven- to fourteen-year-old kids with autism in an after-school enrichment program that sought to foster socialization skills in children with autism and Asperger's syndrome.

People with Asperger's perceive the world differently from most people. Often, they have deep passions in specific areas that are far more important to them than socialization. Consequently, many kids in my class had no interest in theater. Acting did not appeal to them. "Acting out" did.

If I wasn't trying to stop one child from hurling objects or obscenities at me, I was trying to coax another out from under his desk. Of course, I always love a challenge, so I followed their lead and tried to channel their interests into the one thing they all seemed to like: filmmaking. They also liked dark-metal music, which is similar to heavy metal only gloomier and gothic. So we made a film about kids finding ways to make enough money to attend a dark-metal rock concert. The same students who had been unfocused and hostile came together to create this film, which, for better or worse, featured dark, loud music.

I was asked to return the following year to help the kids perform in a live play, provided that I promised to avoid any music that could be viewed as dark or metallic or have any characters with names like "Death-Doggie."

Modeling this new production on my Kids on Stage classes, I suggested that we do an original take on *Peter Pan,* a classic story that I've always found appealing. My new students were ten to thirteen years old, varying in abilities from nonverbals to highly verbal kids with Asperger's syndrome. They loved the idea of adapting *Peter Pan,* and they came up with a concept that was downright brilliant.

"What if Peter Pan's shadow comes to life as his dark side?" one of them suggested. From there, we created Peter Man, the live shadow's name. Peter Man was Peter Pan's nemesis: Peter Pan doesn't want to grow up; Peter Man dresses in a suit and tie. Peter Pan uses enthusiasm to teach kids how to do amazing things like fly through the air; Peter Man uses fear to control kids and force them to become adults.

Wow! This was great. Using the kids' premise, I worked with a fellow actor, David, to create a script that they titled "Peter Pan 2½: The Adventures of Peter Man."

Rehearsals were enlightened, extraordinary. Each week the show became better as we added more songs and props and costumes. Our final dress rehearsal was held an hour before the actual performance, and it couldn't have gone better. I could see it all unfolding: the parents will be so proud, I'll be heralded as a wonderful acting teacher, the show will be a dazzling success. I was excited.

Twenty minutes before curtain time, I began gathering everyone together. Then one of the "Lost Boys," Marlen, locked himself in the bathroom and refused to come out. Everyone tried to coax him out. We tried to bribe him to leave, with offers of delicious food. Nothing doing.

Finally, Marlen's mom showed up with a Superman T-shirt that she promised him for the show. Marlen emerged from the bathroom, and was ready to come onstage. Apparently, he was waiting for his "costume."

Okay. Places everyone! By this time, Marlen was okay, but the rest of the kids had become restless, scared, and distressed. Parents were hurrying into the theater, carrying armloads of flowers and gifts. All this started me stressing. I didn't realize then what I know so well now, that kids with autism pick up on and reflect an adult's energy. So though I was smiling on the outside, they could all sense my inner stress and this made them even more nervous.

Just twenty minutes earlier, I had been so confident that this show was about to be a spellbinding winner. Now I simply focused on the imperative that the show must go on. On it went. And, quicker than you can say Tinker Bell, it descended into chaos.

Marlen walked onto the stage, saw his parents in the audience, lay down, and assumed the fetal position. He held this pose—and groaned and moaned—throughout the entire performance. Our Tinker Bell skipped once, then froze on center stage. I tried to coax her to skip again, but when I reached for her hand, she grabbed me around the throat. I knew not to react, as any response would only make things worse. So I stayed onstage, throughout the entire thirty-five-minute play, with Tinker Bell's hands around my neck.

The other kids forgot what they were supposed to do and did virtually nothing, except for one child who tried to save the day by doing everyone's lines. Ashley played Peter Pan, then Wendy, then Tinker Bell, then Marlen's role, bouncing from one character to another in a way that would have made Lily Tomlin proud. Along with David, who played Peter Man, she plowed through to the bitter end, providing at least some entertainment for the families.

When it ended, I didn't know whether to laugh or cry. I smiled politely, thanked the parents for entrusting me with their children, apologized for the pandemonium, and tried to explain my way out of it.

I felt so sorry for the kids and sorrier for their parents. The play had loaded on them one more disappointment, one more thing that their children couldn't do, one more time when they had to say "it's okay" when it really wasn't. Ultimately, all I had done was give them another reminder that their lives were stricken with autism . . . forever.

Now, when it was too late, I realized the huge mistake I'd made by holding rehearsals in which I was the only person watching. How different things might have been if I'd rehearsed them in front of a live audience so that they could grow accustomed to performing. I vowed that if I was ever to do another show with kids with autism, I would make sure that they played to an audience during every rehearsal.

Of course, I didn't get a chance to do this. The fiasco of Peter Man put an end to my career as an acting coach of kids with autism. Or so I thought.

7.

WHEN I WORKED as a Hollywood acting coach, I noticed that everyone wanted something they didn't have. This was true even on the best sets where the actors had been rewarded with fame, wealth, and adulation. I'd witness supporting actresses who were raking in tons of money in hit sitcoms, throwing fits because they didn't get enough lines one week; I'd see actors who'd landed parts other actors could only dream of, but were miserable because they coveted some other role. I even saw a lead actress throw a Coke bottle at the head writer because she didn't like something he wrote. Everything was "me, me, me." No one really seemed happy or comfortable in their own skin.

Compare that to the special needs world where people dedicate their lives to the less fortunate. What brings joy to these people isn't being admired; their joy comes from being of service. These are the people with whom I am at home, the people whose work is profound and meaningful. Now I am seeking to enter that world.

Another thing that spurs me on is my understanding that a creative arts program for children with autism is not a luxury. It's something that doesn't exist and is desperately needed. I envision a theater program for children with special needs and their typically developing siblings and peers. This inclusive theater program will ease the terrible isolation from which families suffer when confronted with autism.

The program will be founded on the principles that have brought Neal so far. Each child will be accepted for who he or she is; creative people will be trained to join the children's world. Taking from my previous experience, I'll prefilm certain songs and dances so that any child who gets stage fright can still shine during the show, since parts of their performance will be safely "in the can."

The grant seems to write itself. The right words flow through me. I feel as if I'm taking dictation from a higher source. I pour my heart out writing about the need for community that is lacking in my life, about the need for kids with special needs to engage in projects with children who are typically developing.

I truly believe that theater can bridge the gap between the world of autism and the typical world. I believe that creativity makes miracles. I've seen it work for Neal. Why not for other kids?

I COMPLETE A rough draft and send it to Michelle for comments. I also send it to Norma, who went to bed early since she's headed for Disneyland in the morning. Norma and I have long since mended our relationship and she does not let me down. The next day she calls with thoughtful suggestions while she's standing in line for Space Mountain!

At 1:00 P.M. on Friday, I finish. Two hours to go before I need to hand it in. That should be plenty of time to drive over to the Foundation's office. Then I notice that I need to hand in thirty copies and that some of them need to have certain papers attached, and some need still other documents. Oh no! You can't imagine how challenged I am when it comes to this sort of task. For me, it's ten times easier to write a script than it is to go to the copy place, make copies, organize a bunch of documents, and collate them. I am the Lucille Ball of Kinko's.

But I've got to do it. The clock is ticking. At my local Kinko's, I ask for help. I've got to have the copies right away. The staff pitches in. They're all cheering me on. We finish at 2:20.

Now I need to travel ten miles down to Wilshire and past La Cienega—but it's Friday and rush hour starts early. Bumper-to-bumper traffic! At 2:50, I'm still not there. The Foundation is a stickler for their 3:00 P.M. cutoff. Grant proposals that arrive after that are not considered.

At 2:53, I'm stuck at a stoplight. "Oh dear God," I pray. "You wouldn't have had me do all this work and then not let me turn it in. You wouldn't have taken me this far. Or would you?"

I resign myself to the fact that I did the best I could. "Whatever is meant to be is meant to be," I tell myself. I surrender.

The light turns green. I cruise into the Foundation building at 2:57. I race in, along with other grant hopefuls, place my stacks of thirty perfectly collated grant applications on the counter. The digital clock reads 2:59.

I call Norma at Disneyland. She tells me she's just getting off Mr. Toad's Wild Ride. "So am I!" I say.

8.

THE GRANTS WON'T be announced for months. In the meantime, I need to make a living. I write an e-mail that reads, "Returning to the workforce after seven years raising my son. Looking for work as an acting coach, dance teacher, writer, creative arts programmer, or anything else."

I send it to everyone I know, to everyone I used to know when I was in the working world, and to everyone I hope to know, in the near future. To my close friends, I write an addendum: "Just lost all spousal support. Child support reduced to bupkes." ("Bupkes" is Yiddish for "next to nothing.")

Work falls into my lap like ripe fruit falling from a tree. A friend needs someone to substitute for her at a day school where she teaches acting; my former agent gets me some gigs coaching kids on ads for Old Navy, Mattel, and Target; another friend who coaches directors and actors asks if I'd like to collaborate with directors who work with kids. Would I ever!

She introduces me to Doug Atchison, a wonderful guy and a brilliant writer/director who's written a script titled *Akeelah and the Bee*.

I love Doug's script. It's an inspiring tale of a young woman from the inner city who, against all odds, makes it to the National Spelling Bee. Before the project can be green-lighted—Hollywood-speak for getting an okay to move ahead with production—Doug has to cast the movie.

To my delight, he asks me to assist in the process. We go to A Place

Called Home, a dynamic, nonprofit, after-school youth center in South Central Los Angeles, where Doug has volunteered for several years. The kids who attend live in an environment racked by poverty, unemployment, inadequate education. The center offers them free programs that provide positive alternatives to the deadening behaviors and lifestyles that result from such challenges.

I feel privileged to be working with kids who are so creative, so eager to participate. They love acting, love the possibility of being in a real movie. Although we don't find our star for the film, we find many talented kids whom Doug will be able to hire when and if the film gets made.

We discover our choice for the lead through an exhaustive casting process. Her name is Keke Palmer and she's an eleven-year-old African-American actress who's one of the most powerful, talented, and insightful young performers I've ever seen. Doug and I meet with her and her mom to discuss the project. Keke is smart and unusually thoughtful. It's clear that she understands the character of Akeelah from her heart. With any luck, the production company will accept her, and the film will be made.

Doug assures me that once the film's funding is in place, he'll hire me to coach the kids on the set. I know him well enough to know that this isn't just Hollywood chatter. Doug always means what he says.

----------- 9. -----------

EVERY MORNING AS soon as I wake up and every evening before I go to bed, I thank God for my health, for Neal's health, for the roof above our heads. I pray that I will be able to support us. I often hear a voice that comes from my heart and says, "Keep moving. Your life will be better than anything you can imagine."

Jobs keep coming my way; fortunately, none are full time so I can still be available to Neal. This bounty, more than I could have dreamed of, provides me with the profound yet simple joy of sustaining my family. Doing so binds me to millions of other women whose fate and privilege it is to do the same.

No longer financially dependent on any human being, I depend on my willingness to trust in a higher source, to have faith in the abundance of the universe. And, yes, I am willing. As a result, there is food on our table and, slowly but surely, the bills are getting paid.

10.

I DON'T EXPECT Jeff to be a saint. I'm not surprised when the multiple stresses I grapple with take a toll on our relationship. He tries as much as he can, as much as anyone possibly could.

He wants to be supportive and he is. Yet I can see that he's getting cold feet about a long-term commitment. How ironic, I think, considering that I'm the one who originally had the cold feet and that now I've come to love him and rely on him more than ever.

Now he doesn't doubt that he loves me. He says that he admires my fortitude and courage, but he doesn't have my strength. He's seen the challenges of my life. He doesn't think he can handle them.

In the beginning, Jeff was the one saying, "This is forever." I was the one saying, "Not so fast." But I've heard it said that the word "forever" is a girl's kryptonite. Even today, when women are generally considered to be the stronger sex, it weakens us female types and causes us to lose our footing.

Every so often, I remind Jeff of his early declaration.

"Well," he says now, "I meant it when I said it."

YET NOTHING CHANGES. Day to day, as the weeks pass, Jeff is still warm, loving, helpful, fun, and dear to me and to Neal. So I stay silent, until I can't be quiet anymore. Sooner or later, I speak out again. It never goes well.

I understand that Jeff is scared. I'm scared too. Sometimes I think

I should give him an ultimatum: either we move forward or we break up. But I'm not ready for this. It's not that I'm afraid of being alone, I'm afraid of the grief that comes at the end of a relationship.

I heed the advice of a friend who suggests that every morning I ask myself, "Am I ready to leave him today?" If my inner voice says, "No," then—for the next twenty-four hours—I don't question our union, and don't worry that it might end.

11.

"THE BOARD LIKES your grant proposal," a woman from the Jewish Community Foundation calls to tell me. "But the budget doesn't make sense." I'm not surprised. I tried as best as I could, but I'm no MBA. I'm told that if I can put together a budget in which the numbers actually add up, my proposal will be passed on to the next level of consideration. Fantastic!

Jeff's friend Dav is great with numbers. He spends three hours with me on the phone. By the time we're ready to hang up, I've got a workable budget.

"Why are you home on a weekday?" I ask him.

"It's my birthday," he says.

Dav had taken the entire morning of his birthday to help a friend. Yet another kindness. Thanks to Dav, three weeks later I'm walking into a conference room where fifteen members of the grant review board are seated behind tables with clipboards and notepads in front of them. I feel like I'm back in the old days when I used to audition for musical theater.

I don't know whether to talk about the proposal or sing a few bars and tapdance. Since there's no piano in the room, I figure I'd better share my ideas. I ask God for the words, and they come to me.

"I am a single mom with a child who has autism," I begin. "For the past seven years, I've been isolated with my son and without community. My proposal is not just a theater program for children, although theater and creative activities are the means and the children will be guided to express themselves through dance, acting, and music.

"My proposal is about building community. The theater project will provide a place for all family members: there will be parent discussion groups, and parents will be encouraged to help with costumes, sets, programs, publicity. The idea is to create a safe, dynamic, and nurturing space for families of children with special needs."

All eyes are looking at me. Should I go on? They are nodding, approving. This seems a good sign.

"The goal," I continue, "is to create an original musical performance that will showcase the unique and wonderful nature of children who have special needs. Their beauty will come shining through. It will reaffirm two things I deeply believe: that the creative process of theater can transform lives, and that 'different' doesn't mean 'less.'

"The day of the performance, the children will be proud of their accomplishments; their parents will be ecstatic. The children will receive a standing ovation. And there will not be a dry eye in the house."

That's it. The room is silent. No one asks a question. I have no idea if I blew it, or if I blew them away.

At the day school where I teach once a week, I pick up a book of folktales and stories about miracles. The book is full of mystical tales about holy people, tales of their piety, their battles with demons, their ability to heal the sick and comfort the afflicted. I think of how my own life has been a succession of miracles, from finding Neal in Russia, to hearing him say "Mama" for the first time, to coming upon the guy who just happened to be in the hills when Neal was having a tantrum.

To most eyes, these are common occurrences. But the same could be said of the way a flower opens. Think about it: is the opening of a flower something ordinary, or is it miraculous? Take your pick.

Albert Einstein said, "There are only two ways to live your life. One is as though nothing is a miracle. The other is as if everything is a miracle."

It's all a matter of perspective.

I believe in miracles. I rely on them. I see them everywhere, every day. When it comes to miracles, parents of kids with special needs are the lucky ones. Our kids may never attend the best private schools, or elite universities, but we can find a miracle in every one of their accomplishments, however small or great. As I reflect on this, I realize what the theme of my theater program will be. If I am lucky enough to get the grant, the program will be about miracles. Soon, I receive the call that changes my life. I have been awarded a grant to establish what will become known as The Miracle Project.

12.

NEAL'S COACH IS moving back East. Randy has become an integral part of our family. His relationship to Neal is so rich and deep that I asked him to be Neal's godfather.

Finding a new coach won't be easy. It's quite a job. I draw up a list of its many facets:

Neal eats—A LOT—all day. He has low blood sugar and needs snacks between meals like fruit or rice crackers. I keep him on a wheat-free diet as much as possible. He gets hyper on sugar. NO SODAS. NO FRUIT DRINKS. WATER PLEASE.

Neal drinks—A LOT. He will say "ga-gar," his word for "water."

Neal needs to go to the bathroom A LOT. He will not tell you—but take him every hour and a half.

If Neal says "Ruuuu," that is his word for his favorite sitter—Ruth. Tell him, "Saturday."

When Neal poops, he takes all his clothes off. He likes to look in a mirror and see if his butt is clean after he wipes it.

BEHAVIORS

When Neal is nervous, he likes to throw. Give him a ball and let him throw it over a net. He can do this over and over again. He loves basketball, or just throwing a ball through the boughs of trees.

Neal sometimes needs deep pressure and vestibular stimulation. He likes to be swung and spun around.

If Neal pokes another child, he needs a consequence—such as having to sit out his preferred activity.

He is very sensitive to sounds and may tantrum if things are too loud.

If he bangs his head on the ground or whines, say, "I can't understand what you are trying to tell me. When you are ready to tell me, I will listen."

TRANSITIONS

Neal has difficulty with transitions between one activity and another. Five-minute warnings work well, followed by two-minute, one-minute, then all done. If he is doing something that he does not want to stop doing, i.e., playing with a ball, he may get naughty before transitioning. It is good to remind him, "If you stop nicely now, we can play ball again later, or tomorrow."

BALL

Neal loves to play ball with another person or on his own. He likes to kick it at a wall. He can do this for hours. It helps calm him and can also be used as an incentive to get him to do an activity that he likes less.

COMMUNICATION

Neal is trying very hard to talk. He will say, "I waan," meaning "I want something." Sometimes he will take something prior to saying, "I waan." He knows he needs to ask first.

Neal does sign language to convey the words "stop" and "help." He is learning other words to sign. This is a good way to connect with him.

SCHEDULE

Please write down the activities for each day on a yellow legal pad. For example:

> Breakfast
> Walk
> Read
> Snack
> Music
> Lunch
> Recess
> Park
> Dinner
> Bed

Let Neal cross out each activity once it is completed. This provides him with a feeling of control and security, and is very important.

Please have him cross off SUNDAY, MONDAY, etc., at the end of each day on the yellow legal pad. This also helps him calm his anxiety, as he has difficulty with concepts of time.

I INTERVIEW EIGHTY-FIVE people, all of whom are too set in their own ways of behavioral training or too daunted by a job of this intensity. I wonder if Randy can ever be replaced.

In the small hours, I type my fears on my computer. This has long been a habit of mine when I don't know where to turn, as on the night so long ago when I wondered if I should bring Neal home from the orphanage. Now, as always, the typing is both a plea for help and a dialogue with my higher self. Always, a response comes from a calm, centered, knowing place.

"Be patient," it tells me now. "The right person will appear."

13.

I RECEIVE TWO more résumés, one from Zack, one from Paul. Both seem equally qualified. I schedule separate interviews with them for a Sunday morning.

At 8:30 A.M. on Sunday, Paul calls. "The time changed to daylight savings time last night," he says. "I overslept. May I come half an hour late?"

Then Zack calls. "Hi, Elaine," he says. "Just wanted to remind you that it's daylight savings time. I want to make sure you know, so you don't think that I'm showing up too early."

After that call, though Zack didn't know it, he was already hired.

Zack is twenty-five. He was raised in Texas. He's tall, with dark hair, chiseled features, and an endearing modesty and politeness. In the past, he's worked on the administrative side of education. He loves working with kids, but has never worked with kids with autism. I like him. I sense his open mind and loving heart. Jeff likes him too. Most important, Neal takes to him immediately.

Zack trains with Randy, learning how to calm Neal, to redirect his energies, to give meaningful consequences when Neal tests and acts out.

Randy brings Zack to Neal's school, where he learns to help Neal focus and interact with other kids. He also learns to read Neal's cues so he'll know when Neal needs a break.

Zack has an entirely different style than Randy, who believes in tough love and, when needed, rules with playful intimidation and sarcasm. "Neal, if you want to push someone, then push me," Randy would dare him. It was a clever tactic, one destined to make Neal think long and hard before he pushed anyone again. In the end, Randy got Neal to stop pushing.

Zack, by contrast, is cool and calm, playful and fun. He romps with Neal, but knows instinctively how to rein him in. A Southern gentleman to the core, he's strict without being harsh, strong without being punitive. Most of all, he's eager to learn from Neal. They soon form a bond and become fast friends.

Watching them together, I'm struck by the fact that Neal's relationship with Zack proves—yet again—that children with autism are entirely capable of forming meaningful human attachments.

———————————— 14. ————————————

ZACK AND NEAL are ready for school. Neal is scheduled to go to a special day class for half an hour each morning and then go to a regular-education fourth-grade class for the rest of the day. His teacher will be Ms. Linden, a relatively new teacher. She is frail, precise, nervous, and intense. Think Chihuahua.

Upon hearing that she is to be Neal's teacher, Ms. Linden writes a note to Neal's special education teacher. It reads: "I do not want a boy like that in my class."

A boy like that!!! My mind goes to lyrics from *West Side Story*. "A boy like that who'd kill your brother . . . forget that boy, and find another . . ."

I cannot begin to describe the rage I feel. I'm ready to make a civil rights case of it, when I'm called to the school for an emergency meeting. Apparently, another fourth-grade teacher, Mr. Sanschagrin, or Mr. S as he is known, was told about Ms. Linden's remarks. Mr. S is a seasoned teacher, brimming with intelligence and imagination. With no prompting whatsoever, he said, "I'd love to have Neal in my class."

Once again, Neal and I have been saved by the cosmic truth that when one door closes, another door opens. Look at what would have happened had I fought for what I wanted: Neal would have become part of a class where he would never have been welcome. He would have felt the teacher's nervousness, her contempt for kids "like that." It would have been an unholy disaster.

Life is the First Teacher. And life is teaching me to pick my battles. It's taught me that man's rejection is God's protection. For, as it turns out, Neal being taken into Mr. S's class is the best thing that could have happened.

Mr. S is creative and unique. He's special. Funny, those are the same words that people use to describe Neal.

The children in his class learn in a room where the walls are covered with inspiring framed quotes, where desk arrangements are routinely changed just to mix things up a bit and where an indoor basketball hoop looms in a corner.

While other teachers rely on order and rules, Mr. S brings out the best in his students with organized chaos. On Fridays, if the kids have accomplished their weekly class goals, Mr. S takes them to play soccer, a reward for work well done. Each day, when an individual student achieves a personal goal, they get to shoot a soft basketball into the indoor basketball net. Yea! Score!

It's a vital, exciting way to learn and what's most important to me is that Neal is included in every step of the learning process. When Mr. S lectures, he puts kids on the hot seat to make sure they pay attention. Let's say he's talking about the Civil War and wants one of the students to tell him who was the general of the Southern army. He doesn't hesitate to walk over to Neal and extend each hand with a different answer choice.

"Neal, my right hand is Ulysses S. Grant, my left is Robert E. Lee. You choose which one."

Often Neal gets the answer right; sometimes he doesn't, but when he inevitably makes a mistake, Mr. S never makes him feel stupid or embarrassed. When he answers correctly, Neal feels victorious.

Either way, he's thrilled to be included in the class. He's basking in his newfound berth as an intelligent fourth grader.

15.

BY NOW YOU know that Neal can be a handful, and in a typical classroom, he's no different. True, he's come far from the days when he couldn't sit still for thirty seconds, from when his attention was nonexistent or hyperfocused on matchbox cars. Nonetheless, in a regular classroom, he can be a major challenge.

For one thing, he often feels compelled to test the boundaries of what he can get away with. He tests to see how many times he can make noises, close books, or drop his pencil before Zack takes him outside so he doesn't distract other kids. This is an important process. Neal wants and needs to know his limits!

Mr. S understands and trusts Zack to make these determinations. A less confident teacher would have inserted themselves into the situation. I can almost hear them saying, "After all, this is my class!" or "Neal's taking away from the other students."

But to Mr. S, having Neal in his class is important not only for Neal, but for every other child in the class: the class provides Neal an opportunity to learn, while Neal provides the rest of the class with an opportunity to learn that not everyone sees the world as they do.

Because Neal cannot always sit still for the entire class time, Zack takes him outside to run around the track, or walk in the hallway when he needs it. The other kids come to understand that Neal is not getting special treatment, but is getting his individual needs met so that he can continue to participate.

After a while, kids tell Zack, "Hey, I think Neal needs to take a walk. He seems a little restless."

16.

NEAL BEFRIENDS TWO students, Bill and Scott, who happen to be the smartest kids in the class. Bill is a math whiz and natural athlete; Scott, a creative genius, conjures up all kinds of mythical scenarios which the boys pretend play during recess. Bill and Scott appreciate Neal's carefree attitude and mischievous nature. They also applaud his accomplishments and admire how hard he tries despite his disabilities.

After sitting next to Neal and bonding with him, the two boys ask their moms for after-school playdates with Neal. Most lunch periods, the three of them sit together. In the yard at recess, they join Neal in throwing a ball against the wall, and invent new twists to keep the game interesting.

When Neal has tantrums or throws food, most people respond by becoming scared or dismissing him forever. Luckily for my son, Bill and Scott assure other kids that it's okay, that it's just the way Neal is sometimes. They laugh off Neal's behaviors because they've gotten to know him. He does have his difficulties, but for these boys, being friends with Neal is worth it.

I am eternally grateful to Mr. S, who is one of those empathetic, uncommon teachers who can change a kid's life. Any kid really. But especially "a boy like that."

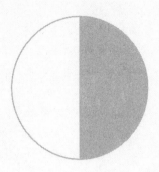

phase seven:
autism: the musical

None of us will ever accomplish anything excellent or commanding

except when he listens to this whisper which is heard by him alone.

RALPH WALDO EMERSON

WHAT IN THE world was I thinking? My ambitious claims for
The Miracle Project are totally overwhelming me. I've committed
to training more than twenty people, to working with twenty kids
who have autism and other special needs, to writing and directing an
original musical for them to star in. How can I do this?

I go to a service where the rabbi tells a story that provides the
inspiration I need: when Moses was carrying the biblical tablets
down from Mount Sinai, he was helped and supported by angels. Yet
whenever he doubted his ability to lead his people, the angels would
vanish and the tablets would become unbearably heavy. But when
Moses trusted in his God, the angels would reappear and the tablets
were suddenly weightless.

This story gives me faith. It tells me that if I trust in God and in
the strength of The Miracle Project, the work will be effortless. My
angels will guide me. I truly believe this.

THE FIRST THING I do is hire an administrator to help with budget
planning, allocating funds, and all those things that I'm not good at.
She does a great job, but then, just as we're about to send out flyers
announcing the project, my helpful administrator vanishes.

I call her. She doesn't answer. I call again and again. I'm increasingly frantic, but she doesn't respond. Finally, I find out from her
husband that she's taken a job that pays more money. I'm left to my
own devices at the worst possible time.

Debra Phillipes, the mother of a nine-year-old boy I've been
coaching, wants to talk with me about The Miracle Project. We
meet at Starbucks. Before the foam flattens on our cappuccinos,
she offers to take over the administrative duties. By the time we've

shared a blueberry scone, Debra is the de facto assistant director of The Miracle Project.

Debra is in her early forties. She's tall, beautiful, brilliant, a Harvard graduate who, like many moms, gave up a career when her child was diagnosed with autism. Debra had been a lawyer, and no doubt a good one: she's extremely organized, incisive, and efficient. She also bakes a mean chocolate-chip banana bread.

The first thing we do is invite a group of friends and professionals in the community to meet with us at her house. We need to find people who would be interested in helping with The Miracle Project.

For the first time in years, I'm in a leadership role. I'm nervous about the meeting, to say the least. Before I go, I change my clothes several times. I want to look official, yet creative; I want to seem confident but not bossy. And I certainly don't want to look showy, as we'll be asking people to join up even though we don't have much money to pay for staff. I settle on a navy blue top, jeans, and a magenta corduroy jacket.

I head out the door, wondering if anyone will care enough about The Miracle Project to even come to the gathering. I'm about to find out.

Twenty-two people come to the meeting. Many have a passionate interest in working with special needs kids. I'm awed by the intensity of their response. Each person is open, willing, and excited to participate in a program that is still only an idea. In this room, with these people, I feel God's presence. Soon The Miracle Project will be up and running.

2.

JUST AS THE Miracle Project is coming together, *Akeelah and the Bee* gets green-lighted, and is ready to start production. I meet with the film's kind and generous producer, Sid Ganis. As Doug promised, I am offered the job of coach for the kids in the film. It's a dream job, but I can't accept it without telling Sid about my situation: I will have to leave early on Wednesdays for The Miracle Project and, if anything goes wrong with Neal, I have to leave on a moment's notice.

I also tell him that I'm available to help in all aspects of production. He seems to appreciate my candor and my passion for the project. He hires me. He also hires Doug's girlfriend, Dalia, to coach with me so that I can leave when and if I need to. This sort of thing doesn't often happen in Hollywood. Talk about a miracle project!

In preproduction, I assisted Doug throughout the rehearsal process as he readied the young actors for the shoot. Now during production, Doug spends much of his time working with the young star, Keke Palmer, and with the adult actors, entrusting me to rehearse the other children before they come onto the set. Since the film is about the National Spelling Bee, I'm also the dialect coach for both kids and adult actors who have to pronounce "big" words like pulchritude and prestidigitation.

I love working on this film. It is a truly collaborative process. At first, I'm intimidated by the lead actor, Laurence Fishburne, a tall, looming, theatrical presence. I call him Mister Fishburne, and keep my distance. But soon his contagious good spirit and wonderful storytelling put me and everyone else on the set at ease.

I'm gratified that Doug seeks out my opinions throughout the filming and invites me to share my years of experience working with kids in order to sensitize other crew members to the children's needs. Doug's gentle, enthusiastic approach brings out the best in everyone and makes this set one of the happiest and most creative that I've ever worked on.

3.

AS DALIA ASSISTS me with coaching the kids, she becomes a dear friend. Outwardly, we could not be more different. She's an Island girl, tall, thin, with almond-shaped eyes and silky black skin. I am—you know—petite, white, round, and Russian. Yet we have so much in common: strong family ties, a love of acting and the arts, and abiding spiritual beliefs.

Dalia is a Christian, but her personal relationship to God is much like mine. She speaks with conviction of miracles, of transformation. Like me, she has a powerful connection to her inner voice. It's Dalia who has taught me the importance of sharing my spiritual journey and truth. In fact, if not for Dalia, I wouldn't be writing this book.

A year that began as one of the most difficult of my life is transporting me further into joyful independence. Having listened to my inner voice, my connection to that voice grows stronger by the day. It's this voice that insisted, "Your marriage is over," that told me, "Teach children with special needs."

In the past, when hearing it, I often dismissed it. Now I am linked to a constant inner dialogue. At times, I feel that it's connecting me to God; at other times, it seems to be connecting me to my personal angels. All I know for certain is that miraculous things occur whenever I have the courage to heed it.

———————————————— 4. ————————————————

JEFF IS SPENDING more time with his friends than he spends with me. Our times together are not only fewer, they're strained. Jeff no longer talks of the future. Instead, he says, "I just don't know if I can do this."

When the holidays come, we receive invitations to a number of parties. Two are on the same evening. One is given by the parents of a child I teach; the other by one of Jeff's grad-school buddies.

We go to my party first. It's in Mandeville Canyon, a magical enclave of Los Angeles where beautiful homes are surrounded by towering trees. My student's home is huge, beautifully decorated, and scented with cinnamon spice that comes from the hot mulled cider being warmed in the kitchen.

A pianist plays holiday music. There is wonderful food and a festive feeling. Outside, in the pool area, they'll be showing a first-run movie.

I love this environment. It makes Jeff uneasy. We're there for less than an hour when Jeff gets antsy and wants to go to his friend's party.

Reluctantly, I leave with him. We drive to his friend's small apartment in the Valley, where guys are sitting around a card table playing poker. Half-opened plastic platters of bologna and dried-out cheese sit on a counter. Songs from the late seventies play on the stereo. There are only about a dozen people. Most are half my age.

I am overdressed and out of place. Jeff is in joy. His friends and classmates are very welcoming. Jeff is hugged by everyone and by one woman in particular, a beautiful artist in her early thirties. She has long flowing hair, wears a flowing skirt and funky jewelry. She smells of patchouli oil.

I learn that she is also a play therapist trainee. She and Jeff definitely have a connection. I can see why he was so eager to leave my first party. I can envision Jeff with this younger woman. I see him pushing a baby stroller, his backpack filled with diapers, baby bottles, and organic fruit. In my imaginings, he is happy, content, free.

After that evening, I begin to pull away. I prepare myself for being alone. Now when I am invited to a single-parent gathering, I go. I befriend some of the men at these occasions. Don't get me wrong: I'm not angry. I'm just looking to survive.

5.

NEW YEAR'S EVE, 1951. Jonas Salk is developing the polio vaccine, *I Love Lucy* recently premiered on television, the radio plays Nat

King Cole's "Unforgettable," babies are booming, and my mom and dad are about to meet.

My dad was one of the most popular and eligible bachelors in their AZA group—Aleph Zadik Aleph, that is, the Jewish boys' alternative to frat clubs. A jitterbug ace, my dad won dance contests throughout Washington, D.C. He hung out with Billie Holiday when she came to town; he went to clubs where he shared a table with Gene Krupa, the storied drummer. Like many of his friends, my dad returned from service in the armed forces and went back to school. He got a degree in psychology, and was now working an assortment of jobs to pay the bills and enjoy life. Shoe salesman, waiter, dance instructor, you name it, my dad did it. My dad was a bit of a "player." He loved to dance, drink a bit, and probably "inhaled" a few times when he was hanging with his jazz idols in the local blues clubs.

My mom was a professional administrator at the George Washington Hospital in Washington, D.C. Having left her small hometown in Virginia, she had completed a secretarial course and moved to the big city. Like many other Jewish girls in D.C., my mom had a crush on my dad.

As solid and responsible as my mom was, my dad was equally free-spirited and carefree. I like to think of him as the pint-size Jewish version of a cross between Frank Sinatra and Fred Astaire. He was handsome, charming, and cool. Way cool. He had a way with women probably because he was raised by three sisters. His stature never fazed him.

"Only five foot three," he used to say. "Any woman over five two is unattractive."

His attitude is probably why my sister and I never had a problem with being petite. He was great for our self-image.

My dad was a bit tipsy that New Year's Eve. Before the clock struck midnight, he got several women's phone numbers, including my mom's. The next day, dad looked at the numbers, the names, and couldn't put faces to them. He called a number at random. My mom picked up the phone. He asked her to join him at a ball game, having no idea who she was. My mom knew who he was and told him that she loved ball games, though she had no interest in sports. That night, she wore a strapless dress outlining her petite, curvaceous figure.

They had a great time at the game, talking during every inning, which was unusual for my dad, who took his sports as seriously as he took his music. He asked my mom out again, and again. They hit it off. My mom was smitten. So much so that four weeks after they started dating, she told him, "I really enjoy our dates together. But I need to know where this is going."

"Going?!" My dad was stunned. "I hadn't thought about it going anywhere. Let's just enjoy being together."

"I'm sorry, Sol. I like you too much to just see you casually. I really can't see you again." And she broke up with him. Just like that.

My mom was so ahead of her time. Conscious, evolved. She wasn't going to settle for anything less than what she knew she wanted. If my dad didn't want more, she was willing to move on. Mom was twenty-six years old. Most of her friends were married or at least engaged. She knew that she needed more than my dad could give her.

For the next two weeks, my dad moped around the house. This surprised him, as he had never been shaken like this before. No woman had confronted him, much less broken off with him for not committing. Even hanging out with his buddies and going to jazz clubs didn't bring him comfort.

"You really like this little girl, don't you, Sollie?" questioned my wise grandfather.

"Yes, Pop. I think I do," my sullen dad admitted.

"Don't let her go," counseled my grandpa.

On Valentine's Day, 1952, my dad showed up at my mom's apartment with flowers and chocolates. They were married four months later.

I loved to hear my mom and dad tell this story. It never bored me. I've heard it hundreds of times. Whenever one of my brother's friends would talk about getting serious with a woman, my dad would caution, "The time to settle down is when you are lonely in a crowd of your best buddies. Not until you're lonely in a crowd. That's how I felt. Lonely without her. I knew I was ready."

The last time my dad told this story, he was sitting on my mom's hospital bed, cuddling next to her. They laughed as he recounted it. They each filled in the details as to what happened next. I can still see them: my mom fading, my dad embracing. Still gazing at each other like newlyweds. Neither ever lonely.

-------------------- 6. --------------------

"DID YOU MISS me?" I ask Jeff when he returns after being away with one of his surfing buddies for a few days.

"Not really," he says.

My heart drops. I stare at Jeff as he launches into the usual: "I don't know if I can do this . . . you are so strong . . . I don't know if I can handle your life."

Ordinarily, I would listen to his concerns, feel terrible, and say nothing.

But tonight I hear myself saying, "You don't have to handle it anymore."

Jeff is stunned. He can't believe what I'm saying. I can't believe what I'm saying, either. It's my inner voice—speaking aloud.

I go upstairs and pack up the shirts that he's kept in my closet.

I say, "Good-bye."

"Let's talk about it in the morning," Jeff insists.

"No," I say. "I'm done."

When Jeff calls the next morning, I tell him, "Please don't contact me."

And I mean it.

Leaving him is the right decision, even though it hurts. Helen Keller said, "When one door of happiness closes another opens. Often we look so long at the closed door that we do not see the one that has been opened for us." I believe that. I just don't like being stranded in that darn hallway.

Yet I recognize that following my inner voice doesn't mean that I will live without pain. It means that I will live with integrity. This seems a worthy bargain: pain fades; integrity is forever.

-------- 7. --------

AS THE FIRST session of The Miracle Project approaches, I set about training my new staff and volunteers with the help of my friend Dr. Sarita Santos. Sarita is a professor of special education at the local college where I once gave a talk in the hope of finding volunteers to work with Neal. None of her students volunteered—but she called me and volunteered for six hours a week—and kept that commitment for three years. We've become family and she is Neal's godmother. She now offers to help me train these new volunteers for The Miracle Project. I plan to teach them much of what I've learned about autism. I have twenty hours in which to do so.

I want them to see autism as something extraordinary. I want them to enter into this world with open hearts, open minds. I want them to be loving, nonjudgmental, and to be the student as well as the teacher. I start out with the most basic principle: I ask them to regard autism not as a disorder but simply as a different way of being.

At each training session, we begin with the centering exercise and meditation that I do at home: we breathe together and let go of all the thoughts and events that occurred prior to gathering. I have found that doing this makes a world of difference when I am with Neal. I tell them how Neal senses if my mind or heart is agitated, or if I'm not really paying attention. I want them to know that it's of critical importance when they work with the kids to be totally calm and totally in the here and now.

I share aspects of my personal journey. I tell them the importance of learning to accept what you fear, of embracing what you dread. I tell them about the freedom that comes when you shake hands with the things that frighten you most.

I want this Miracle Team to accept and love the kids who enter our doors no matter what the kids are doing. So I create exercises to help them become more loving and accepting.

I ask the group to list all the things they do not like about themselves. I give them a minute to do so. Their pens race across the page. I then ask them to choose three of these things and tell them to another person.

Then I ask them to list three things they like about themselves. This is harder for them to do, but finally they do it. It's an important exercise because in order to approach the children from a place of fullness, they first need to embrace what is wonderful about them.

I also want our team to understand the sensory system. For this, I create an exercise through which they'll experience sensory overload. I ask them to pretend that they are one big hearing machine, and to pay attention to all the sounds inside the room, outside the room, and inside their own bodies. Then I guide them to be a smell machine and take in all the smells around them. We go through all the senses one by one, turning up the volume on each of the senses until they experience them in a way that is so intense it hurts.

I then guide them to turn all their senses on to high volume at the same time. Almost every time I do this exercise, the participants experience the same things: they feel panicked, they want to withdraw, they become anxious. I explain that this is how our kids with autism experience the world. From that point on, our staff and volunteers have a deeper understanding of what it feels like to move through the world with extreme sensitivities.

Next, I teach the basics of Floortime, how to follow a child's lead and to playfully challenge kids to expand their abilities. I give them the same exercises that I gave years ago to parent support groups: I ask them to demonstrate "autisticlike behaviors" like flapping their hands or rocking. Each time, they remark on how calming and fun these behaviors are. I then ask someone to try to make them stop. Naturally, the person flapping or rocking feels annoyed. I say, now imagine how a child might feel if they were doing these things to calm themselves and were constantly told to stop them.

The volunteers are getting it. And what do I mean by that? I mean that they are coming to the vital understanding that kids with autism—or, for that matter, those with cerebral palsy or ADHD or Tourette's syndrome—are not all that different from them.

-------- 8. --------

ON THE NIGHT that we are to begin, I lead the staff and volunteers in a meditation. We draw on our own resources of love and compassion. We share our thoughts, our goals for the day. We share our fears.

Most of the team feels excited and positive. Some are apprehensive, worried that they may not be up to the challenge. Others encourage them to trust themselves, to trust their intuition, and when all else fails—to just be loving. We talk about how being loving can be so easy . . . or so hard.

We set an intention for the class and for ourselves. Tonight, our intention is to provide a loving and accepting attitude for the families and the children. That's it. If we get to the singing and the dancing, well, that's icing on the cake.

This first evening of The Miracle Project is chaotic. Fifteen kids take part. Some do not want to leave their parents or enter the room. Others enter reluctantly, holding on to their mothers' legs. Some "momma bears" don't want to let go of their cubs even if the cubs are fine. (I can relate to that one!)

I encourage our team to follow the lead of the kids. One child hides under a table. I guide a volunteer to go under the table with the child. Another child runs around the table in circles. I encourage a staff member to turn this into a playful game of chase and tag. When another child pulls the carpet over his head, I instruct a team member to explore this underworld with him. I smile when I see their interaction turn into a game of peekaboo.

I have become a mini-general, like Wendy Parise, Neal's early preschool teacher, guiding others to be my hands and my eyes. Slowly we bring the group together into one large circle for a group warmup. We tell each other our names, acting them out with movement and rhythm.

"COACH E!" I say, opening up my arms on the word "Coach" and clapping them together on the "E." I ask everyone to repeat it with me.

Each child says their name with a rhythm or a movement. If they are too shy or reserved to do so, we say their names with them or for them. If it is too loud when we repeat it, we whisper their names instead.

Then we dance together, going across the floor with hops, skips, slides, and "silliness." Danny, my friend Michele's son, lets one of our volunteers roll his wheelchair. He glides with glee. I give them all an opportunity to do their own special movement. Kids flap, or walk on tiptoes, or do other "socially unacceptable" behaviors. As they execute these movements, we applaud them. We join them. We turn them into dance.

We break into small groups and learn a song that Rachelle, one of our acting coaches has created. We call it Rachelle's niggun. A niggun is a wordless combination of sounds like "Ya-na-na-ya-na-pa-pa-yaya-ya." It's something that everyone can move to and sing or chant. For the creative dramatics portion, we act out animals from Noah's Ark. The kids move two by two as if they are walking a gangplank onto a boat.

At the end of the evening, we invite the parents in to witness a brief snippet of what the kids did that night. The parents love what they see. The children are happy. Our staff is ecstatic.

We close the first Miracle Project class holding hands, dancing, singing together, with a blessing to send everyone on their way. What a night!

The staff and volunteers gather to share "what worked, what didn't work." We discuss the children's individual differences: the sensory challenges faced by some of the kids, how to help them separate from their parents earlier; we consider the best way to group them.

Then we share our own feelings one at a time, holding hands, using one word only. "Joy," says one volunteer. "Peace." "Excitement." "Love."

Once everyone has shared, we allow these feelings to pass from one to another, then imagine these powerful, loving feelings flowing like a fountain into the world. On the count of three, we all say, "I'm a Miracle!"

As I drive home, I reflect on the class, the grant, my life for the past three years. I am so grateful to be doing this work. I think about the many things that have brought me to this place: my years as an acting coach, the years that I was forced to do my own inner work, the years that I learned about autism from Neal, the many things I learned from our amazing therapists and teachers.

I think back to the day when I had that overwhelming sense that I was being called to teach acting, singing, and dance to children with special needs. Now that is precisely what I am doing. As I felt when I adopted Neal, I believe that everything in my life was designed to bring me to this moment.

--- 9. ---

DURING THE FIRST eleven weeks, we help the children participate more and more with the group. This is not easy, given that most of these children have been successful only in one-on-one therapies. One child strays from the group; another is so afraid of being photographed that he tantrums when he sees the camera; another is hypersensitive to noise and spends most of each session holding her ears and crying.

Our task is to find ways to help them join the others, and we do. We notice that the child who strays loves to draw. We bring in markers as he sits during class and draws cartoon characters. Only eight years old, and he draws like a professional. We marvel at his drawings and, every now and then, encourage him to participate in the group. First, for just a minute at a time, then two, then three—until one day he joins the other students and exults, "I'm participating!"

Our videographer, my friend Kevin McDermott, approaches the child who fears being photographed and teaches him about the inner workings of the camera. Soon, the child's fear fades and he comes to enjoy everything about video.

A volunteer "buddy" stays with the child who is sound-sensitive, letting her know that she can leave the group whenever it becomes too loud for her. He also teaches her to indicate the word "STOP" in sign language. He teaches the group to read her cues. Now, they quiet down when she motions for them to STOP.

As we work on our musical, the children change. The child who had isolated himself is now leading the group in song. Though he has extreme tactile sensitivity, he's able to wear the scratchy prop beard that the other kids are wearing. The child who refused to be photographed plays a lead character in the video portion of our show and is featured in the live performance. I'm so glad that we're filming parts of each child's performance. It's a terrific safety net. Now we all know that if any child gets stage fright, they will still have their moments to shine in the performance. Just knowing that greatly reduces the anxiety levels of the children and their parents.

As the kids rehearse, their parents bond. I introduce them to Rabbi Shawn Fields-Meyer, who has a child with special needs. The rabbi will help these parents see their experiences with their special children as part of their own spiritual growth. In this monthly spiritual support group, we share our joys, our challenges, and our accomplishments—all the while focusing on what is good and positive and right with our children. Soon, we parents become family. We share birthdays and holidays; our kids have playdates. For all of us, that persistent sense of isolation is assuaged. We are no longer alone.

Finally—the performance. The audience witnesses what we have been observing during the weeks of rehearsal: special children and typically developing peers singing, dancing, acting together. As their director, I have lost track of who has special needs and who does not. Now we are all simply members of The Miracle Project Players, a tight theatrical ensemble.

The child who covered her ears stands center stage and sings to the audience, her face beaming. In the audience, her parents beam back at her. What's happening is that they, and the other parents, are also undergoing a transformation. Until now, these parents watched their typical children in plays and sporting events and musical recitals and took their child with special needs only to therapies. To see their special child acting and singing and dancing in front of an audience was a dream that these parents never dared envision.

I am one of those parents too, and I will never forget the sense of joy and gratitude that overwhelmed me upon seeing Neal's angelic, glowing face on film as he hit his mark and hummed sweetly.

Everything I imagined that fateful day that I wrote the grant for The Miracle Project has come to pass. Our feelings of joy and accomplishment are profound. As I had promised, the kids take their bows to standing ovations, and—if you'll forgive the cliché—there's not a dry eye in the house.

That night taught me, as a parent of a child with autism, that all such parents can and should raise our expectations of what is possible. It proved that in an environment of creativity, love, and acceptance, miracles can and do happen.

—————————— 10. ——————————

MY HEART STILL belongs to Jeff. The mention of his name can send me into tears. I figure that he must have moved on by now. But he hasn't, I learn through mutual friends, who also tell me that he isn't happy, either. In any case, I need to get over him. I never will if I don't look somewhere else.

Friends tell me to go on the Internet to find a date. I figure, Why not? I found Neal's best coaches on the Internet—why not find someone for me? Perhaps I can find an older, mature man who, like me, comes with some baggage.

I exchange e-mails with a few men. I try to sense their priorities, to see what has meaning to them, to ascertain whether they're open-minded or closed and prejudicial. I ask key questions, among them: Did you like your mother? (I've found that men who love their moms and have worked out their mom issues are kinder to women—don't you think so?)

One guy sounds pleasant and appealing, but as we continue to correspond he reveals that he only likes people who are white, upper class, and who think like him. Bye, bye.

After many "no thank you's," I narrow the meager field to one man who seems kind and interesting. He's divorced. Successful. Has one son. Coaches the kid's soccer team. Definitely loves his mother.

He takes me to a lovely restaurant. We chat. It's pleasant. But throughout the evening, I think about Jeff. How he would have laughed at the $22 pasta.

"It's just noodles," I imagine him saying. "I could make that dish for under five dollars."

I think about how he's understated and cool and so comfortable in his own skin. That night, after three months of not hearing from Jeff, I return home from my date and find an e-mail from him.

11.

I'VE HEARD IT said that if you want to know what a person is really made of, break up with them. If they go crazy and act needy, run like the wind. If they respect your wish to be left alone, they are a pretty decent human being. Up to this moment, Jeff has honored my request for no contact. As suspected, he's a decent human being. Also, possibly a clairvoyant one.

How else to explain that he gets in touch with me on the very night that I go on a date with someone else. He's writing to say that he misses me. He asks about Neal. He misses him too. He's done a lot of soul searching and he's ready to commit. He's ready for us to be together. "The pain of being without you," he writes, "is greater than the fear of being with you."

I want to write back, "Come over! Now!" But that inner voice dominates my fingers.

"It's nice to hear from you," I write. "We are well, thank you."

Still, when my date calls and asks me out again I feign being busy. For the next hundred years.

Another e-mail arrives from Jeff. It reads like a Shakespearean sonnet. I call Norma in a panic, "He's 'theeing' and 'thouing' me!"

I want to laugh at this emotional outpouring, but in fact it terrifies me. I do not want to open myself up to being hurt by Jeff again. I don't want Neal to open up to him. I am not stupid. Still, would it be wrong to see him just once?

I agree to meet Jeff for coffee. So I won't stay too long, I bookend our meeting with obligations that give me only an hour to be with him. I dress in tight jeans and a black V-neck top. You can see that my attitude about seeing him is kind of mixed up. We meet. It's awkward, but nice.

He says again how much he misses me, misses Neal. His car, "Greeny," our sofa on wheels, was stolen. He misses it too. He wants me to go with him to his best friend's wedding in London. We'd planned to go months ago. He still has the tickets. I'd like to run into his arms, go to England, Tahiti, anywhere with him.

Instead, I say, "I can't get away."

We're silent for a moment.

"But we can be friends," I say finally.

Jeff proves to be a very good friend. He helps me with Neal again; he helps with The Miracle Project; he helps me in every conceivable way.

It's great to have him around again, even though I'm convinced that if I surrender to his professions of love he'll become afraid again, and run away. Besides, I really don't have time for a romantic relationship.

———————— 12. ————————

I KEEP MEETING parents who tell me how much fun their kids with autism have at sleepaway camp. A good camp might help with two issues I'm having:

Neal needs to learn to thrive away from home. I need to let go a bit.

It turns out there's a camp that also accepts children with developmental disabilities in Malibu, some twenty miles from where we live. The camp's directors assure me that they've worked for years with kids who have Neal's challenges.

If Neal comes here this summer, I say, I'd like to bring a one-on-one aide for him. They don't understand why I can't trust their capable staff.

"Because Neal is nonverbal and needs help to communicate," I tell them.

"He'll be fine," they assure me.

I'm doubtful. But they're the professionals.

I drive Neal to the camp and stay there until I've gone over the list of his needs with all the counselors and see that he's happily tossing a ball back and forth with one of them. He doesn't mind seeing me leave. I'm relieved as I proceed up the coast to visit Julia and her husband in Santa Barbara. Within an hour, I call the camp.

"Neal is doing fine," they tell me. "He went on a hike this afternoon with the other campers and is swimming in the pool now. Relax; enjoy your time away."

Just as I'm unwinding after dinner, the camp's director calls.

"Neal is out of control," he says. "You have to pick him up right now! He didn't want to go to bed. He's pulling the blinds up and down in the cabin. I'm afraid he's going to hurt himself."

It's 8:30 P.M. I couldn't get back to Malibu for at least an hour and a half. I call Jeff, panicked. Luckily, he's just finished kite surfing about five miles from the camp.

"I'll get him. Don't worry," Jeff comforts. "I'll bring him home and stay with him tonight. You can drive home in the morning. Try to get some sleep."

As soon as Jeff arrives at the camp, Neal calms down. Jeff takes him home, getting into the town house with the key I recently gave him. There, they both sleep soundly.

I return home early in the day. Jeff has prepared a beautiful breakfast for the three of us. Neal is peaceful, happy, relieved. After breakfast, I ask him to write out for me what happened. In school, he's been writing, now that we've discovered that putting a little pressure on his upper arm helps regulate his central nervous system and keeps him focused. I touch his upper arm as he writes, "Because of my apraxia."

His apraxia! The inability to talk! He wanted to tell the counselors something and he couldn't express it. I feel horrible. I hold him and tell him that I will never again leave him without someone who understands him.

That day Jeff takes us on a beautiful hike in Malibu. Neal has become quite the mountaineer. He smiles happily as he leads us up the steep hill. As the three of us stand on a cliff that overlooks the glistening Pacific Ocean, Jeff hugs me. That night, after Neal goes to bed, we embrace.

"Thank you for helping us," I whisper. "I missed you."

We are a couple again.

On New Year's Eve, Ruth babysits Neal while Jeff and I go to Malibu. We sip champagne as we watch the moon reflect on the ocean waves. At midnight, Jeff reaches into his pocket and reveals a "Wizard" finger puppet on his right forefinger. The puppet is holding a ring. At first, I think it must be a fake ring, like the kind in a Cracker Jack box. But then I look closer. It's a diamond engagement ring.

"Well, will you?" Jeff asks.

"Will I what?"

"Will you marry me?" he whispers, in the most loving voice I've ever heard.

"Ah, yeah, sure," I gasp. "Why not?"

--------------------------------- 13. ---------------------------------

JEFF'S PROPOSAL LEAVES me terrified. What if it doesn't work out? I've already walked down that aisle, only to tumble through a trapdoor. What if Jeff truly can't handle my life?

I'm also not sure that I'm ready to relinquish my status as a "Single Working Mother of a Child with Special Needs." I wear it like a medal of honor. Wouldn't marriage mean surrendering my duty? Would I be court-martialed?

How can I add a marriage to my life? Like every parent with a child who has special needs, I feel that no matter what I do, I'm never doing enough. Each night, I go to bed with a sense of inadequacy and failure. Then I wake up and jump into my "to do" list. The Energizer Bunny, that's me, getting as much done as possible in the vain hope that I might go to bed without feeling that I've let

Neal down in some way. No, I'm not trying to "cure" him. My efforts are all to make him as independent as he can be, and to make him happy.

If Neal cannot speak, it's my fault; if he still throws tantrums, I'm to blame; if he's not socializing, it's my problem because I failed to find him the opportunities. I am consumed with making his world right. And yet, no matter how much I race during the day, time remains my enemy. I never get it all done. So here I am, an about-to-be wife (if I can ever decide on a date for the wedding), a fiancée to whom marriage signifies more opportunities to fail, to not be enough.

At The Miracle Project's parent group, the rabbi speaks about the Passover seder and of dayenu, a Hebrew word that means "it would have been enough." Dayenu is a word chanted at the Passover table in response to statements of praise for all that God has done: "If God had brought all of us out from Egypt . . . dayenu . . . it would have been enough."

"If he had brought us out of Egypt but had not split the sea before us . . . dayenu . . . it would have been enough . . ."

THE RABBI ASKS us to share our gratitude to God, to consider the things that comprise our own Dayenu. What are we grateful for? What abundance has been given to us? How have we been brought out of our own personal Egypt into freedom?

I have so much to be grateful for. Wonderful friends, work that I enjoy, my health, my family. I just wish that I didn't have this terrible, nagging sense of inadequacy. God's works are great. It's me that is flawed and never doing enough. But then, in a moment of quiet, I feel Neal's soul say "Dayenu" to me.

I listen again. And there it is, as clear as day: Dayenu . . .

Mama, if you had just brought me out of Russia from that orphanage—Dayenu

If you had brought me out of the orphanage, but didn't heal my physical illnesses—Dayenu

If you had healed my illnesses, but not found doctors and coaches to help me with my autism—Dayenu

If you had found the coaches, but not quit your work for seven years to focus solely on me—Dayenu

If you had loved me so much, but not put me above all else in your life—Dayenu . . .

For the first time in all the years that I have been with my precious son, I finally feel that I am doing all that I can do. I am doing enough. If that is so, perhaps I can open my heart to marriage.

phase eight: celebrations

The more you praise and celebrate your life,

the more there is in life to celebrate.

OPRAH WINFREY

I FEEL SILLY, oh so silly! I'm standing in front of a three-way mirror holding a virginal white lace wedding gown. I'm shopping for a wedding dress, accompanied by Leah, a friend who's twenty years younger than I am. Everyone thinks the dress is for her and that I'm the mother of the bride.

The last time I waltzed down the aisle I was wearing a white silk gown with yards of beaded train, and an intricately beaded lace jacket all of which I designed myself and were handmade by Dorothy's personal seamstress. Now I pack up that gown, still beautiful after all these years. I take it to the place where I will find my gown this time, Brides Against Cancer, a nonprofit organization that recycles wedding gowns and donates the proceeds to grant dying wishes to women who are losing their fight against cancer. The money they raise pays for a videocamera to tape last words, a final trip with loved ones. Whether you donate or purchase a dress there, you help other women profoundly.

Moments after I donate my gown, a volunteer calls out. "I found your wedding dress!" And she has. It is gorgeous: a beaded halter gown in a size 4 that fits as if it were made for me. I believe it was, by the Fates. I look at myself in the mirror. I see a woman full of joy.

I AM ABOUT to say "I do" again. For the second time and hopefully the last. If I no longer believe in Forever, I wholly embrace the day-to-day power of For Now. I am going to walk down that aisle again. The one I walked down naively almost twenty years ago. What will be different this time? I ask myself. Everything, I know.

I am a different person, having gained—or so I hope—more than just age and pounds. Wiser now, I want simply to love and be loved. This time when I say "I do," I am not expecting a fairy tale. I am entering a union that will merge my son, my past, my baggage, my strengths and imperfections. This is what I bring to our perfectly imperfect love.

I have proven that I can be happy and successful on my own, a good mother and friend. I am not looking for someone to complete me. I have found my soul mate, someone to meet me.

This time, I don't want to be the "wife." I like the title "partner." Partner is just that, an equal. For me, the term "wife" conjures up generations of subservience, of giving up "me" to be loved by "you." I have worked too hard, too long, to give up even a smidgen of my long-fought-for identity. Partner, I am. Partner, he is. Partner, we do. My task, and my privilege, is to cherish my partner for exactly who he is.

2.

FOR A MONTH before the ceremony, Jeff and I purposely spend most of our time apart. I give up chocolate—and every kind of sweet. I'm determined to fit into that dress! I've also had no caffeine because my brother the dentist just whitened my teeth. I'm not sure what I miss most: the chocolate, the caffeine, or Jeff. I think it's the chocolate!

For weeks, I have feared that I wouldn't be pretty enough, worthy enough, skinny enough for such a grand occasion. Yet, as the day approaches, any concern or worry is melted away by the boundless warmth that Jeff and I feel for each other and share with friends and family whose love and good wishes for us are unmistakable.

Ours is a spiritual union and I prepare accordingly. I go with my cousins and a few close friends to the mikvah, where I am immersed in a bath of holy water. Under water, my body seems weightless, breathless, as if I have returned to the womb. I release the pains of miscarriages, the loss of my first marriage, the loss of my mother. I let go, I pray. I emerge renewed and purified. I put my clothes on and, with my cousins, enact a joyous dance in a circle. I am elated, on another plane, enraptured. I feel in step with our tradition, in which the bride and groom are like Adam and Eve, newborns, without history, without sin, two individuals, each with a clean slate.

Everything involved with our wedding will be personal and full of meaning. The date is January 14, 2007: lots of sevens there, Jeff and my favorite number. Jeff designs the wedding invitations and we print them ourselves. They depict a three-dolphin family embedded in a delicate heart-shaped sunburst.

The ceremony will be photographed by my friend Rebecca's husband, the renowned photographer David Hume Kennerly. It will take place in a meadow at Temescal Canyon, the lush, verdant, hilly place where Tom carried Neal on his back high into the hills to help him overcome his fear of hiking. Rabbi Shawn Fields-Meyer, who led the spiritually based parent group at The Miracle Project, will officiate along with Jeff's friend Dav, who helped me write the original budget for my grant.

Jeff wants to cook for our guests. I talk him out of this one. Instead, we turn to one of Neal's coaches, who has a catering company, to create our favorite dishes: ceviche, the dish that Jeff brought to the sing-along on the night we met. Also poached salmon, baba ghanoush, hummus, olives, platters of cheese and fruit.

Jeff's sister, Evette, designs and bakes a gorgeous chocolate-rum wedding cake that she covers in pale beige marzipan and decorates with white chocolate seashells and starfish. To top it off, Jeff and I contribute a kitschy but whimsical luminated glass heart augmented with kissing dolphins.

Two days before the ceremony, the wedding party, friends and family, gather to decorate the canyon hall, which was built in the early 1900s, to be a chapel. We hang tulle over immense windows that look out onto giant sycamores and vibrant patches of wildflowers. Norma and other friends collect the wildflowers and place them in huge round pots. Other friends stand on enormous ladders to hang sparkly lights from the rafters of the thirty-foot ceiling. I can hardly watch.

Before sunset, we practice how everyone will walk from the chapel to the meadow. The rabbi and Jeff's friend Dav lead the procession. Our nieces, the flower girls, practice throwing petals. I playfully skip down the path, *Wizard of Oz* style. We are all laughing. It still feels like a game to me.

On Shabbos, we rest, reflect, prepare spiritually for the ceremony which will take place the following day. We follow the custom of fasting before the wedding.

I dress for the wedding ceremony in a small cabin adjacent to the meadow. As I look into the mirror, I see my mother's eyes looking back at me. I thank her for teaching me to love. I thank her for giving me a model of what a loving marriage is. I am soothed and comforted by her presence. I know that she is here with me.

In the chapel, I am seated like a queen, with Dorothy to my right and my future mother-in-law, Madeleine, to my left. My friends and family greet me, and as they do, I give them blessings. This is another custom, one that stems from the belief that on her wedding day the *kallah,* or bride, is closer to God than on any other day in her life.

"You are beautiful," I say to one friend. "You give so much."

"Take care of yourself," I tell another.

I feel as if I have gained an extra soul, an extra spirit on this sacred day.

Jeff is entertained by his buddies in another reception called the Tisch, or table, where his friends and family have gathered to discuss a meaningful topic. Every time Jeff begins to speak, his friends interrupt him with noisemakers, jokes, or music.

Soon, a dancing clarinetist escorts him to meet me. He enters the room, with all our friends and family joining in dance and song. Jeff puts my veil over my face. He whispers, "I love you, always."

We sign the ketubah, the marriage contract. Then we start our walk to the meadow. As I walk, it feels surreal. I gaze into the loving eyes of my friends and family. I feel as if I am walking onto a cloud.

Jeff's mom and dad walk him, as do Grandpa John and his new wife (he remarried at ninety-five years old!). Our ring bearer is a beaming Neal, dressed just like Jeff in a black tuxedo and a gold bow tie. Our assorted nieces and nephews join in the procession, scattering petals before us. Jeff's friend Stu is his best man. My maid-of-honor is Debbie, my best friend from high school. Ida is deemed our "Angel of Honor," since it was at her gathering at the Hollywood Bowl that Jeff and I met. Before we walk down the aisle, one of the children I've worked with sings "Miracles."

My dad is now too fragile to travel, so my mother-in-love, Grandma Dorothy, "gives me away" to my brother and sister, who walk me down the aisle to the chuppah, under which the ceremony will take place. The chuppah is a canopy supported by four posts. Ours is made of a gorgeous prayer shawl that Neal's godmother, Sarita, gave us. Waiting beneath that canopy are everyone who ever held me, and helped us, through the good times and the darkest ones. Among them is Julia, who insisted, after my divorce, that I would find someone to love again.

We are our own "shtetl," huddled together in the canyon of the Pacific Palisades. We are the wedding scene in *Fiddler on the Roof*, though thankfully without the Cossacks!

I walk around Jeff three times, he walks around me three times, we hold hands and walk together in a circle as we're serenaded by my friend Vida, who shared summers with Neal and me at the beach.

Rabbi Shawn tells of Moses seeing the burning bush and how, instead of being horrified by it, he was in awe. She likens this to the union of Jeff and me and Neal. She says that Jeff is Moses—he did not run from Neal and me. That I am Moses—I did not run from Neal's challenges. That Neal is Moses—embracing his own disabilities with courage. How everyone present on this day is Moses—sharing the vision and embracing our love.

Then seven blessings are offered by friends, among them Greg and his wife, Alice, who adopted her daughters just before I adopted Neal

240

and later saw how much I needed to be part of a community. Another blessing is given by Dalia, who encouraged me to express my spirituality.

I feel the spirits of my ancestors, my aunts and uncles, my grandparents, my mom. Jeff and I are united. Our souls are one. It is a lovely, perfect ceremony, a gathering of our village that is as much a reminder of the past as it is a lovely harbinger for our future.

Following the ceremony, Jeff and I observe the custom of taking time to ourselves. We withdraw to a little cabin. We feel so at peace. If the day had ended there, we would have been content. But there is much to come.

We enter the reception and are heralded with tons of confetti, blowers, and an incredible fanfare that culminates in a group circle dance that lasts forty-five minutes. We show a videotape of my dad that makes us all feel as if he is actually with us. He offers his warm, sweet blessing and reflects on his love for my mom. Love abounds. We are seated with crowns, like a king and queen, while our friends and family entertain us and dance around us. The dancing and celebrating continue through a glorious sunset, into the small hours.

—————————————— 3. ——————————————

TOWARD THE END of the first season of The Miracle Project, we're approached by a group of filmmakers from In Effects Films. They're endorsed by Cure Autism Now, which is currently part of Autism Speaks, a worldwide organization whose goal is to better the future for all who struggle with disorders on the autism spectrum.

They have hired a director, Tricia Regan, and are looking to make a documentary about autism, but with a difference: the film they are looking to make will show kids with autism engaged in an activity—for instance, putting on a show where autism is not the issue, but rather the obstacle to a successful endeavor.

They're intrigued that The Miracle Project is helping kids with autism do things that "experts" deem cannot be done, from basics like tolerating noisy environments and making easy transitions from one activity to another to socializing, being spontaneous, sharing feelings, working together as a group toward a common goal.

The filmmakers come to our rehearsals, and are deeply moved by what they see. At the performance, they're as ecstatic as everyone else in the audience. They ask if I would be willing to host another season of The Miracle Project and let them document it.

Before I commit, I want to be sure that we're all on the same page. To me, it's essential that this film show the ability within the disability of autism, that it make the point that while autism poses great challenges, the rewards it offers can exceed them.

The primary mission of The Miracle Project has been to use theater arts to foster creativity, community, and joy. The children learn to express their true selves, their parents get to revel in who their children are, we all come to believe in the life-changing power of the arts and of the human spirit.

I tell the filmmakers that if they agree to focus not on the horrors of autism, or the so-called cures, but on the real-life rewards and challenges, then, yes, I would love to participate.

Fortunately, Tricia Regan is a thoughtful, insightful individual, as are the four producers, two of whom have children on the autism spectrum. We are all in accord: we will create a documentary that will help make autism a condition to be understood rather than a diagnosis to be feared.

I'm excited about what this film could do for the common reaction to autism. I would like the world to know how special kids with autism are, and that it is we, the so-called normal folks—or neurotypicals as we've recently been deemed by the autistic community—who need to educate ourselves and grow to be more compassionate, appreciative, and understanding.

After all, we live in a world that is too loud, too hurried, too toxic. Our kids with autism recoil from it; we adjust to it. Doesn't this suggest to you, as it does to me, that they know the TRUTH and respond to it? Perhaps they are the "canaries in the coal mine."

How I would love it if Neal could go to Starbucks and, instead of getting dirty looks when he covers his ears because the coffee grinder is so loud, the other customers would nod in understanding. Wouldn't it be wonderful if, when a little girl is having a bad day and throwing a tantrum in a grocery store, folks wouldn't judge her mom as a bad parent but would ask, "How can I help?" Could a film help to bring this about? I think it could.

Because of The Miracle Project, I have been able to reach people in a way that I could never have imagined. In the grant, I promised that I would have an impact on a hundred people. If this film gets made, the possibility exists of having an impact on thousands.

The producers want an entirely new cast of children for the film. Tricia says that having kids who've succeeded in the program would take away the suspense and urgency and authenticity. I agree to this, but I will also keep the original Miracle Project troupe going. I can't abandon it now that we've grown together and melded into a family. The documentary will follow the new kids from their initial meeting with me, to their first, inexperienced forays into dancing and singing, to the performances they give in the final production. The issue at the heart of the documentary will be: Can they do it? Can this group of kids overcome the hurdle of autism and come together to create and perform a live musical?

The filmmakers agree to help me recruit the new kids. We also need new volunteers, so one of the producers approaches the Carter Thor Acting Studio, a local acting school. From them, we get a slew of professional actors, models, musicians, and dancers who are eager to work with us. A few have siblings or relatives with autism or other special needs, and jump at the possibility of merging their art with their private life.

Again, I lead a twenty-hour training program. This time, it's videotaped. At first, it's disconcerting to have a camera follow me.

Am I making sense? I worry. Am I slurring my words? Did I brush my hair? But soon I forget about the cameras.

Dalia comes to one of the training sessions. "You may think you are coming here to help these kids, and you are," she tells the volunteers. "But truly you are changing yourself. You are changing the world we live in. YOU are creating miracles."

—————————————— 4. ——————————————

IT TAKES NINE months to find nine families courageous enough to put their lives in the lens. They're willing to do so in order to change the perception of autism. We gather them together to meet the staff and volunteers.

"I have no idea what's going to happen," I tell them. "The first few weeks will be chaotic. Your children may want to run around the room. They may want to sit in a corner. But what I can tell you is that they will be loved for exactly who they are."

One family, the Isaacs, are still not 100 percent sure about committing to the documentary. Are they ready to "out" themselves as living with autism? Are they ready to go public with the diagnosis of their son, Wyatt?

Diane, Wyatt's mom, is reserved and unpretentious, with a warm, beautiful smile. She's an award-winning television and independent film producer, though to see her in her sweatpants and T-shirt, sitting on the floor stretching, you'd never suspect that she could pick up the phone and have her call taken by pretty much anyone in Hollywood.

Like many parents of kids with autism, Diane has spent a lot of time hoping for a magic cure. "I used to dream that I would someday uncover a hidden protocol," she tells me, "that it would miraculously transform my son to normal.

"I envisioned telling everyone about this treatment: some powerful herb, revolutionary diet, or electromagnetic stimulation. This was my happy-ending story. It was science fiction."

She decides to let Wyatt try out the class. "He lives so much in his imagination," she says, "that he really might enjoy it. Though he's had no acting, singing, or dancing experience, this could be good for him. He definitely needs something that's purely enjoyable, something more than therapies and homework."

Here are Diane's impressions of Wyatt's initial experience with The Miracle Project.

"We were greeted by Elaine Hall, better known as Coach E!— the dynamic, bright-eyed founder and creative director. She was like a colorful court jester in the wild kingdom of unique children. She moved around the room like a graceful butterfly, joining each child in whatever they were doing.

"Two kids had burrowed under a rainbow parachute. Another was leapfrogging across the floor. Others were singing, coloring, flapping like birds, drumming a pot. One was under a table, another spinning in her own private orbit.

"The most memorable impression of that first day was that the children with autism, their siblings and peers, the volunteers and staff, and the parents and Coach E! all sparkled. There was a kinetic charge to them. I realize now that it was the frequency of human joy."

After that first day, Diane asks Wyatt if he wants to be in the class.

"Yes," he says, "it's fun!"

She tells him that our sessions will be filmed and shown to a lot of people. They will all know that he has autism.

"Mom," Wyatt responds, "if it can help other kids with autism, then I want to do it."

Wyatt is gentle, with dark blond hair and freckles. At first glance, he looks like the boy next door. He's shy, self-conscious, a little anxious. But he has an old-soul wisdom, a knowingness and sensitivity far beyond his years. "Your head tells you what you want," he says, "but your heart tells you what you need."

I often refer to him as the little Buddha.

Wyatt grows orchids. He teaches me that flowers have feelings.

He doesn't like cut flowers because the cutting hurts them. Another thing I come to love about Wyatt is how beautifully he relates to Neal. Children with autism don't need words, he tells Neal, because God hears their voices through their hearts.

When Diane asks him how he knows these things, Wyatt says, "It came with the package, Mom."

—————————————— 5. ——————————————

AS THE MIRACLE Project progresses, I take a few students aside each week to work with them on improvisational theater games. It's a wonderful time for me to get to know each of the kids. The exercises we do are quite similar to the Floortime work that I used to do with Neal in the playroom.

While I'm working with one group, another group works with Karen Howard, our warm and loving music therapist. Still another small group huddles with our musical director, Katiana Zimmerman, who teaches them to sing and write songs

We're all overseen by our assistant director, Simon Hamlin, who's an organized, efficient, natural leader.

What I enjoy most is that every child with autism is different. It reminds me of something Neal's pediatrician, Dr. Ricki Robinson, says: "If you meet a child with autism, you have met only one child with autism."

What I have found is that, while every child is different, they all respond to love, acceptance, joy, and community. Like anyone, each of these kids has specific strengths and weaknesses; they have specific interests. The therapeutic community dubs these interests "perseverations" or obsessions. We call them "passions" and make them the basis of our show.

Henry is passionate about dinosaurs. He knows everything about them. He's extremely insightful, articulate, and bright. Henry has light blond hair and is always in motion. He's either pretending to be an Acrocanthosaurus and "eating" one of his fellow actors, or he's lecturing the group about evolution. His dad is Stephen Stills, the legendary rock star, but Henry's not interested in rock music.

"It's too loud," he says. "I'm old-fashioned."

For kids with autism, especially those who look "normal" like Henry and Wyatt, childhood, adolescence, and the teen years can be exceptionally difficult. These kids are on the cusp: they don't fit into special education classes, but they don't fit into regular classes, either. Other kids can be really mean to them. And teachers often don't get it.

I can picture Henry becoming a leading science professor at a major university just as I can picture Wyatt being a great religious leader or teacher. If only they can get through childhood.

------ 6. ------

WYATT IS VISIBLY upset. He tells the group that a kid at school has been teasing and bullying him. This, in itself, is "progress" for Wyatt, since it shows that he trusts the group enough to open up to us.

I ask the others if they've ever been bullied. I always do this when a child brings up something personal, so they will see that they're not alone. Three other children jump at the chance to finally tell others their personal experience of being picked on at school, and being called "weird," or "baby," or "stupid." They're pleased that they can share these things—possibly for the first time ever.

I tell them that I was bullied when I was a child for being Jewish and for being so small and so ethnic-looking. "Your nose is bigger than you are!" I was teased.

As I relate this, my mind flashes back to the day I asked my mom, "What is a kite?"

"A kite is something that flies in the air," she answered.

"No," I said, "not that kind of kite. The bad kind."

You see, I had been called a "kike," a nasty word for Jew. But I don't tell this to the children. Nor do I tell them how awful I feel that a child as sweet and loving as Wyatt is picked on, or that someone as smart as Henry is called "stupid."

Instead, I say, "They do not know who you are. If they truly knew you, they would see what wonderful people you are."

I want to tell them so many other things, but Henry blurts out, "Let's get on with the acting, Coach E!"

"Sure," I say, following his lead, "how about we act out a scene where a kid is being bullied?"

They love this. We cast someone to play a bully, someone to play a teacher, someone to play the kid being bullied. Wyatt chooses to be the bully!

"It's fun being a bully!" he says.

To see Wyatt act as a bully that day was a revelation, for me and for him. For me, it was a window into Wyatt's immense creativity. For Wyatt, it was powerful to be on the other side. Though later, asked if he'd rather be bullied or be a bully, he says—not surprisingly—that he'd rather be bullied.

Wyatt understands the difference, and what that difference implies. Just as he would never hurt a plant, he would never intentionally hurt another human being.

7.

THE TOPIC OF bullying becomes the central theme of our musical. This is how it goes: throughout the ages, there have been bullies. We've mistreated each other. We've bullied the Earth. Now, humans are in danger because the Earth is in danger. We need to go back in time and find clues that can save the Earth. We'll call the show *Who Am I: A Time Traveler's Tale*.

The main character will be a highly sensitive child who can actually hear Mother Earth telling him the Earth is in danger. He and his friends find a hi-tech remote control that zooms back and forth through time.

As they time-travel, they meet renowned "sensitive" people who help them find clues that ultimately save the Earth. We discover these renowned people through a book that one of the parents brings in. *Different Like Me: My Book of Autism Heroes* is designed to introduce children to inspirational historical figures whose behavior deviates enough from the "norm" that they could, possibly, have had autism. Among them are: Albert Einstein, Lewis Carroll, Vincent Van Gogh, and Sir Isaac Newton.

Our tale will include "little Albie Einstein," who's teased for staring all day at his compass, and young Vincent Van Gogh, whose poor mom worries that he only wants to paint.

To get a script together, I call a dear friend and colleague, Elaine Aronson, a professional comedy writer, who's one of the best in the business. She was one of the first female writers on *Night Court* and went on to write for *Roseanne, Cybill, The Gary Shandling Show,* and many more. Some of the funniest lines in modern TV came from Elaine's brain and computer. She's always been generous with her time and talent. I give her the basic story line, as determined from scenes we've created during our group improvisation sessions, and we write a first draft of a script. She takes it home and adds her magic.

Each of our children is finding their place to shine. Lexi is echolalic, which means she repeats reflexively what others say. Now she's letting go of that a bit and is improvising spontaneously. Lexi has perfect pitch. She loves to sing Joni Mitchell songs and feels all music so intensely that each song she sings is becoming an expression of her unique musicality and of her sweet and caring self.

Jacob, who's minimally fluent in speech and types to communicate, is producing sweet poems, one of which will become the lyrics to a song sung in our show by Lexi.

Giancarlo, whose eyes rarely focus on others, is a visual artist with a phenomenal sense of color and light. The drawings he creates each day will become part of the stage sets and will grace the cover of our program.

Adam is prone to tantrumming and has difficulty participating in group situations, yet he, like Lexi, has perfect pitch. He also plays the cello with authority.

Neal, more athlete than performer, surprises us each week by dancing and becoming involved in our group improvisations.

As the kids reveal themselves more and more, the volunteers are evolving in consciousness; the parents are bonding. Everyone is thrilled, except the filmmakers. From their perspective, things haven't been going well . . . they've been going too well. The documentary has no tension, no drama. It is important, Tricia says, to show the full picture—the good, the bad, the ugly of autism.

"No drama?" I ask, exasperated. "Didn't the camera catch the way Jacob was glancing over at Lexi? Or when Adam finally told Wyatt, 'I like the way you sang that song'?"

These things, to me, are dramatic. But this is a film production. They want an arc, Tricia keeps saying. In other words, they want to see someone or something fall apart and get put back together again. That I haven't been able to accommodate their wish is good for The Miracle Project, and bad for the documentary.

Each evening after everyone leaves, Tricia interviews me. She films me as I share amazing stories the kids told that day, and speak about how each child is growing. But then, Tricia surprises me.

"I need to interview you," she says.

"You've been interviewing me for weeks!" I say.

"No," she says, "I've been interviewing you as Coach E. I want to see Elaine the mom. Elaine and Neal at home."

Oy! I didn't know that this was going to be part of the project. I thought it was about my work, my methods, about the way kids relate to each other in class. I had no idea that she needed to see my private life, which up to now has been just that: private. I'd really like to keep it that way.

"I'm so tired by the weekend," I tell Tricia, "I just want to be with Neal alone. Without cameras, without any stress."

This is true. Also true is that I'm not the best housekeeper, and that I see private clients on Sundays so I can pay my own bills and that, in the time remaining, Neal and I just hang out and don't do anything filmworthy. But Neal's birthday is coming up—so I invite her and the crew to his party.

Neal is about to turn twelve. He's almost as tall as me, with long limbs, a slender torso, and the face of a mischievous angel. He's always active, running in circles like a pony discharging excess energy. He fidgets a lot, and either makes intense eye contact or seems unfocused. If you saw him, you'd think he was a typical kid with ants in his pants.

I've invited his entire school class to Douglas Park, the little park where Neal and I go in the mornings to hang out after we get my decaf cappuccino and his scone. If four or five kids actually show up at the party, Neal will have a fun day.

The morning of the party, I race to the 99 Cents store, buy up tons of party favors, cups, napkins, all with a soccer theme. I love the 99 Cents store.

As it turns out, every kid in Neal's class comes to the party. They love Neal and want to be part of his celebration. I also invite his coaches, his grandma Dorothy, my friend's kids, and the camera crew that is making the documentary.

It comes to about forty-five people. I can't believe it. I just wanted to make sure that someone would be there! As the party gets into full swing, I am overjoyed. Neal is overwhelmed.

I'm so caught up in serving food and cutting cake that I don't see that the party is too much for him. At times, Neal leaves the group and goes off to swing on the swing set by himself. At other times, he plays in the park with one of his coaches.

One of his classmates has brought his little brother along. Throughout the day, the little boy grabs the other kid's cake, and pulls on Neal's balloons. When Neal plays catch with one of his coaches, the little boy wants to play too. The coach encourages Neal to play with him. Neal really doesn't want to. He makes a face. He turns away from the little boy. He tosses the ball over his head. Now his coach insists that he be gentle and play with the child. Neal still doesn't want to. But he does. The camera crew films them.

As the camera pans into him, Neal looks mischievously into the lens, as if to say, I'll show you! Then he pushes the little boy to the ground, sending him into tears. The party, which moments ago was a marvelous success, is abruptly over. Neal feels bad that he couldn't control his impulses. His coaches and I feel terrible that we failed to read Neal's cues. A beautiful day, interrupted. But the filmmakers got their drama. My drama and Neal's drama, that is.

One of the wonderful things about our director, Tricia, is that she keeps the camera running after an intense moment to see the further subtleties of a given situation. Fortunately, she stays on Neal's face as he goes from laughing at the incident, to sadness, to remorse, to apologizing to the child. Still, I'm worried. We've not had a situation like this since that dreadful night at Norma's.

After the party, Neal is distant. I need to know what's on his mind. At home, he refuses to type about the incident. I take him to see Darlene, hoping that in her presence he'll be able to talk to me freely. At first, he doesn't want to. Darlene encourages him.

Finally, Neal types, "Mom, I want to put you on the spot."

I smile. "Okay," I say.

He then types five words: "Be more of a listener."

I take a deep breath.

Wow. He's right. The day of his party I wasn't listening. Nor have I been listening as attentively as I should. I've been so busy keeping all my plates spinning that I allowed the most important plate to crash.

"Thank you, Neal," I say. And I mean it.

Once again, Neal has taught me to listen to the child who does not speak.

———————————————— 8. ————————————————

IN THE FIRST Miracle Project, we filmed parts of the show in advance, so that any child who experienced stage fright could still be part of the performance. This greatly lessened the tension for the kids and for their parents. It was our safety valve, and it worked. Now, three-quarters of the way through the rehearsal process, Tricia insists that this time the entire show be performed live. This means that the kids will be flying without a net.

"Listen," I say to Tricia, thinking back to my "Peter Man" fiasco, "what if some of the kids just can't do it? What if they get too anxious in front of a live audience?"

"Don't worry," she says. "Whatever happens will be what's supposed to happen."

That's usually how I see things too. But not this time. My job is to uplift the kids, not to risk causing them damage. But at this point, I've given away my power. I hate being in this situation, but I can't turn back now. It'll work, I tell myself, because the kids can do it, and because it has to work.

Four weeks before the performance, we begin rehearsing in the Odyssey Theater, thanks to the kids and their parents who raised the funds to pay for this perfect venue. "I'm in a fun acting group," Henry wrote in his very own fund-raising letter. "We want to perform in a real theater."

Now, at their first rehearsal in that theater, the kids are excited. Too excited. They run all over the place. They dart behind the stage, into seats in the audience, behind the sets, into the green room. Look anywhere in the Odyssey Theater and you will find a kid with autism.

I think it's hilarious. Sort of like a Marx Brothers movie . . . but in terms of putting on a production . . . boy, is it not working! Jeff comes to help out and to assist the volunteers in gathering the kids together.

Henry is having a tough time. Though he's focused, funny, and a terrific actor when doing his lines, he gets fidgety when he has to wait for other kids, and the bright lights hurt his eyes. Jeff loans Henry his sunglasses and stays close to him, helping him stay focused, taking him outside to run around when he needs a break.

Wyatt takes performing seriously, and embraces the significant demands of being onstage. I don't rehearse him or any of the kids over and over as I would with typically developing children. As soon as you give these kids their lines, they get them down pat and you better not change them!

Neal participates easily with the group, especially since all the songs are also taught in sign language. In our skits, he takes the part of a primordial being and then of a dinosaur; he dances with scarves while Lexi sings Jacob's song, "Fly."

It goes,

> *If you look long and hard*
> *Maybe you'll see why*
> *Everyone has a talent*
> *And they can learn to fly*
> (lyrics by Jacob Artson)

Somehow, it's coming together.

Before the official dress rehearsal we have what's called a "tech rehearsal" where we work out the myriad details pertaining to lighting, scenery, sound cues, musical cues, when to enter and exit. Tech rehearsal is slow and painstaking: hours pass as we go through each scene, making sure that everyone knows what's expected.

Adam and his one-on-one aide miss the tech rehearsal. This is a problem, since in the show he's playing "Twinkle, Twinkle Little Star" on his cello, and we need to work out with them where we'll put his instrument on the stage, and who'll set it up and take it away. Although it sounds simple, this setup is actually a complicated proposition that can take a while to work out.

During dress rehearsal the following day, the kids are onstage singing and saying their lines, and there's no time to stop and work out Adam's setup. So I ask Adam's mom, Roseanne, if, just for the dress rehearsal, it would be okay for Adam to sing "Twinkle, Twinkle Little Star" instead of playing it.

"We'll have time to rehearse his entire setup," I tell her, "prior to the actual performance."

Roseanne misunderstands. She thinks I'm refusing to let Adam play the cello altogether. She becomes unglued—in front of me, in front of the kids, in front of the cameras. As she erupts, so does Adam. It's that umbilical cord thing, that overwhelmingly strong tie between parents and their children with autism. This untimely mess pleases only one person: Tricia, the film's director! Finally, there's drama and dissension at The Miracle Project!

In the wings, Adam is screaming, Roseanne is yelling at me, and I'm responding by shutting a door in her face.

As this chaos unfolds stage left, Henry, Wyatt, and the others continue their dialogue, glancing now and then at Adam, at me, and at Roseanne, but never ceasing to rehearse. Suddenly Adam runs away. Roseanne and several volunteers search frantically for him as, onstage, Lexi is singing, "Something got lost along the way."

I love these first-time actors! Intuitively, they're observing Broadway's tried-and-true dictum, "The show must go on!"

We can't find Adam. Then someone spots him in the audience, calmly enjoying the rehearsal from a seat on the aisle. When it comes time to sing "Twinkle, Twinkle Little Star," he's still in the audience. His mom encourages him to join in on the song, but he shakes his head, no. The other kids sing.

Then suddenly Adam jumps from his seat and calls out, "Wait! Wait!"

Everything stops as Adam races to the stage. They begin the song again. Adam sings. His voice is light and sweet. The other kids join in. It's a lovely moment.

Roseanne and I embrace. We recognize that both of us are mothers who only want the best for our children. In the end there is only love.

———————————— 9. ————————————

ON THE MORNING of the show and the filming, I wake up with a start. "Can we pull this off? What if we don't?"

I've done everything in my power to make the kids comfortable: I've rehearsed them in front of an audience, I haven't judged them. I've allowed them to be themselves. They all know their songs, their choreography. There is nothing more I can do except let go and pray that the theater gods are in our favor.

As the seats in the audience begin to fill, the kids and I gather backstage. From this moment on, it's essential to have absolute quiet in the wings. To silence them, I say, "Pretend you're invisible." After that, not a single peep is heard and the children stand in the wings, tugging at their costumes, little professionals preparing themselves for their big moment.

As the house lights dim, I walk onto the stage and ask the audience to be open and willing for whatever happens. I invite them to reach down inside themselves and find that place of unconditional love: love of themselves first, then love of others. I invite them to be part of our miracle.

Then the stage lights go on, and I walk Lexi onto the stage. She is calm, centered. She has so much love and music inside her that she literally bursts into song.

> *Open your eyes, unplug your ears. Take a deep breath and*
> *   smile . . .*
> *Hear all that's good. Hear the music in each day.*
> *Miracles happen everywhere. Yes, miracles. Open your eyes*
> *   to miracles.*

To live and breathe, and be.
(written by Karen Howard)

Her soprano is pure and true and clear. Lexi sings with her eyes closed, but her face shines. It's as if she's channeling the voice of an angel.

Henry strides onto the stage. He moves with assurance in his power. He's focused, disciplined, charismatic as he delivers his lines like a true professional. He pauses in all the right moments for audience laughter. And he can improvise. When they reach the part in the play where they warn the government that the Earth is in danger and the government does nothing, Henry adds the line, "Okay you guys—lollygag around . . . me and my friends will just have to take care of it." Henry, it seems, can take care of anything.

When Wyatt takes to the stage, he's confident and charming. He's not just a fine performer, he really has star power. When he's "bullied" by the mean kids, he makes the audience feel his pain, just as he enables them to share his joy when he joins the group and goes back in time to save the planet.

He sings the song "Sensitive," which Katiana and I have written for him.

Sensitive . . . Am I too sensitive?
Is it something about me?
Or is something really there?
(written by Elaine Hall and Katiana Zimmerman)

It's a plaintive song and Wyatt sings it with an endearing earnestness. His performance is so engaging that later he'll record "Sensitive" with Stephen Stills and Jack Black for a CD that combines the talents of special needs kids with those of professional performers.

Adam is calm throughout the show. He's relaxed, now that we've had time before the performance to rehearse the placement of his cello. Though he's able to play difficult and sophisticated pieces by Mozart, he now approaches "Twinkle, Twinkle Little Star" like a virtuoso, and with touching seriousness. As his bow moves over the strings, he gets real emotion out of that simple childhood song. When he finishes, he turns to the audience and exclaims, "I did it!"

Neal is anxious backstage. One of his aides comforts him as he joins in the group songs, sometimes with his hands on his ears to mute the sounds. He dances like an Egyptian for the Pyramid scene, then looks out into the audience and, using his sign language, asks if I will take him to the "little store" after the show. I nod yes. Satisfied, he rejoins to hold the sign that reads "ONE PLANET ONE PEOPLE ONE SONG."

The kids sway to the music, singing their hearts out, thrilled to be onstage and to have gotten through the entire performance with such energy and fervor and joy. Their faces shine as they join in the final song, a rousing, hand-clapping number titled "I'm a Miracle!"

> . . . *it's time to part, we leave with peace in our hearts,*
>   *so now we say good-bye.*
> *We are miracles, we are stars!*
> *I'm a miracle you're a miracle, we're all miracles . . .*
> (written by Elaine Hall and Katiana Zimmerman)

On and on they sing, brimming with confidence and that unconditional love for one another and for themselves. The audience sings too, and the theater is elevated into a rollicking yet sacred space. The transformation has taken place. The miracle has occurred before our very eyes.

-------------------- 10. --------------------

OVER THE SUMMER, In Effects Films sells two hundred hours of footage to Bunim-Murray Productions, who make reality shows for TV. With Tricia at the helm, they begin the lengthy process of editing.

I call Tricia occasionally to keep up with things. I ask her not to include the birthday scene—in which Neal pushes the little boy. I pray that it will end up on the proverbial "cutting-room floor."

I'm invited to see an early cut of the film. I'm happy and excited until I see Neal pushing the boy. I can't believe this scene is in the film.

I am terrified of what people will think when they see it. I'm afraid of what my in-laws will think. They've come to love and embrace Neal just like their other grandchildren. If they see him push another boy down, will they refuse to have him around the other kids? I'm afraid that Neal will be singled out as "dangerous." That people will again encourage me to put him in a home. Will Neal be viewed like Lenny in *Of Mice and Men*? I cannot sleep. I cannot eat. I'm a mess.

I even call a pro-bono attorney to see what my legal rights are. I have some. I can withdraw the scene, if I want. I meet with DanaKae, my longtime mentor, who believes that showing a child pushing another child can be helpful, if handled properly. It can show other parents that they're not alone, that their child is not the only one who acts out physically when overwhelmed. She encourages me to tell Neal that the filmmakers want to show that scene, and ask his opinion.

Neal listens solemnly, and considers the information. Then he types: "We are emissaries."

Because showing the scene is all right with Neal, I am willing to compromise. I tell the producers that if they insist on keeping that scene in, it has to be given context. They have to explain that nonverbal children with autism are apt to react physically when they cannot express their needs. So we compromise: they will show Neal pushing, and they will include an interview with me in which I talk about communicative intent.

-------------------------- 11. --------------------------

THE TRIBECA FILM Festival in New York City was founded by Robert DeNiro and is one of the most prestigious film festivals in the world. You can imagine the delight that everyone associated with *Autism: The Musical* feels when we learn that our documentary was chosen to be shown there. The film's producers fly Jeff and me to New York with some of the other families featured in the film. While we're away, our wonderful babysitter, Ruth, stays at our town house to take care of Neal.

We stay in a beautiful hotel overlooking Broadway. It's unbelievable! But the day of the opening, I am anxious, feeling withdrawn and shy and experiencing far more anxiety than I do in most situations. I am not accustomed to being in front of large crowds.

This would have been my dream come true in my early twenties, when I was pursuing a career as an actress and dancer. But for the past twenty years, my work has been behind the scenes, encouraging others to be front and center, to shine their light and be highly visible. I am uneasy about being front and center myself. I am not ready to have my image projected on a huge screen with hundreds of people watching! Ahhhh! Help!!!!

I call my friend Dalia, who is not only one of my spiritual buddies, but also an actress quite accustomed to being in front of audiences.

"Just show up and be of service," she says. "Be an example of God's light working in your life. You are where you are today because of God's work."

This brings me such peace. I am there, I tell myself, as proof that when we follow our inner voice miracles happen.

At the opening, I sit on an aisle seat with Jeff by my side. During the film, I get up periodically and walk up and down in the foyer. How will it be received by a New York audience? I watch the audience as much as I watch the film. I see people smiling, laughing at the right places, visibly moved at others. But how will they react to the scene in which Neal pushes the little boy?

When this moment plays out on the screen, a loud gasp is heard in the theater. Everyone seems horrified. My worst fear realized.

I leave the theater again and pace around outside. Jeff comes to find me, and brings me back in. It's time for the scene where Neal is typing with Darlene, on the day that he tells me "Be more of a listener."

At this, the audience gasps again, surprised that Neal has a level of consciousness they didn't suspect he had. As the film goes on, the audience continues to laugh at the funny parts, and clearly enjoys seeing the kids come together for the performance.

As the lights come up, I see people wiping tears from their eyes. They are applauding uproariously. Tricia beckons us down to the front of the auditorium. We are given a standing ovation. Can this be real? Again, I feel that I am in a dream.

During the question-and-answer period, I feel quite comfortable in front of this audience. We are asked many questions about the film, about our lives. Most of the people want to know how to have The Miracle Project in their own community.

As it turns out, the scene in which Neal pushes the other child is especially helpful.

The comments about it put my mind at ease:

"What parent has not had a situation where their child hurts another child?"

"It is apparent that he feels remorse, it is handled well in the film."

As DanaKae predicted, parents who have children with autism are actually grateful to find that they are not the only ones who have a child who acts out when overwhelmed. Tricia, too, was right.

I feel blessed beyond belief to have been part of something as wonderful as The Miracle Project and *Autism: The Musical*. People line up to shake my hand. To hug me. Families want their photos taken with us. Best of all, many children with autism have attended the screening. They are smiling.

The next day, the producers show me the reviews. *Autism: The Musical* is receiving unbelievable accolades: " . . . as riveting as it is revelatory . . . downright joyous . . . eloquently attesting to the transformational power of theater . . ." We've done something good.

————————————— 12. —————————————

AUTISM: THE MUSICAL is purchased by HBO to air for Autism Awareness Month and will go on to win two Emmys. I receive literally thousands of e-mails from people around the world who want to establish their own Miracle Project. Wyatt's mom partners with me to create a template that will help others create this program in their own communities.

As the documentary plays in film festivals around the world, it garners awards wherever it goes. When Autism Awareness Month comes around, I'm asked to speak on radio, TV, CNN International. I'm interviewed by the *New York Times,* the *Los Angeles Times,* the *Wall Street Journal,* the *Seattle Post,* the *Boston Globe.*

The day that the *L.A. Times* piece comes out, Neal and I go to the grocery store to buy the paper. We open it up and there's a huge picture of the two of us. Neal's eyes bug out of his head. He's so proud and happy that he dances in the aisles.

I attend screenings around the country. Sometimes Jeff comes with me. He's a loving if reluctant presence, walking with me down "the red carpet." Most of the time, he stays at home, helping out in the house so I can travel.

After each screening, I'm asked to speak about The Miracle Project and how it got started. I talk about autism and advocacy and awareness. No longer shy about speaking in public, I love to share my passion about autism. It moves me to see that the film profoundly touches its audiences.

* **

GRATEFUL AS I am to be a messenger on behalf of autism, I am also aware that I still have my own private challenges.

"I love the autism that is Neal," I say to a woman I meet in Toronto, Canada, at an International Conference on Disabilities. She has an adult child with autism and has been influential in establishing housing for adults with autism. She is someone I can confide in.

"I let go of the idea of curing Neal long ago," I tell her. "Since then, my goal has been to make him as independent as possible. My fear is that he'll need support for the rest of his life. My public life is taking off but privately I worry that I've done something wrong."

"You're not God," she says. "Neal has his own path. You've done everything that you could humanly do."

Then she asks an interesting question, "What is it that you want most of all?"

"I want Neal to be happy."

"And is he happy?"

"He types it all the time," I say. "H-A-P-P-Y!"

I think about it. I consider the "benefits" of Neal having a one-on-one support for the rest of his life. At least, I joke, that would mean that I wouldn't have to worry about him drinking and driving or hanging out with the wrong crowd.

This makes me feel better, but the concern remains.

———————————————— 13. ————————————————

NEAL IS DOING so well in school that the school district wants to replace his longtime, relationship-based, one-on-one aides—Zack and another terrific aide, Craig—with a district aide. This sets off alarm bells in my head. I remember when Neal was in preschool and "doing so well" that I let the district make decisions that caused him to regress seriously. I refuse to let this happen again. And, after the debacle at sleepaway camp, I promised Neal that I would never again leave him with someone who does not understand him.

Yet I have no options. Legally, I have to let the school district hire a district aide and see how they do before I can fight to have Neal's own aides reinstated. In other words, I have to let Neal fail miserably in order to keep what is working in place.

Reluctantly, I let Zack and Craig train this new person, Anderson. I don't want Neal to fail, so I do everything I can to help them. The school district assures me that this new aide has been trained in Floortime, and is trained in the augmentative communication Neal has been using. I learn quickly that he has not been trained in either.

The first day with his new aide, Neal takes off all his clothes in front of the principal's office. He's never done anything like this before. The next day, he hurls dangerous items in class. He's restrained by Anderson, and then forcibly taken out of the classroom.

Apparently, Neal had tried to express to Anderson that he needed a break from class. But Anderson was told by the district's behavioral team to keep Neal in class no matter what. Neal's goal was to get out of that class. He knew how to achieve it.

"You have to bring back Neal's trained aides, Zack and Craig," I tell the school behaviorist. "This is serious. It's not working!"

But the behaviorist won't listen.

Jeff speaks with Neal before he goes to school. He encourages Neal to embrace his best behavior and maturity and tells him that he needs to "take responsibility for his own education." Neal nods in agreement.

At 10:20 that morning, I hear a knock on the door.

"Who is it?" I ask.

Another knock, this time accompanied by loud pounding. I get scared and double-bolt the door.

"Who is it?" I demand again.

Then I hear, "Me, Nea."

I open the door to reveal Neal, backpack on shoulder, looking a bit frazzled but confident.

"What are you doing home?" I ask. "Where is Anderson?"

I assume that Anderson is right behind Neal. I step out the door and look. No Anderson. Thinking he must be on the sidewalk, and that Neal just ran ahead of him, I call his cell phone.

He answers instantly. "Have you seen Neal?" he blurts frantically. "We've lost Neal. We've been looking all over for him!"

"Neal is right here with me," I say.

"Oh, good," he says.

"Where are you?" I ask, assuming he's close behind Neal.

"I'm at school. We've got security guards out looking for Neal. Can you bring him back?"

"No!" I answer incredulously. "I don't think so."

I hang up. I look at Neal. He does the sign language for "All done."

"Neal, did you walk home from school?"

"Uh-huh." Neal nods.

"By yourself?"

"Uh-huh."

I don't know whether to laugh or cry. I laugh. I am actually proud of Neal's resourcefulness. Neal has never been left alone. Never. He's never walked home or anywhere by himself. It's a miracle that he's okay.

Then the "what ifs" hit me. What if I wasn't home when he got here? What could have happened? Where would he have gone? What if he had gotten hit by a car or kidnapped? What if he got lost? I am hysterical. Neal looks at me, annoyed, as if to say, "Get over it, Mom."

I try to calm down. I can't. I call DanaKae. She's always there when I need her most.

"Look at Neal," she tells me. "Look at him right now."

I do. He looks like a deer caught in the headlights.

"He's standing right beside you," she continues. "He's fine. Just be in gratitude that everything is okay. You do not need to give him consequences. Tell him that you are so proud of him that he knows where to go to feel safe."

I hang up. I turn to Neal. "Nealie, you did the right thing," I say. "You took care of yourself. I'm so glad you found your way home."

I plead to have Zack and Craig reinstated. I plead with the head of special education, with the superintendent of the school district, with the City Council—all without success. Then I discover Cogwheels, a program that homeschools several kids using a common philosophy.

Cogwheels was founded by Portia Iverson, who, with her husband, John Shestack, established the organization Cure Autism Now, the first organization to raise millions of dollars for autism research.

Their son, Dov, has autism. Like Neal, he's extremely smart and nonverbal. It was for Dov and other nonverbals that Portia established a school that would encourage these kids to express themselves through typing, writing, and other forms of what is called "augmentative communication."

The school has academic courses taught at age-appropriate levels. It is perfect for Neal. He attends classes with Zack or Craig by his side. At Cogwheels, learning with other kids with autism, Neal is happy, secure, safe. His sensory system is more regulated. He's less distracted and able to focus for four to six hours a day on academics and life skills. He's getting good at sign language, which is opening new doors for him as he becomes able to communicate to more people.

Again, I learn how life leads us where we do not know to go. Had I gotten my way and forced Zack and Craig on the school district, we never would have found Cogwheels, where Neal is thriving. When I ask Neal why he likes this school, he types, "They don't discount my intelligence."

Funny, what I wanted was for Neal to be independent and to be happy. That has happened, but in Neal's way, not mine.

14.

PEOPLE ASK IF I'm planning to start up another Miracle Project.

"I just don't know," I say.

The truth?

I've loved every minute of it: working with the kids, creating the plays, sharing our personal stories with the parents. I pray that I can find a way to continue. Yet the fund-raising and grant writing, the begging parents, friends, and strangers for money have taken their toll. It's an exhausting process, especially given the hours that need to be dedicated to administrative work and having to work extra jobs just to pay my own bills.

"If only some big nonprofit would adopt us," I tell Jeff. "It would be so much better if The Miracle Project was under someone else's umbrella and I could just run the program, and not have to do everything else myself."

This is my dream, but I can't conceive of a way to bring it into being.

But miracles happen. A grant is awarded to Vista Del Mar, the place where I took the first steps that led to my adopting Neal. This grant is targeted toward developing a bar mitzvah and bat mitzvah program for children who have autism and other special needs. Now they ask me to be the program's director.

Bar mitzvah and bat mitzvah are important passages in the Jewish tradition. They are ceremonies that occur at age thirteen for boys and age twelve for girls, the point at which young people are deemed able to observe the commandments of the Torah and to signify their willingness to do so. Most Jewish children celebrate this "coming of age." Many children with autism do not.

I am thrilled to combine my love of autism and creativity with my love of God and Judaism. I feel certain that the qualities we drew on for The Miracle Project—love and acceptance, creativity and joy—

could be applied to a religious education. The people at Vista see this link too. To my amazement they also invite me to bring The Miracle Project there. This Miracle Project will take on a whole new life, complete with a development department, a space to rehearse for the first time in my life, and an office! My mom would have been so proud! I use part of my fee to hire an assistant, Naomi. And guess what, she's an expert at budgets! I am thrilled and thankful. My prayers have been answered.

Curiously, I'll be creating the bar mitzvah program during the year that Neal will turn thirteen, the year that he should become a bar mitzvah. There are no accidents.

For years, my cousin Gloria has sent me articles about kids with special needs becoming a bar/bat mitzvah. She e-mails me about the importance of building a spiritual community for Neal. She often suggests that I take Neal to synagogue. I thank her for her care, but I know in my heart that I won't follow through. Neal and I have our own spiritual connection. We pray each night, every morning, and before meals. We celebrate Shabbat together and I speak to him often of his own relationship to God. But I attend my weekly synagogue service on my own. Since my early disastrous attempts at taking Neal to a religious service, I have given up the dream of sharing a communal religious experience with him. Until I find Koleinu.

The word *koleinu* means "hear our voices" in Hebrew, and is a Shabbat service designed specifically for children with special needs. It is held in a small classroom, converted into a mini-sanctuary within a large synagogue in Los Angeles. Like any Jewish temple, the room has prayer books, prayer shawls, and an ark that holds the Torah scrolls. But this is not like any other Jewish temple. Within its walls, kids with all sorts of developmental disabilities gather with their families to sing, pray, discuss—here again: a community.

Neal becomes an active participant in the service. He opens and closes the ark; he helps to carry the Torah; he borrows a talking machine from one of the other kids to recite blessings. He responds powerfully to the Koleinu service. He types, "God helps me find patience with my autism."

At this service, I feel as close to God as I have ever been in a formal religious setting.

—————————————— 15. ——————————————

"MY BAR MITZVAH is going to be a happening, a great celebration," Neal types with Darlene, during one of their communication therapy sessions. "It is when I make a commitment to the Torah."

"Is that right?" asks Darlene, whose expertise does not particularly include Jewish studies.

"Exactly right," I say.

I have not been certain that Neal is ready to be a bar mitzvah. I want to make sure he understands what he is doing. Clearly, he gets it, and far more so than do many twelve-year-old boys. Most kids his age think that bar mitzvah is synonymous with "big party." It isn't.

When the bar and bat mitzvah classes begin at Vista Del Mar, Neal will be one of its six students, and one of the two who will have bar mitzvah celebrations this year. We bring in the Miracle Project team to help create the class, along with a rabbi and a cantor. We call the class Nes Gadol, which means "great miracle."

For the past six years, I have recited the Shema (pronounced She-MA) with him every night before he goes to bed.

The word "Shema" can be translated as "hear" or as "listen." How perfect that the one word that Neal is to utter at his bar mitzvah celebration is "listen," the word he put forth to me, a word he knows so well.

We teach him to say it. We show him how to place his finger on his lips and whisper, "Sh," then press his lips together to make the "ma" sound. Just like "Mama" we say.

I've come to believe that a spiritual life is essential for ALL children. At our Nes Gadol classes, the same young people who, that day at school, have kicked, bitten, or thrown a tantrum are able to come together and quietly share their deepest feelings.

They talk about love, friendship, about taking care of the Earth. They talk of God. They seem to have an intuitive grasp of spiritual concepts like generosity and gratitude. When we ask them to define the Neshama, the Hebrew word for "soul," one nonverbal, severely autistic boy types the word "Radiance."

FOR HIS BAR mitzvah ceremony, Neal wears a colorful prayer shawl that he painted himself. During the ceremony, he literally dances his own prayers, moving with grace and joy across the bima. He takes my hands. As we did when he was three and four years old, we spin together in swooping circles.

For the Torah blessing, we input the blessings into Neal's talking device. He pushes the appropriate buttons before and after the Torah reading and points to the passage in the Torah.

Suddenly, with 150 pairs of eyes fixed on him, Neal becomes overwhelmed. Standing on the stage, he starts to cry. I take him out into the lobby, hoping for his sake that he'll be able to continue. I know how much this means to him.

We are joined by Wyatt and Leven, my friend Vida's son. Both boys have always regarded Neal with sweet compassion and interest. Now they stand beside him, concern on their young faces.

"Neal, you're doing great," they tell him, "you're doing great."

We sit a while in silence. Neal eats some apple slices and takes a sip of water. Finally, he gathers himself and returns to the synagogue to complete the ceremony.

For weeks, Neal has been working with Darlene typing his Torah speech. Now he chooses to sit with the congregation as Jeff, standing at the podium in front of the Torah, reads it aloud.

Jeff says, "Neal's Torah portion is about Miracles, gifts from God, leadership and humility. Neal typed his speech on these subjects." Jeff then reads what Neal wrote and typed:

"To be Jewish is to take the Torah as the word of God and live your life as God has said. The people of God live by the Torah. They are to be rewarded.

"The greatest gift is my mother. She rescued me from a different life. I know that everything I have started that day. God put us together so I could have Mom. The greatest gift is my mom.

"I am a leader of my thoughts and decisions. It is the right and responsibility of a boy to learn what God wants and expects of us. Then to listen and set an example. I get to be smart and teach people about differences.

"To pick a humble act I have to say it is how I show patience to my life each day. I have to be humble to God when I am challenged with autism. My humility comes in my love and humor.

"Thank you to Rabbi Avi for being real and being a great teacher. Thank you to my mom and Jeff. Perfect love is what they give. Thank you to all the people who support us."

It is over. Neal's face is lit by his glowing smile. As a klezmer clarinetist plays, the congregation leaves their seats and dances through the aisles.

coda

It is good to have an end to journey toward; but
it is the journey that matters, in the end.

URSULA K. LE GUIN

A FEW WEEKS after Neal's bar mitzvah, Bridget returned to Los Angeles after many travels and experiences. One night, she dreamed that she saw Neal. The next day, she was driving down Wilshire Boulevard and there he was, walking into Koo Koo Roo's with one of his coaches. She ran in after them. Neal seemed to remember her—but was distant.

She wanted to work with him again, though it took a few months before I felt comfortable about it. I wanted to make certain that she was ready to make such a commitment. I didn't want Neal, or myself, to go through what we went through when she left years ago.

Bridget made the commitment. Today, she's as great with Neal as she was before. She's a strong taskmaster when it comes to teaching him manners and how to be gentle in the world.

She couldn't believe how independent Neal had become. The last time she saw him, he was in the playroom, fearful to go anywhere. The other day, she joined Neal and Zack at Six Flags Magic Mountain and Neal convinced HER to go on a roller coaster!

As I survey my life, I am filled with gratitude for all that I have been given. All the things I wanted—the things that everyone wants—have come to be: a loving marriage, meaningful work, a child who is happy and on his way to his own sort of independence.

Another thing that has come to pass is my dream of being like the Old Lady Who Lived in a Shoe and had so many children she didn't know what to do. The Miracle Project has given me those many children, and every bit of progress they make counts as among my greatest blessings.

Even my craziest dream about speaking at the United Nations came to pass when I was asked to speak at the U.N: "Autism: Celebrating the Ability Within the Disability." I was joined by moms and kids from *Autism: The Musical* and kids from Vista Del Mar. I spoke to a full house. We showed the film, the kids performed, and people from countries around the globe lined up to speak with us and share their stories! What a celebration!

Through my journey into autism, my beliefs have taken me full circle. Before Neal's diagnosis, before I knew that he "had" anything, I saw Neal as whole, as extraordinary. Then, he was labeled autistic and I made it my job to "fix" him and "cure" him with various interventions and therapies. We still do the therapies. They remain essential. But the reality is that he was never broken. He is and always has been whole. My responsibility to him has been the same as the responsibility of any parent to any child: to help him be the best person that he can be given his particular assets and liabilities.

* *

ON A RECENT day, I go on a hike with my friend Ida. We hike up the hill at Will Rogers State Park where years ago Neal became so upset by the sound of the tractor. On the way down, I take off my sun cap to feel the wind blowing through my hair. I race under the trees, making sure I feel the leaves on top of my head. I jump, skip, and do cartwheels through the meadow's wildflowers and tall grass.

I reflect with Ida on the way my journeys with Neal have restored my own childhood playfulness. Neal has become my favorite hiking companion. His sense of direction is much better than mine; he finds lovely new pathways and creates his own at times. Sort of like the way Neal does life.

I am no longer concerned about what is "normal." Though I once yearned to fit in with everyone else, I have come to realize that the "normal" that I was seeking was actually a search for self-acceptance. Through the rigors of life and the grace of God, I have found that acceptance, and taken from it a sense of peace. Beyond that, the "normal" that I so desperately craved has been trumped by the miraculous.

Mine has been a journey to successive miracles, as expressed though Neal's growth, the growth of the children in the program and my own metamorphosis into a stronger, more compassionate, understanding, humane being.

I have come to understand autism as a gift that can uplift everyone it affects, for autism teaches us the highest values: to accept and cherish others for who they are, to revere rather than dread the differences between us, to acknowledge that there is no right or wrong way—that there is only your way and my way and that both are valid.

Above all else, I have learned that the more I see the world from the perspective of Neal and other kids with autism, the richer and more meaningful my own life becomes.

** *

MAY 6, 2009. Neal's birthday. He is fifteen years old. He is tall, slender, fair, and a fusion of opposites: poetic and soulful, yet sparked by nervous energy, capable of seeing and taking in everything, except when he's tuning out.

Neal is handsome, with the easy physicality that you see in athletes and dancers. People often respond to him with deference, sensing somehow that they are seeing a "personage." It's the same attitude that I first saw exhibited by the Canadian prime minister on the day that we brought Neal out of the orphanage.

To celebrate the day, I take his Cogwheels class to Koo Koo Roo's for lunch. We sing "Happy Birthday" over a carrot cake. With a wry smile on his face, Neal blows out his birthday candles. Later, when I wonder what he wished for, he types out the words "For my body to be still."

That evening, I ask him how he is feeling about being fifteen. He types, "Not that much different. More responsible. Happy."

For dinner, Jeff cooks Neal his favorite foods, quinoa pasta and asparagus. Neal says the blessing before the meal. He does this in his own—"Neal speak," we call it. Usually Neal is quite rushed, but tonight he takes his time with the blessing. In his own way, he says thank you for our food, for Mama, Paba (his name for Jeff), and then he points to himself, Nea.

After dinner, he asks to go for a walk. He leads Jeff and me back to the place that is so symbolic for him: the big house where he once lived. The next morning, when I wake up, Neal runs in my room and signs, "Walk to Starbucks." And we do. Neal skips happily the whole way there. He gets a gluten-free cake and we sit in the park and eat.

It's the same park we've been going to for thirteen years. It's the park where Neal learned to go down the slide with our dog, Luckie, where Grandma Dorothy taught him how to play in the sandbox, where my dad gently pushed him on his first swing. Looking at

Neal, it's hard to imagine how this tall, lanky fifteen-year-old was once the tiny toddler I pushed in a stroller.

Later that day, Neal and I go to the beach. He runs down to the shore, and I watch as he heads out into the waves, eager, commanding, and fearless, his terror of sand and sea long gone.

I recall times when Neal couldn't set one toe in the sand, much less dive through the crashing surf. I remember the week we spent stuck on the porch of the beach house in Delaware, when Neal poured water into a wading pool and bonded with my mom, who, like him, didn't want to get "sandy." I remember how I carried him on my back to a beach towel, where he refused to move. Those times seem long ago. And they are.

Now I have memories of Neal and me picnicking at the beach, watching the kite surfers, and seeing fireworks spill their profusion of colors out over the ocean and across the sky. These are memories of the two of us together, feeling God's presence.

Now, as the sun begins to set and the moon begins to rise, I watch my son run and jump and dance in the waves and I know that the journey we have taken together was the journey we both needed to take. Now we are blessed and we are happy.

There have been hard times and frightening times. I lost many things, but I never lost hope. Everything worked out the way it was meant to work out. My barn burned down. Now I can see the moon.

acknowledgments

WHAT A JOURNEY this has been.

I have been blessed beyond measure to have found the right team to make this book a reality. First, thank you to Elizabeth Kaye, for her dedication and commitment to this work. Elizabeth's integrity and experience infused *Now I See the Moon* with depth and understanding, and her probing questions and expert "weeding" brought out the best in me and the best in this book. She is a very talented writer. Thank you to my insightful, gifted editor, Julia Cheiffetz, who held the vision for this book so high that we needed to fly to reach it. Thank you to my esteemed publisher, Bob Miller, who took a chance on an "unknown" simply based on tales of my "huggability"! Thank you to Katie Salisbury for all her assistance. I am so fortunate that *Now I See the Moon* was nurtured and published by HarperStudio.

I extend tremendous gratitude to Irene Webb, my "tough love" agent who is known and respected as the kindest and best in the biz and whose support and belief in this project held us like an angel. Thank you to those who helped so much in the early stages of the book: Wendi Niad, Jennifer Graff, Linden Gross, Michael Levin, and Tom Fields-Meyer. To Mim Eichler Rivas, the godmother of *Now I See the Moon,* thank you for encouraging me to "just start writing."

This book would not exist without the documentary *Autism: The Musical,* and I am forever grateful to Sheila Nevins and Nancy Abraham from HBO; Jonathan Murray and Sasha Alpert, Janet Grillo, Kristen Stills, Perrin Chiles, David Glynn, and director Tricia Regan. I am in awe of the impact this little film has made all over the world. I have utmost admiration for the courageous parents and children who chose to put their lives in the lens. Thank you to Simon Hamlin and all the staff and volunteers who helped make this film so special. Thank you to the original Miracle Project staff: Karen Howard, Katiana Zimmerman, Aaron Feinstein, and Rachelle Friedman.

Thank you always to Dr. Stanley Greenspan for his incredible contribution to so many. Thank you to Dr. Barry Prizant, Dr. Stephen Shore, and Portia Iverson for their help with this work. Thank you to DanaKae Bonahoom, Sharon Lowery, Shelley Cox, Susan Corwin, Dr. Leonard Donk, Cynthia Lloyd Darst, Dr. Eric Dolgin, Cari Derbise, Beth Galanty-Blaney, Peggy Garrity, Dr. Robert Gramlich, Julie Grass, Wendy Haines, Jenivieve Joshua, Dr. Harvey Karp, Dr. Margaret Paul, Stephen Marks, Melanie Segal, Clara Sturak, Beth Tishler, Elle Walker, and Tami Walsh for their guidance and protection. To Daniela, Mark Kretzmann, Jami Carter, and Sheryl Paul for hours in the playroom, we thank you. And we bless the memory of Kathleen Zundell. Thank you to the staff from the Son-Rise Program. My appreciation to all the clergy who inspired and supported me through the years. I am extremely grateful to Rabbi Bradley and Elana Shavit Artson for their encouragement and wisdom. They all took us to new levels of understanding.

Thank you to the many professionals and organizations who supported us: Michelle Wolf, Sally Weber, the Jewish Community Foundation, the Culver City Playhouse, Breeyah, T.I.P.S., Autism Speaks, Autism Society of America, TACA, The Daniel Jordan Fiddle Foundation, The Donner Foundation, The Doug Flutie Jr. Foundation, the HollyRod Foundation, The Chaka Khan Foundation, and Kids on Stage. Thank you to everyone at Vista Del Mar for choosing to see the ability within the disability of autism and taking a chance on me to create Nes Gadol and the Vista Inspire Program. And thank you to all the staff, volunteers, and families of The Miracle Project, my first families—the Felders, the Goldbergs, the Finns, and the Lohmans; Vista Inspire Program; Nes Gadol; and Rabbi Jackie Redner and Rabbi Avi Taff for being such blessings in our lives.

To say that it takes a village to write a book is an understatement at best. It has taken many villages to write this one. Many of the people who helped me along the way have been named throughout the book. Some names were changed for privacy. To everyone who has ever touched Neal's and my life—all of the doctors, teachers, and friends—I am eternally grateful. To list all of their names would be a book in itself.

There are others who must be named: I could not have finished writing this book without their help. Among them are Neal's coaches: Zack Wimpee, Craig Martin, Ryan Berman, Bridget Walsh, Lisa Johnson, Paula Riff, and James Fair. Thank you for keeping Neal so terrifically engaged and growing this past year while "Mama was busy working." Thank you to Ruth Salazar and her children, Ruthie, Maria, and Roberto, for their love and support. Thank you to Naomi Salamon and Jenn Brook for all of their help and support during busy times.

Thank you to Tracy Columbus for her boundless energy and generosity and helping to make the seemingly impossible possible. Thank you to my Miracle Project partner and dear friend, Diane Isaacs, for her creative brilliance and strength. Because of Diane we will one day create The Miracle Project in every community. Thank you to Wyatt for his incredible heart. Thank you to all of our donors and the foundations who supported our mission.

Thank you to Lynn Angelet, who, whenever my life became more challenging, would make me laugh by saying, "Your story just keeps getting better." Who would have thought then that it would become a book?

Thank you to all of my friends and family who showed me kindness and understanding for all of the missed birthdays and dinners throughout the creation of this book. Special thanks to Cathy Dinovitz, Gloria Golbert, Lauren Katz, Norma Meyers, and Ilene Weingarten for reading early pages and encouraging me to keep on writing.

Thank you to all my in-laws, my in-loves, and my family(s) for loving me through the challenging times, embracing Neal and me with open arms, and celebrating with us now.

Thank you to my son, Neal, who inspires me daily. Thank you for allowing me to share this story to help others. You are my hero.

Thank you to my amazing husband, Jeff, for his love, support, and unwavering patience through this year of writing—from preparing his nightly gourmet meals, to staying up all night with me to help meet deadlines—for taking care of Neal, and for comforting and believing in me. Because of you I can fly.

Lastly, which is actually always first, is my gratitude to the God of my understanding for sustaining us, enabling us, and bringing us to this joyous time.

Many blessings,
Elaine

appendix

a list of resources

HERE ARE SOME of the professionals, organizations, programs, and media that are mentioned in *Now I See the Moon*. Visit The Miracle Project website at www.themiracleproject.com for additional resources, which will be continuously updated. Please let us know of resources in your area so that we can add them.

OTHER RESOURCES WITH ELAINE HALL

Autism: The Musical
   Directed by Tricia Regan; DVD can be purchased through www.themiracleproject.com or at www.newvideo.com

The Miracle Project
   Where Miracles Happen Every Day; www.themiracleproject.com

Fly: Into Autism
   Album pairs celebrity artists such as Jack Black, Chaka Khan, and Holly Robinson Peete with children who have autism; www.flyintoautism.com

7 Keys to Unlock Autism for Educators (Spring 2011, Wiley)
By Elaine Hall, Diane Isaacs, and Lisa Johnson

Who Am I: The Play Within Autism: The Musical
Music, lyrics, and DVD available at www.themiracleproject.com

Unlocking the World of Autism: 7 Keys to Becoming Miracle Minded
DVD and CD-ROM series produced by Concept Media with
Elaine Hall and Diane Isaacs for first responders and medical
professionals; www.conceptmedia.cengage.com

ARTS: A Film About Possibilities, Disabilities, and the Arts
Film directed by Keri Bowers; www.normalfilms.com

Fly Away
Directed by Janet Grillo; distributed by New Video,
www.newvideo.com (in production)

SERVICES AND PROGRAMS MENTIONED IN
NOW I SEE THE MOON

Autism Speaks: www.autismspeaks.org
Autism Society of America: www.autism-society.org
Autism Today: www.autismtoday.com
Autism Treatment Center of America: Son-Rise Program:
www.autismtreatmentcenter.org
Beth Shir Sholom: www.bethshirsholom.com
Broadway Gymnastics School: www.broadwaygym.com
Camp JCA Shalom: www.jcashalom.com
Cogwheels program via the Strange Son website: www.strangeson.com
Conscious Weddings: www.consciousweddings.com
Doug Flutie Jr. Foundation: www.dougflutiejrfoundation.org

Dr. Eric Dolgin: www.osteohome.com/SubPages/eric.html

Dr. Stanley Greenspan: www.stanleygreenspan.com and www.icdl.org

HaMercaz: www.jewishla.org/divisions/ha_mercaz/ha-mercaz.cfm

Darlene Hanson, MA CCC: www.darlenehanson.com and www.wapadh.org/

Inner Bonding: www.innerbonding.com

Inner City Arts: www.inner-cityarts.org

Jay Nolan Community Services: www.jaynolan.org

Jewish Community Foundation Los Angeles: www.jewish foundationla.org

Jennavieve Joshua: www.timetothrive.com

Jill Strauss Dance: www.jillyjazz.com

Dr. Harvey Karp: www.happiestbaby.com

Kids on Stage: www.kidsonstage.com

Koleinu at Temple Beth Am: www.tbala.org/page.cfm?p=51

Making Lemonade—The Single Parent Network: www.making lemonade.com

Nes Gadol: www.vistadelmar.org

Ozreinu: www.ozreinu.org

A Place Called Home: www.apch.org

Step By Step: www.stepbystepeduplay.com

Talk About Curing Autism Now: www.talkaboutcuringautism.org

Therapy West: www.therapywest.org

United Nations, UN Works: World Autism Awareness Day: www.un.org/works/sub4.asp?lang=en&id=8

Vista Del Mar Child and Family Services: www.vistadelmar.org

Vista Inspire Program: www.vistadelmar.org/services.php?recordID=6

Zero to Three: www.zerotothree.org/